CW01304998

VOLLEYBALL COACHING WIZARDS

VOLLEYBALL COACHING WIZARDS

Insights and experience from some of the world's best coaches

JOHN FORMAN & MARK LEBEDEW

Wichita Falls, TX

Volleyball Coaching Wizards
Insights and experience from some of the world's best coaches
by John Forman & Mark Lebedew

For information, address author@volleyballcoachingwizards.com

Cover photo courtesy of John Forman

DEDICATION

This book is dedicated to all the volleyball coaches out there at every level and in all corners of the globe who are dedicated to their players and who maintain a learning mindset. May you always retain your passion for the sport and your role in it.

CONTENTS

	Special Reader Bonus	ix
	Acknowledgements	x
	Foreword	xi
	Introduction	1
	In Recognition	7
1.	Carl McGown	10
2.	Giovanni Guidetti	35
3.	Ruth N. Nelson	59
4.	Jefferson Williams	108
5.	Teri Clemens	138
6.	Garth Pischke	172
7.	Tom Turco	196
8.	Craig Marshall	228
	Conclusion	265
	About the Authors	267

SPECIAL READER BONUS

THANK YOU FOR BECOMING A READER OF THE FIRST VOLLEYBALL COACHING WIZARDS BOOK!

We'd like to show our appreciation for your interest in our work and for supporting the Volleyball Coaching Wizards project by offering you a special readers-only free bonus. Just use the link below.

volleyballcoachingwizards.com/bookreader/

ACKNOWLEDGEMENTS

Volleyball Coaching Wizards would not exist were it not for all the amazing coaches we've interviewed so far. Without their willingness to give their time, attention, experience, and insight, the Wizards project – and by extension, this book – simply could not have been developed. Everyone thanks you for your contribution to the education and development of volleyball coaches everywhere!

FOREWORD

Coaching is a practice more than a profession.

Nowhere is this clearer than in the journeys described by the eight people in this book whose sustained success has earned them the designation of 'coaching wizard'!

You will discover that their paths to wizardry are diverse, yet the outcomes are remarkably similar.

Some are readers, researchers, and seekers of scientific insights about the sport; others are former players and rely on experiential knowledge and intuition; still others came to volleyball through serendipitous circumstances and studied coaching from the outside in; several were the beneficiaries of the uniquely American experiment called Title IX which made the sport of volleyball available to vast numbers of females in the United States and spawned thousands of coaching opportunities.

You will find that hard work, opportunity, and luck are so intertwined in their stories that they become indistinguishable.

So what is the lesson of these tales of wizardry?

That excellent coaching, while not easy, is not magic.

Each coach provides clues about aspects of training and motivation that shape their individual approach. They detail the emergence and development of their distinctive coaching philosophies.

All share a fascination with the sport of volleyball, yet the varied ways they distinguished themselves provides models for other coaches no matter the gender, level, or age of the team.

Kathy DeBoer, Executive Director
American Volleyball Coaches Association (AVCA)
August, 2016

INTRODUCTION

What is Volleyball Coaching Wizards?

Back in the late 1980s a man by the name of Jack Schwager authored a book titled *Market Wizards*. In it he shared material from a series of interviews he did with great financial market traders and investors. These individuals traded in several different markets, they had a variety of methods, and their backgrounds were diverse.

Thousands upon thousands of traders and investors consumed the original *Market Wizards* book and the follow-up editions Schwager developed over the years. They became an often re-read source of inspiration and information for a whole generation (or more) of traders. Readers could identify with the people profiled in the books and see a path to success for themselves in those pages.

The *Market Wizards* books also share some of the history of the markets through the eyes of those who participated in them. In that way they helped develop a trading literature above and beyond technical and tactical manuals, which are easily found.

The **Volleyball Coaching Wizards** project was conceived to fill a similar role for volleyball and volleyball coaching.

We want to give volleyball coaches the same kind of inspiration and information. We want to show how great coaches come from a variety of backgrounds. We want to show that there are great coaches operating in a wide variety of coaching arenas. We want to show that while there may be some similarities among great coaches, there is still an array of philosophies and methodologies underlying their success.

Great coaches can be found at all levels

One of the things we feel very strongly about is that coaching level does not equal coaching mastery. There is a very strong tendency to look at coaches of top national teams, outstanding professional clubs, or powerhouse college programs and say they are the best of the best. Similarly, there is a tendency to think that coaching a U18s team is higher status than coaching a U12s team because you're working with "better" players.

In other words, there's an attitude that better coaches work with better players. That leads people to think, "He/she coaches the best team, so they must be the best coach," and anyone else is less worthy of respect.

From a career perspective it leads people to think that coaching better players equates to being a better coach, which creates a ladder-climbing mentality. That isn't inherently a bad thing, of course. Moving up the ladder to bigger clubs or to universities in stronger conferences tends to mean better pay, among other things. The problem is when coaches think that because they coach at a higher level than someone else it means they are a better coach.

Coaches should be measured first and foremost by the impact they have on their players and their program or club. They should also be judged on their influence on other coaches, though admittedly those in higher profile positions will tend to have more opportunity to impact others.

A major part of being a true master coach is understanding where you can best have that influence. For some it's at the top level of the sport. For others, though, it is at a development level.

Ruth Nelson is a perfect example of this. She mostly coaches very young players these days. If you ever get to talk with her, though, you'll quickly realize she knows more about the sport and coaching than most. That's why she's got a steady stream of coaches seeking her mentorship. Try to tell them that since Ruth is working with a bunch of 5 year-olds she can't possibly be considered a great coach. They'll laugh you out of the gym!

It's also a simple numbers game. There are far more coaches working with youth athletes and in low level college and club programs than there are coaches working at the elite level. There are far fewer full-time paid volleyball coaches than there are part-timers and volunteers. And when you look at places where volleyball is not as big a sport as it is elsewhere, coaches just lack the opportunity to coach elite level players – or to get paid, in many cases. They simply coach the players in front of them because they have a passion for it.

We have examples of just that among the interviews in this book. Jefferson Williams has done most of his coaching in England where volleyball is a minor sport. Tom Turco coaches in one of the weaker volleyball regions in the U.S. From that perspective it would be easy to overlook them both. If you judge a coach on championships, however, few can come close to matching them. Equally, both have been highly influential on coaches around them.

Throw Garth Pischke in there as well. He's won more men's college volleyball matches as a coach than even the legendary Al Scates. He's done it in Canada, though, so hardly anyone has ever heard of him.

The point is, just because someone works at a lower level of the sport – either by choice or because of circumstances – it doesn't mean they should be considered a lesser coach. They should be judged on their impact and influence.

Contributing to the volleyball literature

The first thing to be noticed about volleyball literature is how little of it there is. In football, or basketball, or cricket or any number of other sports, the stories of the giants of the sport have been documented over and over again. For the most part, the lessons that can be drawn out of those sports, have been drawn out.

In volleyball – except in some small pockets – those stories have not been told. Those lessons have not been passed on. Coaches in different countries largely work on their own, seeking their inspiration from those in their small circle, or from other sports.

Our goal with the Volleyball Coaching Wizards project (and this book) is to expand those small circles into one large circle. By doing so, we can help improve the level of coaches everywhere, and grow the sport.

How do we intend to accomplish these ambitions?

So, what are we doing to highlight great coaching at all levels and contribute to the volleyball literature? Simple. We're interviewing great coaches from all over the world at all different levels of play, then sharing the results of those interviews with our fellow volleyball coaches across the globe.

This book is part of that process. It is meant for most readers to be an introduction to the Volleyball Coaching Wizards project. At the time of its publication we have completed about 40 interviews with coaches from a number of different countries and levels of the sport. We decided to provide a cross-section of them here to give you a flavor for what the project is about.

In these eight interviews we have:

- 4 coaches who have coached at national team level
- 4 coaches who have coached in professional volleyball
- 4 coaches who have coached college or university volleyball
- 4 coaches who have coached youth volleyball

They combine for:

- 2 CEV Champions League gold medals and an FIVB World Club Championship
- 18 collegiate national championships and over 2500 match victories
- 20 high school state titles
- More than 50 club level (professional/adult) championships
- Numerous Coach of the Year awards and Hall of Fame inductions

You will find in this book coaches who have worked mainly with men and boys, coaches who have worked mainly with women and girls, and one coach who has worked a lot with both genders. Half the coaches are American, and the other half are non-American. Some have worked primarily as part-time coaches with day jobs, while others have been full-time coaches.

Two of the interviewees are pretty well known to volleyball coaches around the world. One, in particular, is among the most respected in the world for the influence he's had on coaching. The other is coming off unexpected success at the Olympics. The rest don't have the same profile. In some cases they are only known in a relatively small area, while others do not have the same spotlight they once did.

Like we said, this is a group selected to be diverse and thus representative of the coaches we have already interviewed, and those we will interview in the future. It is a merely a sample, and just one way we are getting the experience, insights, and expertise of these great coaches out there for everyone to learn from and enjoy. This is the first of what is expected to be a series of books.

A note on the interviews

What you will see in the chapters to follow are transcripts of the conversations we had with each coach. If you've ever seen a transcript of a conversation or interview you know that it's not always an easy read. We all have our conversational quirks in terms of how we transition between thoughts. We're all guilty of running on our sentences, or starting on one thought, then shifting to another midway through. That's usually easy to follow in conversation, but can make for difficult reading.

For the sake of readability we've edited each interview as we felt appropriate. That means while what you see will mostly be word-for-word what the Wizard coach said, in places we've smoothed things out in terms of grammar, punctuation, etc. We always looked to maintain the interviewee's voice and tone, and we definitely did not alter the content of what they said.

John interviewed five of the Wizards here, while Mark handled the other three. While we did have a group of subjects we generally tried to make sure got addressed, we did not run the interviews off a script. That allowed us to let them be more conversational and organic in nature. It also allowed us to follow along on subjects specific to each coach, which is an important part of the project's aim.

Share your thoughts and opinions

We'd love to hear what you think about this book. Definitely leave a review on the website of your favorite book seller.

You can also reach out to us directly at: volleyballcoachingwizards.com/contact-us/

And now, on with the book!

IN RECOGNITION

Unfortunately, some of the most influential and respected coaches the world of volleyball has known are no longer with us. Their impact, however, lives on in those who follow in their footsteps. It's impossible, of course, to mention all of them here. In keeping with the theme of this book, we've selected two notable names – one American, one non-American.

Jim Coleman

If you followed the lines of coaching influence among U.S. volleyball coaches – and not a few non-U.S. coaches as well – you'd find a great many of those threads trace back to Dr. Jim Coleman. Both Carl McGown and Ruth Nelson among the interviewees in this book worked directly with Coleman during their careers. His name comes up frequently among the senior U.S. coaches when you ask them who influenced them in their development. And coaches not directly influenced by Coleman have been influenced by coaches who were.

Former USA Men's National Team coach Doug Beal is quoted as having said, "I can't think of any coach that hasn't been touched by Jim Coleman."

Coleman was involved in the USA national teams from the mid-1960s until his retirement in 1998. He did three stints as head coach of the Men's National Team: 1965-1970, 1979-1980, and 1990. He also assisted with the team from 1971 to 1972, and then again from 1987 to 1990, along with being an advisor and staff member in the 1984-87 period, among other contributions. Overall, Coleman was part of seven

Olympics Games, eight Pan Am Games, five World Cups, six World Championships and eleven NORCECA Championships.

At the collegiate level, Coleman started the volleyball program at the University of Kansas in the 1950s and made it one of the strongest of the era with Top-3 finishes in 1957 and 1958. He coached the George Williams College men's team in 1973, 1974, and 1976, winning the NAIA National Championship in 1974. He also coached the women's teams at Whitman College and Washington State University from 1981-1984, then coached the Minnesota Monarchs in Major League Volleyball in 1987.

One of Coleman's major innovations was in the collection and usage of statistics in volleyball. To quote the Volleyball Hall of Fame, in to which he was enshrined in 1992, "He and his wife, Lee, created volleyball statistical systems, which are now used worldwide."

Coleman was also highly influential in how the game is played as a 25-year member of the FIVB Rules commission. Little known fact: He invented net antennae.

Unfortunately, Coach Coleman passed away 15 years ago. If he was still alive, he might very well have been the first person we contacted to interview for Volleyball Coaching Wizards.

Vyacheslav Platonov

From 1977 until 1983, the Soviet Union Men's National Team was untouchable in world volleyball. In that seven year period they won one Olympic gold medal, two World Championships, two World Cups[1], and four European Championships. Only the Eastern bloc boycott of the Los Angeles Games prevented them from attempting to add to that streak.

The coach of this dominating team was Vyacheslav Platonov. When he took over, the Soviets were in a period of disarray following consecutive losses to Poland in the World Championships and the Olympic finals. He transformed the team and the game, and helped to turn blocking into an art form.

Sadly, Platonov's influence is not widely recognized outside his home

1. That was in the era in which it was a stand alone 'major' tournament and not part of the Olympic Qualification process

country. That absence of recognition is one of the inspirations for the Volleyball Coaching Wizards project. Luckily one of his books, *My Profession : The Game* has been translated into English.

Platonov passed away in his beloved St Petersburg, where he is remembered with an annual tournament. Along with Jim Coleman, he would have been one of the first people contacted for this project.

1

CARL MCGOWN

When it comes to influence on volleyball coaching, few can match Dr. Carl McGown. His advocacy of training specificity, among other concepts, through his work with the USA National Team program, Brigham Young University (BYU) and Gold Medal Squared has changed the thinking and training methods of many coaches all over the world.

Among Carl's personal coaching credits is 225 career victories, nine Top-10 finishes, and a pair of NCAA men's national championships while head coach at BYU. Twice he earned National Coach of the Year honors. He also won league and cup titles coaching professionally in Switzerland.

As a member of the USA coaching staff, Carl helped guide teams to four gold medals, three of which came at the Olympics. Overall, he's been with the program for seven Olympics and seven World Championships.

In 2010 he was inducted in to the AVCA Hall of Fame.

This interview was conducted by John in June, 2015. At this point, Carl's son Chris has just resigned as BYU Men's Volleyball coach. Carl was Chris's volunteer assistant for four years, so his future with the program was uncertain. He was getting ready to do some women's coaching in Hawaii, though.

Can you document your coaching biography?

It might be a long and wandering path. I grew up in Long Beach, California, and for a large part of my youth we lived on 1022 East 1st Street. When I was a little guy – twelve or something like that – I went to this place where they had volleyball courts on the beach. It was about three blocks from my house and some guys one day said, "Hey little boy, do you want to play?"

I started playing on the beach at Long Beach. When I got older, a church that I belonged to – the Mormon Church – had this thing that was called All Church. If you were good in your area you could go to Salt Lake City and play in the All Church Championships. You could do it with basketball. You could do it with volleyball. You could do it with softball. You could do it with a lot of sports.

I played church volleyball, and then I went to BYU and John Lowell had just retired from the Army – Major John Lowell. He became a coach of our club team that we had at BYU. When I graduated from BYU with my masters degree I got a job at the Church College of Hawaii [BYU-Hawaii], and I was assigned to coach it. I begged to coach it. John Lowell ended up being good friends with Jim Coleman, so Jim invited John to be an assistant coach, and later on Jim needed somebody to go to the World Championships in Bulgaria in 1970. John Lowell told Jim Coleman that I would be good, so Coleman hired me in 1970. I don't know if he hired me is the right word, but he said, "Come and be my assistant coach."

So in 1970 I went to the World Championships in Bulgaria with USA.

Coleman was the coach of our men's team, and then he stepped down, so USA was looking for a men's coach for our national team. From '73 to '76 I got to do that. I coached Doug Beal, and I coached Fred Sturm, and Marv Dunphy was an assistant coach. During those three years I got affiliated with Doug, who would become our greatest coach, and Marv who was terrific, and Fred who was terrific. I got to go to lots of places with those guys- to the Olympic Games, among other things.

Then I was teaching school at BYU. I didn't ever plan to be a volleyball coach. When I was going to school in the '60s there weren't really volleyball coaches. There wasn't NCAA volleyball. There wasn't NCAA women's volleyball. There was just people having a good time together. I'm at BYU teaching school, I'm in the professorial rank, and in 1990 some kind of miracle happened. BYU added a men's NCAA volleyball program, and it was right in the middle of Title IX. It was one of the most unlikely things that you could ever imagine – that a school would start a men's volleyball program in the middle of Title IX – but they did. I was a full professor at the time, had a pretty good job. After a while the athletic director and the dean got together and said, "Carl, we want you to coach this team at BYU."

So I became an NCAA volleyball coach in 1990. I did that until I retired in 2002.

When I had retired, just about that time, Doug needed an assistant coach for the 2004 Olympic Games, so I got to be his assistant coach. In 2008 Hugh McCutcheon became our Olympic coach and he was a player that I had coached at BYU. He dragged me along to be part of the Beijing Olympics. That's that, and now I'm getting real good at golfing and skiing.

Basically from 1970 to 1990, the only coaching you were doing was with the national team?

Yeah.

You were just being the consummate professor and focusing on your students.

Yeah, I got to be a full professor, so you had to research, and publish, and have graduate students, and do all of that stuff that goes on in most universities. Teach and research.

The thing that I feel a lot of people who are aware of your history and involvement with the national teams and whatnot think they understand about you and your contribution is that you brought specificity into volleyball, from a coaching and training perspective. First off, is that a relatively fair statement to make?

I don't know if I brought it in, but certainly it's a really important thing to know if you're going to coach. Yeah, from way back when, we've talked about the specificity and motor programs. We talked about it with Doug, and Marv, and Fred, and all of the coaches in USA volleyball have heard about it a lot.

Where does this come from in terms of your own development?

Was this something that was part of your education or did you pick it up along the way?

I went to graduate school at the University of Oregon and studied in the department of physical education there, but I also studied in the psychology department. They had a degree at the University of Oregon in motor learning, and they really got support from the psychology department. When I graduated from the University of Oregon my very first job was at the University of California Berkeley. I took over the position of Franklin Henry who had just retired. Franklin Henry is often called the father of motor learning. One of the things that Henry talked about way back in the '50s is the specificity of motor programs. I knew about him from when I was a student at Oregon, and I also knew about Henry when I was at Berkeley because he had an office in the basement and I'd go down and sit at his knee every chance that I got. He would just tell me stuff.

In the 1970s, when I was with Coleman, and in 1968 when Coleman and Lowell were together, we didn't know anything, I could say. We knew very little about what it meant when we said motor programs are specific. That's something that developed after I was a graduate. We started, this applies, and there isn't much transfer unless you do it this way. That's stuff we learned starting in the early '70s.

On that subject, you just brought up transfer. Can you drill down on that a little bit in terms of how that applies for multi-sport athletes, which these days is a big talking point in terms of youth overall development and sport retention.

There's a lot of work being done on long-term athlete development, LTAD, and whether you should specialize early or not specialize early. Transfer has an influence on what you believe you should do to have the best long-term athlete development that you can get. We know simply that if these motor programs are so incredibly specific, and there is reason to believe that they are, then one of the things that we would predict right away is that if you're playing basketball, it's not going to transfer very much to your ability to play volleyball, or any other kind of thing that you want to talk about. If you're playing softball, it's not going to transfer all that much to tennis, or even baseball, or what have you.

Once you have a belief in specificity, then you also have to have a belief in lots of other things. In transfer, and in whole versus block practice.

What else? There's still other things, progressions, and state dependent remembering, all those things essentially say the same thing if you study them experimentally. In my class I used to say we've got this broad base that you can't ignore it, there's just too much research support for this idea.

If I were putting together long-term athletic development programs in my country, which I'm not, I would be happy to have people specialize early if they wanted to. I'd have some kind of program there for that, but I'd also have programs for people that get into the sport when they're fourteen or something, and now they're going to learn to play volleyball. There are some things to be said for getting in early, and there are things to be said for no, don't get in so early. You'll get burnt out, and you'll get hurt, and what have you. I don't know what else you want me to say.

That's reasonable. Staying on the transfer side of things, it makes intuitive sense that at the fine motor skill level things are not going to transfer. You're not going to be able to take a jump shot in basketball and apply that to basically any other sport. On a more gross level, movement or anything like that, are there things which do transfer?

I suppose you could say everything transfers, but the question is how big is the transfer? Is it small, medium, or large amounts that we're getting from doing these different activities that we do? There's a bunch of stuff now that comes out about the neurological pathways that are going to be used when you do this movement, and it looks like it's just like this other movement. For example, in our country baseball guys hit balls off of a tee. I saw a thing on ESPN the other day where a guy was hitting balls off of a tee, a major league baseball guy. Hitting balls off of a tee and hitting a moving baseball are grossly very much alike, but the neurological commands that you need to put in place to do hitting a ball off a tee are just not the same as hitting a baseball. We would expect transfer to be very, very small.

There have been lots of studies that have done big motor things, not just little fine motor things, but big motor things, and what they find always is the amount of motor transfer is tiny. There's some there, but it's tiny. If you really want to get ahead, you can't be wasting your practice time on tiny little things, you've got to spend your practice time on the things that are really big and important.

Let's take that to coaching the BYU men. At the starting level you've obviously got to recruit and select players. Did any of this, the motor learning stuff, or the specificity, or any of that play into how you selected players for the squad, and if so, how?

We know that it doesn't have to do with specificity necessarily, but we know that initial ability and final ability are very poorly correlated. There's a guy right now in the NBA, you probably pay no attention at all to the NBA, but they just had the NBA championships and there's a guy there named Stephen Curry that was the MVP of the NBA. Now they're doing little articles about Stephen Curry and how when he was in high school he couldn't do this and he couldn't do that, and when he was in college he still couldn't do this and he couldn't do that. Finally now with all of his development he's the most valuable player in the NBA.

There are, I don't know, thousands of stories like that where these kids weren't very good and they got to be great. I coached at BYU for I think thirteen years, and during that time there were nine [particular] guys that came into my gym. Most of them were not recruited. They just showed up because they were Mormon guys and they wanted to go to school at BYU. They weren't very good and we would put them over on what is called, in our gym, the dark side because the lights weren't very good over there, so it was literally the dark side. We put them over there when they weren't good enough to be with us on the light side, and nine of them in twelve years ended up being first team All-American. If I'd have known they were going to be first team All-American I wouldn't have put them on the dark side in the first place, "Come and be with us, you're going to be an All-American."

How that influences the way you recruit is you're trying to get people. I don't guess I want 5'6 middle blockers. There's some body configurations that have to be there. In terms of who's going to get to be good, you don't really know. I actually wrote a paper for the FIVB one year where we talked about this, and I talk about all kinds of other professional athletes. Tom Brady, and on, and on, and on. What it says to me is coach as many as you can for as long as you can.

If you look at our national team, there are guys that won a gold medal. Riley Salmon, he was never good enough to play college volleyball. All kinds of Olympians in our country who were not very good when they were in college. What that means is what I just said. Okay, get a bunch of guys, get them in the USA gym. We do a pretty good job training people in the USA gym. Let's get them in and see what happens. Reid Priddy is an example. Just lots and lots of guys. Rich Lambourne is a libero. He was an outside hitter, and on and on.

Right, of course in Karch's case with the women he's got the advantage of having a vast pool. He can run fifty players through his gym in a year and barely scratch the surface.

If you look at the USA women in our country, there's been an immense player pool forever. The player pool for women is enormous in our country. But it's not until Karch became the coach, and Hugh became the coach, that they started training these girls like we train men in our country. I've had dinner with Karch on more than one occasion where we talked about specificity. Karch knows that stuff, and of course he was trained by Marv. Marv was not so focused on specificity because we didn't really know about it as much as we'd have liked, but we knew some.

The men in our country have got this tiny little player pool. My guess is there are more male players in Germany than there are male players in the United States. We've had a lot of international success because we train the guys better than we train the girls, who have not had international success until now.

Let's drill down on that. What was the difference pre-Hugh? What were the women doing that just wasn't working, or wasn't effective enough given the vast pool that they had available to them?

Way back in the '60s the Japanese were the best in the world, and they had a coach that was crazy, and he trained all these girls that won a gold medal. The Japanese women were gold medalists back in, maybe, I'm going to say '64, but I don't remember. It could have been '68. [The Japanese women won gold in 1964, and silver in 1968]

Anyhow, the women in Japan were really good, and a lot of coaches from Japan ended up coming to the United States to coach. I don't know exactly why that pipeline got opened, but maybe just because they were good and the people from the USA asked them if they would come and help us. Very much through our women's history we had Japanese and Korean [coaches]. Moo Park was our national team coach once upon a time, and we had a big influence from Asia, a big impact. They'd been doing that. The coach before Hugh was Lang Ping, I think. That's Asian of course. They'd been doing that since the '60s, and '70s, and '80s, and '90s, and 2000s.

If you come in a men's gym in the United States and watch practice, and come into a women's gym in the Unites States and watch practice, you're thinking, "Oh, my gosh, this is very different."

I've got a little handout thing that I give when I do coaching clinics, of how BYU won a conference a couple of years ago and they won fifty-two percent of the available points, and a team that finished eighth in the conference, in the Mountain Pacific Sports Federation, won fifty percent of the points that were available. It's not such news that we knew there were a lot of 25-23 games, and how slim the margins were for winning and losing. We think everyone knows that, but when you start looking closely you think, "Wow, it's even slimmer than I thought."

If I'm in a gym where I get one hundredth of a percent more transfer today than you get, I'm better than you in a hurry, if I'm getting one hundredth of a percent more out of practice than you are.

Without necessarily getting too specific, it sounds like in the women's gym there was a lot of block-oriented training. What they would have considered very technical training – not super game-like – whereas in the men's gym, much more game-like, much more random. Is that what was going on?

Yeah. In 2004 both the men and the women trained in Colorado Springs at the Olympic Training Center, and I was Doug Beal's assistant coach then. Toshi Yoshida was the women's coach, and there were lots of times where we would be in the gym at the same time. There were three courts in the main gym, and so we'd be on a court, the women would be on a court, and maybe there would be an empty court for whoever wanted to use it for a while.

Lasting impression is Toshi and Kevin Hambly would be up on tables hitting balls at their girls, and they would do it in some form that looked really impressive. They would hit this way, and they would hit that way, and then here comes one from here, and here comes one from there. You'd look at it and you're thinking, "Wow, this is really an impressive practice," but what's going on is they're standing on tables hitting balls at their girls, which isn't of course what we think learning how to dig is all about.

We'd be over on our side of the curtain and we'd be playing volleyball in one form or another, and they would hardly ever play volleyball. They would just dig balls that their coaches hit at them. Yeah, it was lots different.

Going back to what you were doing with the BYU guys, because some may not understand how the men's structure works. You get the players in the Fall when they start school, but you only have them for a minimal amount of time because of the NCAA rules. You don't really get them full on until January, and then the season runs through basically the beginning of May when the finals are. How would you set up your training over the different phases of your season?

There is a phase where you get all your players twenty hours a week. When the season starts in January you get your players twenty hours a week all the weeks, but in the Fall you get twenty hours a week for usually six weeks. They keep changing the NCAA rules. There was a time time when you could only have them two hours, and you could only have four of them. That was what you got for ten of the weeks. Say that a semester is sixteen weeks, so for ten of the weeks you can only have them two hours a week. What you're going to do then is you're going to have these individual and small group sessions and you're going to do everything you can to get the fundamental skills exactly the way you want the fundamental skills to be performed. It's not so bad.

Actually, the NCAA regulation ended up being some kind of a Godsend. Now you've got to pay attention to how the fundamentals work, you can't just start playing all of a sudden. You've got to make sure they know how to play.

I had a guy named Mike Wall who ended up being a two time All-American and a two time National Champion. He's now an assistant coach for the men's team. When he was a fifth year senior I was telling him, "Mike, this is the way I want you to hold your hands when you pass." Here's a guy, it's a fifth year guy, 42 inch jump [about 107cm], really a good player, and I'm making sure that he knows how to hold his hands when he gets ready to pass or dig a ball.

The fall semester meant our guys were going to have the fundamentals exactly the way we wanted the fundamentals to be. Maybe not the way Marv wanted the fundamentals to be, or how Scates wanted them to be, but the way we wanted them to be. They could learn that in the Fall, so it was a blessing, I think, that it was like that.

Of course in women's volleyball it's not like that. They're going to start practice in the middle of August and they're going to play volleyball at the end of August. They get the same rules that we have in the Fall. They get those same rules in the Spring or the Winter, whatever, and then they take Summer off. By the time they get back they're out of shape and they've forgotten how you're supposed to hold your hands. The way it is, men's volleyball in the United States is better than the way it is for women.

This is going to be a little bit of a detour, but I think we're going to get to this point anyway. You talk about having a very specific way you want your players to execute a given skill, and I understand you've been quoted as saying there's one correct way. Obviously, you just mentioned that Marv Dunphy might have a different way, and Al Scates might have a different way, but I'm presuming that when you say, "There's one right way," it's based on bio mechanics. Is it something where you're trying to teach every single player the exact same technique, or is it something where there's at least a little bit of adaptation from player to player based on their own physiology?

That quote that you just stated, I never said that.

That's good to know.

I play golf, and if you go down to the golf course, or if you go to the US Open that they just had, you can see the swing mechanics of pretty good pros. Mostly they look the same. This guy swings like that guy swings. What I do say is I think that some ways are better than other ways. I think this way is better than that way, and so I want you to come in my gym and play this way, because I think it's better. I'm worried about two percent. I can tell you a couple of stories about liberos. I guess I will tell you a story about Erik ... Who's Erik, jeez, I can't remember his name...

National team liberos?

National team libero.

Sullivan?

Yeah, Erik Sullivan. In 2002 I went with Doug to the World Championships in Argentina, and while I was there Doug said, "Carl, go coach somebody."

"Doug, what does that mean?"

He said, "Just go find somebody and coach them."

I'm wandering around and I see a libero. He's our libero so you know he's pretty good, or he wouldn't be our libero. Somebody else would be there. He's got a little thing that I don't like very much that he's doing when he's passing and digging. I tell him, "Erik, can I coach you?"

He looks at me kind of, "Sure, that would be okay."

I start changing the way he passes.

We're at the World Championships and this is a good player, and I said, "Okay, I want you to do this instead of that, and also we'll do this instead of that."

We start doing stuff and part way through the tournament I hear Doug say to Hugh, "Erik is playing better," so that fires me up.

When I get ready to leave and we're walking on the tarmac on the way to come back home out of Buenos Aires, Erik Sullivan comes up to me and says, "Carl, you really helped me. That's the best I've ever played."

We changed some little things and he played better.

In 2009 I'm with Hugh. He's coaching the women now and we're in San Juan Puerto Rico for a zone tournament, and Hugh says to me, "Go work your magic on Stacy Sykora."

I say, "Okay."

I go to Stacey and I tell her, "Stacy, I've come to coach you. Let me tell you about Erik Sullivan."

We talk about Erik Sullivan and she says, "Okay, let's go."

I'm coaching Stacy and she starts playing better, and she tells me when we're leaving, "That's the best I've ever played. I'm never going to change the way I do things."

We changed some little things and she played better.

My son, a couple years ago, was the AVCA Coach of the Year at BYU, and I went to the convention in 2013. I went to the banquet and I'm sitting at a table listening to him speak and Stacy comes up with her cell phone and says, "Carl, I just want to show you my cell phone. These are all the things that you told me back in 2009 and I still have them and I still use them when I play volleyball."

She was in Brazil playing and got hurt in a van wreck, and if she hadn't been hurt she would have played in the 2012 Olympic Games and I think they'd have been gold medalists because she was way better than the girl that played instead.

I could send you a spreadsheet with the BYU record in their conference for the last five, ten, fifteen, and twenty years. They were quite a bit better than all the other teams in the conference for the last five, ten, fifteen, and twenty years. I've fooled with Erik Sullivan. I've fooled with Stacy Sykora. I'm coaching BYU. I went to Switzerland not so long ago – 2007, 2008 – and changed the way they played. All of those things with Erik, and Stacy, and BYU for the last five, ten, fifteen, twenty made me think that some ways are better than other ways.

I ski with a guy who's the bio-mechanics instructor at BYU. We skied together all the time I was at BYU. We're both retired now, and we would talk about the bio-mechanics, "Should I do it that way?" Or, "That way's better than that way."

You can see that I have a strong belief that some ways are better than other ways. So I will be in our gym in August and be an assistant coach at the University of Hawaii [Hilo]. The coach there has said to me, "Carl, I already know how I want to play. You can coach the team. I want to find out how you want to play."

We're going to go teach those girls this way is better than that way. I'll sell that. We've already given them a book by Carol Dweck, and so they've read that and we're going to sell them that this way is better than that way, and that's what we're going to do. It makes sense to me. We haven't been crummy doing it this way.

How are you, for lack of a better word, defining the better way? Presumably there's a motor learning or mechanical aspect to that.

You're looking at the athlete and saying, no, if we adjust this position or this movement slightly, we're going to get, as you said, the two percent.

Yeah. We have some principles that we think for example, if we're teaching you to forearm pass we're going to say to you do you think the laws of physics apply to this skill? You're going to answer. The answer is ...? I'm waiting to hear it.

Yeah of course.

The laws of physics apply, and here's another thing we think applies – simple movements. It's better than if you make a complex movement. What do you think about that? Would you agree with that?

Yeah.

Okay, so we're two for two so far.

Let's add one more principle. We think that the ball will do unexpected things when it comes over the net to you, and the thing that you can respond best to unexpected events with is with something that has to do with hands and arms, better than legs, better than facing. Your hands and arms are very malleable, very adjustable. Let's use them to try to get a nice platform out there, to try to get the laws of physics in place.

We operate with those three principles, and if you can make guys and girls believe that these principles make sense, then what follows is if these are the principles, then we have to do these things to adhere to those principles. These things being, now we'll have some keys that we tell you about because motor learning says you need to have keys, and you need to have certain kinds, and you need to have them in certain orders and what have you.

Now we believe in our principles, and these keys are going to make it so that you look like this when you pass and dig. That makes perfect sense to me and to most of the people that we get to coach.

Being over in Europe, the culture of coaching, well, the culture of volleyball in general is interesting because obviously they don't have the education link that we do in the States – whether it be high school or college. Most things are run in the club system. So many aspects of it are different. There tends to be a more of a

pragmatic approach to things than may be the case for a lot of us coaches coming from the US system. The bottom line is the bottom line. Does the ball go where I want it to go? If so, then that's the technique that we need to use, or this player needs to use, or whatever.

I'm assuming that your argument would be that okay, yeah, that's fine but if you want to close that two percent gap that you mentioned before, then that's where you need to start getting into the finer elements and the finer details.

Yeah. We can argue successfully, I think, there are a lot more volleyball players over there than there are over here. Over there being Germany, or over there being almost all the countries over there. There are more boys playing volleyball than in the United States. Yet, USA has won lots of gold medals with a little tiny player pool.

I'm talking about the BYU team in the conference for the last twenty years, and it's not like everybody wants to come to BYU and have all kinds of rules and regulations placed upon them, and it snows here. A lot of boys are from California and they don't want to go over. It's not like UCLA and everybody's dying to come to our school. We're BYU and no one's dying to come to our school, but we're way better than anybody else for the last five, ten, fifteen, twenty years. What does that mean? I think it means what I'm telling you. What we're doing here must be good.

Let's circle back to how you handle the progression of the season. We talked about the Fall stage where for a certain phase you get them for just the two hours, and then the four hours in the weight room, or whatever, and you can work a lot on the mechanics. Once you get them into the traditional season, as they call it, in January, where does the focus go to at that point?

We focus on a couple of systems. We want our block and defense to get in place, and we'll start on that. We've already got them moving the way we want them to move, the footwork patterns, and the arms, and all of that stuff. That we could do with small groups. Now we get everybody for twenty hours, the whole group. Now the first thing we're going to put in is our block and defense, and once we get it so that we like it pretty good- maybe it takes us two or three weeks to get the foundation in place – then we're going to put our offense in place, and then we're going to try to just get better. Maybe we'll have a week or so to just get some good 6-on-6 stuff going on.

I know you've got non-conference competition at the beginning and then conference play before you get into playoffs and the NCAA tournament. Is there any sort of peaking idea throughout that progression, where you want the team to peak at certain points?

No. In the beginning, in January, I always wanted to schedule some wins. I'm never going to play some of the teams that BYU played the last two or three years. They're playing teams that are too good for them, and teams that ended up winning NCAA championships and stuff, but I didn't want to do that. I wanted my guys to get some wins under their belt, and then we just talk all the time about, "Okay, we want you to get better today. We want you to get better today."

That's the primary focus, get better today. You're going to have a list that you're working on that we've worked on together. When I tell you to get better today I'm talking about you doing this. I'm talking about that other guy doing that, and we're just going to keep going until it gets to be the end of April and we're starting to get ready for playoffs, and starting to get ready for the NCAAs. Now there's going to be some peaking going on. Mostly we're just trying to get better every day.

There will be times... I had a little form that I would give to the guys and they would fill it out telling me how they're doing, physically and mentally, and there would be times when I'll make practices shorter and what have you. There have been lots of times we had a day off and I went skiing. I don't think of those as tapering, or peaking, or anything. It's just like we need to have a day off. I guess you could think of it as tapering, but I didn't ever think of it as that. They were tired, okay.

How did you set up your typical week? You were playing mostly on the weekends, I presume? How would you structure the progression of training over the course of the week leading into your competition?

Monday would be not a heavy day. Tuesday would be a little bit heavier. Wednesday we'd get after it pretty good. It's going to take two and a half hours to do all the stuff we're going to do. Thursday it's going to take maybe a couple of hours, and then Friday and Saturday we're going to play.

You basically built intensity through the week up to match day.

Yeah. Thursday is, we're going to play really hard, but just not very long.

What were the guys doing in the weight room during the regular season?

During the Fall there would be a period where we would lift four days a week, and mostly we were doing Olympic style high, fast twitch kind of stuff. They have standards that we expect them to reach, and what have you. I had a team where I had four guys with 42 inch or greater jumps. I played my whole life and I never saw anybody with a 42 inch jump, and I had four of them on my team. We would get in the weight room and we would lift hard, and we worked hard in practice and the guys got better. There would be six, seven inch gains from when they were freshmen to when they were seniors.

At some point we're lifting four days a week, and then when we start with our twenty ... Then we would only lift three days a week. When we got to the regular season in January, we would lift one day a week, and usually on Monday morning.

I was talking with Mick Haley the other day and, this is probably something they're going to try and do this year. They're looking at during the season lifting every training day but only doing two exercises each session, and doing it after training. Instead of doing one longer session as I'm assuming you were talking about for your Mondays, it would be a series of much shorter sessions, I'm assuming.

I know this. We have the data, that you can get stronger if you're lifting one day a week. I also know that if I just had a hard practice, and practice should be hard. I don't want to come in and just screw around in practice. We're here to practice. The duration may vary, but we're trying to get better and we have to work hard to do that. I know that if I just had that kind of a practice I'm in no way interested in being in the weight room after.

With the national team, obviously the whole structure is very dif-

ferent. You're talking more training camps versus a sustained period where you've got them like you do at the college level, and you can work with players from freshmen on up. What's the philosophy at that stage in terms of approaching player development and approaching technical and tactical work?

I'm sure it varies. I can tell you what I think. I became Doug Beal's assistant coach on 2003. The guy that was his assistant had just got a new job at Arizona State University – Brad Saindon – and I had just retired. Doug said, "Do you want to come and be my assistant?"

I said, "I would love it. If I come over there I want to do some things. I want this to happen, and that to happen. I don't just want to have nothing to do."

He said, "Come on over. We'll spend four days in April and we'll talk about what you want."

I got over there and it was a Monday, and I said, "Well, I want to do this," and he said, "Okay."

"I want to do that," and he said, "Okay."

By the time the morning was over Doug had said, "Okay, you can do everything you wanted to do."

So I did it.

I got in the gym with all the guys who were going to be 2004 Olympians and we talked to them about, "We're going to change the way you play volleyball. We're going to play like this, as opposed to like that."

In the gym when I was there with Doug Beal we were all about playing volleyball with these fundamental movements, the stuff we've been talking about, you and I. We did that. We did that, we did that, we did that, and when we started we were ranked twelfth in the world at the time. We ended up being ranked fourth in the world when the Olympic Games were over in Athens.

Hugh, who was an assistant coach with me and with Doug, Hugh got the job. Hugh had played volleyball at BYU. Hugh knew what we were doing on the way to Athens because that's what he was used to as well. Hugh got to be the coach, and Hugh just kept going doing the same kind of stuff. This is the way we're going to play. He just kept going. You know, of course, that in 2008 the men won a gold medal. If you look at them, if you go watch them play, you're going to see they look a lot like BYU, the way they're playing, with the same passing movements, with the same blocking movements, with the same attacking movements. They look a lot like BYU looks.

That was it. Hugh was over in 2009. The Long Beach State coach became the coach [Alan Knipe]. At Long Beach State they don't play the way that we play at BYU. It was the first time since 1984 that the USA wasn't playing the same way they've been playing all these years. First there was Doug as the coach, and then there was Marv as the coach, and then there was Fred as the coach, and then there was Doug as the coach, and then there was Doug as the coach again, and then there was Hugh as the coach. All of those Olympic Games we had basically the same kind of stuff going on. We said, "This is the way that we play in this gym."

You're talking about making technical changes with players. These are guys who are either playing professionally overseas for the most part, and/or are college athletes who obviously are playing under different coaches. I'm sure there was some resistance – whether from the player themselves or their coach on the other end – to changing them to reflect the style that you guys wanted them to play in the USA gym versus what their professional club or their college team was doing. How did you overcome that sort of thing?

I think that in the first place, we can tell them stories about how much better people get when they come in the USA gym because we're going to play a certain way. We can tell them stories about Erik Sullivan if we want, about he just changed. We can tell them stories about the guys that were on that team in 2004, how they changed. The way that men play in our country is mostly the way that we play in our national team. It's much more alike than it is different. It's not that way in women's volleyball, it's much more different than it is alike in women's volleyball. In men's volleyball you don't have to change the world to get these guys to do some of these things you want them to do.

Kevin Barnett was a right side player in 2004 and I told him once upon a time, I told him, "Kevin, you're going to get cut from this team because you can't block on the right side. You're a real good blocker on the left side, but you don't know how to pass. There's no place for you on the right side, there's no place for you on the left side, you're going to get cut. What if we do this? What if we teach you how to pass?"

Of course he was all for that, and we taught him how to pass. He ended up being maybe our best passer and our best outside hitter in Athens. If you phoned Kevin Barnett and asked, "Did you change the way you were passing on the way to the 2004 Olympic Games?" he would tell you, "Yeah, I did, and I'm sure glad I did or I wouldn't have made the team."

For the moment, let me rewind things a little bit. You mentioned some of the names of coaches you've worked with. Who's been involved in terms of helping you develop as a coach over the years, and are there people or things that you continue to follow from your own developmental perspective?

The guy, of course, that got me going was Jim Coleman. He's the father of volleyball coaches in the United States. Then, of course, I got to hang out with all these guys that all had a big influence. I had to hang out on my own, too. When I first started coaching at BYU we were in the Mountain Pacific Sports Federation, everybody was terrific and we were terrible. There was a whole bunch of you better figure out how to do this yourself. John Lowell, Jim Coleman, those guys had a big influence. And of course Doug, Fred Sturm and Marv Dunphy. All of them. It's been wonderful.

Mark and I have managed to create a couple of heated debates having to do with a couple of different things. One of them is hitting and setting close to the net or not close to the net, which I know is research that has been done. I'll get to that in a second. One of the other things that we talked about was the value of digging versus the value of transition points. In other words, digs are not all created equal. The story that come up is that at one point, and this is, I think, when Erik Sullivan was still libero for the national team, he was fantastic at digging in six. Got lots and lots of digs, but the team discovered that they actually did worse, they scored fewer points.

We didn't discover that.

You didn't? All right, what's the true story?

The true story was he was good in the middle, and we put him there and he stayed there for the whole tournament.

There was no drop off in production from the pipe, for example?

No, we don't know that. We don't have that data.

Okay, inconclusive then.

No one knows that, but I do know what happened to Karch. He put his libero middle back, and their point scoring efficiency went up four percent.

Okay, interesting. Women versus men, so there may be a causality there. The women's pipe isn't as strong as it is in the men's game. That's interesting. The reason I brought up the whole tight set, not tight set is because there was a study that was done on the BYU women's team, I believe in 2006, where all the different facets of the game skills were examined for that season, and one of them was the distance from the net that the set was executed at and its impact on point scoring.

I've seen that report, and I know there are others that have been done in a similar vein. I haven't been able to go through them just yet. You being a researcher yourself, one of the issues that I've got with a study like that is it's not cross sectional, it's a single team in a single season, which introduces some potential biases into the results. One which actually came up in a discussion, was expectations. If a hitter is expecting the ball to be at a certain distance and it's set at a different distance, it may not be that the set at the alternate distance is any better or worse. It's just that the hitter can't hit the ball there because that's not where they're expecting it. Have people actually tried to do more broad based studies of these things?

That was a masters study that was done. The guy that chaired the study is Gil Fellingham, who knows quite a bit about volleyball and an awful lot more about statistics. One of the data points in that study is that hitting the ball out of the back row was one of the least efficient things you could do. When I look at that study, we talk about it in our coaching clinics, actually. This is maybe just because she was no good, not because hitting it from the back row is no good. I know, and the people I talk to know that, yeah, this is just BYU that we're looking at here and there's all kinds of reasons why the data can turn out the way they turn out.

We've got a guy now that's working for BYU volleyball, Giuseppe Vinci, that has VolleyMetrics as his little company. He now has the ability with the way he's charting – he's charting all these women's teams and all these men's teams, so he's got a really wonderful database. He's just now putting his company together, so I don't know what questions he's looking at or what answers he's giving, but I know pretty soon if you want to know something about men's or women's volleyball, Giuseppe Vinci is going to have great data.

Yeah, he's collecting a massive amount, isn't he?

Yeah, and it's done correctly, with Gil Fellingham supervising the whole thing because Gil knows.

Switching gears a little bit, you've stayed involved with the sports and involved with coaching for a considerable amount of time here, part of which, for a lengthy stage it wasn't even your primary focus. What's kept you motivated?

I like being in a gym. When I was little I liked to play. I got big and I couldn't play anymore, and if I was going to have anything to do then I had to be in the gym coaching, and I like it.

How involved do you stay these days?

I was Chris McGown's volunteer assistant coach for the last four years. There were plenty of perils to deal with, father/son kind of stuff. I didn't ever think it was my team to coach. It was his team to coach, so I was just doing what I was told, mostly. Now he resigned, and I'm going to go coach at the University of Hawaii Hilo Campus. My wife and I like Hawaii, so it'll be a chance to be in the gym having fun.

And away from cold Provo.

Yeah, but I'm going to go home. They're going to be through in the end of November, so I'll be home in time to strap my skis on.

Just in time to get going with the men's season in January.

Yeah, no. I've got to get asked, now they have a new head coach.

While I'm thinking about it, do you have a recommended reading list? You mentioned *Mindset* by Dweck. Is there anything else that you recommend to coaches?

I like *The Sports Gene*, I think. *The Genius in All of Us*. Have you read that?

I haven't yet. I think I've heard of it.

The Talent Code. I don't know if you've read that.

Yep, I have.

A book that's way old is *The 7 Habits of Highly Effective People*. That changed my life.

Yours and a lot of other people's.

Yeah, he sold millions of copies. Have you read *Moneyball*?

I'm literally reading it right now. I've seen the film and I know the basic story, but I'd never gotten around to reading the book.

The *Five Dysfunctions of a Team*.

I've heard of that one. I think that one's on my list.

You know Bill Walsh? He wrote a book *The Score Takes Care of Itself*.

I think somebody else mentioned that. I know Walsh has been mentioned before, but I'm pretty sure that book came up as well.

He wrote two. One of them was kind of all about football, and the other one was just more about coaching. *The Score Takes Care of Itself*. I quite like the fact that he says, "We're going to do things perfectly."

That was his standard, perfection. I wonder what's the definition of perfection? There must be something that you want to have exactly the way you want to have it.

Did you read *Outliers*?

I haven't yet, but again, it's on my list. I know the basic idea.

Yeah, that's all that's going to come off my head right now.

That's fine. Complete shift of focus here. You spent a season or two ... was it two seasons in Switzerland, or just one?

I spent a season, and then they made me their national team coach and I coached in the World University Games in Shenzhen, or however you say it. They were trying to get somewhere in the European Championships, and I coached against Croatia, and we lost against Croatia in a five set match. My outside hitter blew his ACL out to start game five. I was in Switzerland for two different summers and a regular league season from whenever, October to whenever we were done, April.

How did you find that experience in terms of coaching players from different cultures?

Like lots of things it's a long story here I'm going to tell you. When I retired as the coach at the university, Mike Wilton, and he was a former graduate student of mine. His assistant coach was his son. His assistant coach left to go chase a girlfriend to the mainland. Wilton called me and said, "Carl, I've got a job opening. Do you want to come and be a coach?" [This was at Hawaii]

I said, "I'll do it for the fall semester because during the winter semester I want to be skiing in Provo, Utah.

He said, "Okay."

Fall semester of 2005, I guess, I was his assistant coach, and he said to me when I went there, "You do what you want, I'm going to listen." That, of course, is attractive.

There was a guy on the team named Lauri Hakala and there was another guy, he was from Finland. He's now the assistant coach of the Fin men's team, and another guy, Matt Carere, who was a Canadian. They both ended up making All-American after I was there, and they weren't any good at all before I went there. I did that, and then he wanted me back a second year, so I did it again, and then I had a chance to go to Switzerland.

I'm telling Lauri, we were just talking on the phone, he hasn't graduated from school yet. I'm telling him, "Hey, I'm going to go to Switzerland and coach."

He phones me back the next day and says, "I want to go."

I said, "Well, it turns out we need an opposite."

Lauri is 6'2 but he can get on the ball in a hurry. So I said, "Yeah, that's good, we'll make you an opposite."

Two days later Matt Carere called and said, "Listen, I want to go."

We needed an outside hitter and Matt was an outside hitter, so those two guys came to Switzerland with me. They told the other guys when we got there and were having our meetings, "Just do what Carl tells you and it will work out just fine."

If you watched the Swiss team that I coached you would look at them and you would say, "Gee, that looks like BYU."

I had help. I had Lauri and Matt telling these guys. Some of them... There was a 32 year old Polish guy. There were some Swiss guys that were in their thirties that had been playing for a long time. Switzerland is not Italy, of course, or Russia. Anyhow, there were professional volleyball players there and I changed the way they played and it wasn't hard at all because Lauri and Matt said, "Just do this. Just shut up and it will be fine."

It's always great when you can have your own players evangelizing your philosophy.

Yeah, it was wonderful.

You've coached women a little bit, though not nearly as much as you've coached the men. Is there any difference in how you approach coaching them at all?

Not really. You don't have them hit out of the back row, so that's different. The women want to get better and they can play. The fundamentals are basically the same, some of your systems are a little different.

You talked about how in the collegiate game in the US these days everybody basically plays a very similar system to the way the US national team plays, and Mark made the observation that when he scouts teams he knows without even having to look at them, on the men's side, that about eighty percent of what they do is the same. There's only about a twenty percent variation from team to team, whereas if you look at women's teams – this isn't the US but it's

globally – the styles of play are considerably different. Not even just necessarily from country to country, but even within countries, as you say, with the US. Do you have any theories on why that would be?

No, no theories. My basic one would be Japan got here way back when, and now we've still got a lot of Asian stuff going on. If Karch keeps coaching, a bunch of that variability is going to go away.

2

GIOVANNI GUIDETTI

Italian Giovanni Guidetti increased his international coaching credibility up another notch by leading the Netherlands Women's National team to the medal round of the 2016 Olympics in Rio. The success of the Dutch women surprised many, though probably not those who have followed Giovanni's career. After all, this is a coach who previously led the German women to some of their best performances. And that's just on the international side of the sport.

Giovanni coaches professionally in Turkey where his women's club team at VakıfBank has won both the CEV Champions League and the FIVB Club World Championship. Of course, he got his start coaching in Italy, both in the professional leagues and in the national team set-up. He was twice named Coach of the Year in his native land.

This interview was conducted by Mark in September, 2015. Though English is obviously not his first language, Giovanni speaks eloquently (with the occasional colorful language) on the subject of volleyball and coaching.

To begin with, can you tell us about your background in volleyball and how you came to the place you are now.

My father was a volleyball coach. He wrote probably the best volleyball book that there is still in Italy right now about to how to teach volleyball, from a young player to the most experienced player. But, in his time he didn't have the chance to be only a volleyball player because the money for volleyball was not enough. So he was, in the meantime, a volleyball coach in schools, and tennis coach, and so on.

I just started very young with volleyball, and I played a lot. When I was around 18, 19, I realized that I was not going to be a player of a high level. At 21 years old, I became an assistant coach of a Second League team. At 23, I became head coach of a Second League team. At 25, I became head coach in the First League in Italy. Always in women's volleyball.

From that, they called me, because at that moment I was a coach and I was still able to play good volleyball, so they called me to be an assistant coach of the Italian National Team. I was in Sydney [Olympics] as an assistant coach of the Italian National Team. And in these three or four years I learned a lot. Meanwhile, I was also coaching the youth Italian team and the Club Italia Project.

Then I had an experience outside Italy, in a project in America called USPV, United States Professional Volleyball. They were trying to introduce a professional league in America, and I was running tryouts, and just teaching some volleyball, and promoting volleyball.

Then, I came back again to Italy. I did some work again in the First League. And then I started with Germany. Sorry, I had one summer in Bulgaria [National Team]. And we played in the European Championship. After Bulgaria, I went to Germany, where I stayed 8 years. And, meanwhile, I started also in VakıfBank, Istanbul, where I will coach for my 7th season, this season, if I'm not wrong.

The Germany experience is with the National Team?

Only the National Team. Women's National Team from 2006 until last summer, in 2014. In 2007, I started in VakıfBank, in Istanbul. And I'm still there. From this summer, I took this new job of Holland Women's National Team. This is pretty much my career.

The reason why I started is very clear: because I'm in love with this sport from when I was really young. I don't know if this love came naturally or because I was used to seeing a lot of volleyball. When I was 3, 4 years,

I was hoping for the match of my father would finish so I could go hit some balls on the wall and try to make some attacks. From there spending all summer just playing volleyball and beach volleyball. I really fell in love with Karch Kiraly, Pat Powers, [Aldis] Berzins, [Craig] Buck and the Doug Beal [1984 Olympics] National Team.

It's just what I love to do most, and I was pretty lucky for the chance that I got.

Most people probably won't be very familiar with the Italian system. Can you describe briefly how the Italian system works, where Club Italia fits in to the system, so other people have a little bit of an understanding.

I think it's different than many other countries. Sport in Italy is totally separated from the school. In schools you just have two hours sport a week. All the sporting activity is outside the school and so there are millions of clubs. People don't believe me when I tell them my town, Modena which has less than 200,000 people, has 50 volleyball clubs or maybe around 100.

Each one of these clubs has a minimum three, four teams in many categories, or maybe even five or six or seven. We have two great teams in the First League – Liu Jo [women] and Casa Modena [men] – they are both playing First League in men and women. Then there are really millions of these young little clubs that are competing in a lot of different competitions from amateur to professional.

So the Italian Federation has a big amount of players and a big amount of clubs. Of course they have the national team program that runs during summer, and they created this program [Club Italia]. Actually we were part of the beginning of this program. Because this idea started with Julio Velasco and Angelo Frigoni, but Velasco left early for Lazio [the soccer club]. That's where I came in.

When we started Club Italia, the idea was to pick the best players of Italy that were not good enough to play in the first league, but good enough to play in the national team [in the future], and just train them.

The Club Italia program is a success, because we have players who are at a stage where they are talented and need professional training, but are not good enough to be professionals in some clubs, or would go to clubs where they know they don't have a chance to play. That's why Club Italia was created.

I built most of my career outside Italy. In Italy I had great club experiences, and was fortunate to get experience with the national team, but it is in the last 10 years of my career working outside Italy where I have had the best achievements in my career.

I guess that your father was your first influence as a coach, but who were some of the other influences that you had in the beginning and as you gained experience and continued on this travel?

I can tell you about couple of influences. For example, for sure, I fell in love with the American National Team and took a lot of inspiration from American volleyball. One time I had a couple of weeks free, I just emailed Doug Beal and asked him, "Can I come visit you and ask questions?"

It was a kind of weird email, but then he replied "with pleasure", and so he invited me to his office. He gave me four, five days of his time off to just listen to my questions and answer them in a very honest and very full way. That was one of the greatest experiences that I had.

Still a very big inspiration of mine, as well as a very good friend of mine, is Julio Velasco. These are the two people that I had the chance to talk a lot to and to get real inspiration. Together with them there is my father. These are the three people I am lucky to talk to more. After that I really admired a lot of the work and passion of Ze Roberto and Bernardinho [the Brazilian Women's and Men's National Team coaches respectively]. These are pretty much the coaches that I admire and really take most of my inspiration from.

Are there some things you can think about your training philosophy, how it has changed from when you began when you were 21 to how you are now?

I think that the training philosophy didn't change much. I think from the beginning I always was very attracted and passionate about teaching volleyball. Maybe because I came from a family of teachers. Both of my sisters are teachers. My mother was a teacher, my father was a teacher. I mean I'm the stupid one of the family because I don't have any of their very high academic levels.

I mean I always have this passion [for] teaching and I think I didn't lose this for sure. I think it's still the same like when I was 21. Just of course now I can teach better, I can find the solution to the problem quicker. I can find the right focus for any player quicker.

Basically my philosophy of working was always the same. It is a mix of learning and to give to the player all the instruments they need. So give to the player all the, how to say, bullets in their gun that they can use. Then combine them in the game of the team. It was always a big combination of how much they can become better as an individual player, how much they can learn, and the skill.

I have always focused on teaching as much as I can to the player. I know that for some coaches maybe this is even wrong. They say, "Okay there is [a short] time you just have to use what they have." I agree, but also I want to give them what they don't have.

I always try to give them everything to try to make them as perfect as they can be. Then of course combining this with fun, so I think I didn't lose that. I liked to have fun in the gym when I was 21. I like to have fun now, so the atmosphere in the gym and the way of working is very near to a family system or a group of friends that are there to achieve the same goal. Then of course to try to put the team together and to make it the best that it can be to win.

I don't believe this philosophy of work has changed a lot. It is my behavior that changed a lot. If I watch myself 10, 12 years ago, I was not the coach that I am now and maybe I changed. I became too angry, I was too irritating for my players from the bench, and I was reacting most of the time in a too aggressive way. That then was fun for the people watching me, it was fun for the journalists, but it was not helping the players.

That's what I learned this year. I also had the good fortune to work with a very good sport psychologist and mental trainer for three, four years with the German National team. They just helped me a lot to focus on my behavior. I am still, of course, very passionate, but I think I am able to control much more. This has been the biggest change on myself in those years.

What about in terms of methods of training, methodology?

It's difficult to put a classification on my methodology. I think I am a good observer and I am a good learner and so with the fortune that I had to travel so much in the last 10-15 years of my volleyball life, I really tried to take the best from every philosophy. I'm telling you that I admire a lot of the American Volleyball philosophy, but if you see the way I'm working maybe I'm closer to the Brazilian way of working.

Also, I had the fortune of having the assistant coach of Japanese National Team for two years at VakıfBank. This also gave me a lot of insight about the way they are teaching technique, how they are seeing the skills in Japan. This gave me a lot, combined with my big Italian background.

I hope I am a good mix of all of them, and I always make this point in every coaching clinic. I always say, that after I have the chance to see so many players, so many coaches, so much high level volleyball, I took this and that from them. I don't know if it's the best way, because there is not one way to do the things. There are many way to do the things and that is what I think is better for me.

If you listen to the Americans, I mean, I saw your website and in your website you have [Carl] McGown. When McGown speaks about volleyball, he's showing the six, seven coaches on boxes attacking on the net and he is saying in America "we never do this". Then you go to Brazil and you go see the training of the Bernardinho and you see for 3 players, 10 coaches all on the boxes and they are training like this.

Then you look at the history of volleyball, I don't have the exact number, but let's say United States has 20 gold medals, Brazil has 20 gold medals. You can say "they are wrong they are right, they are right they are wrong". They are seeing volleyball in a very different way. If you look at the Russians, they see it a different way again, and they are winning.

I think this is the key of our job. It's stupid, I think, to just marry a philosophy and just go with it, because there is not one philosophy. There are many, many ways to achieve the result. It's according to what we think is correct. Because I believe that the first thing that we have to be like as a coach is that we have to be authentic. I don't know if it's good English, authentic. I think you understand what I mean. We have to be ourselves every time. We have to do something that we believe, and there is no truth about nothing. That is what I think, mostly.

I saw in the press this week, I think, that next season in VakıfBank

you'll work with an American assistant. Is this deliberate to have a different influence?

Absolutely. I told you I had a Japanese assistant two years ago. Then this year I really pushed to have this Jamie [Morrison, assistant coach to Karch Kiraly in the US Women's National Team], American assistant, actually was first assistant with the men's team when they won the Olympic medal in London. In London, I guess so, no, the previous one.

In Beijing.

Beijing yeah. He was an assistant with the men team when they won the gold in Beijing. He was an assistant with the women when they won the silver in London. I think I can learn a lot from him. I already met him and just the idea is to have a different way to see volleyball. I will put three coaches on the boxes and he will tell me, "We don't do that." That way we start the fun, "Okay, I will tell you why I like it, you tell me why you don't like it."

Then we have to see if we can find a rule about that, we can find something that you convince me or I convince you, or maybe we are both right. That will be my season. I'm sure I can really learn a lot and maybe also he can learn a lot and we can really share our experience to both become better.

That's a great philosophy. You often choose your staff in this way? Do you have a philosophy for choosing your staff or it just works out this way?

No, that's the way I try to put [together] my staff every time. The first rule of my staff is that everybody — I try — that everybody should be able to handle a volleyball because I need a lot of people helping me, attacking and serving and just putting the ball [into the drills]. I want people that can handle a volleyball. That is the first thing.

The second thing, I want the best staff that I can have. I just try to pick the best person I can have and I force them to say to me every time that I'm wrong and they are not agreeing with what we are doing. That is what I'm really searching from my staff. I was never scared to have people too good near me, so no, that's totally opposite. I want the best people I can have because I really want to become better.

I really think that the most difficult part in our job is to improve and to become better. Especially with the life that I've got, that I love it because I really love [it] ... I'm thankful for all the coaching life and the life that I'm having.

In 12 months I have maybe two weeks free. Normally these two weeks free, I don't spend these two weeks free to become a better coach. I just use these two weeks free just to relax and have fun and to escape volleyball. How can I become better? How can improve if I don't go to university every day?

Of course I try to do everything to learn new things, because I cannot travel to see other coaches and to see other volleyball programs. What I can do, because sometimes I have the means, is just to try to have a very different kind of assistant coach that can help me. Mostly they can tell me that I'm wrong in what I'm doing, in what I'm saying. I always try to have great people near me.

I mean this Japanese coach, my assistant coach, became head coach of the Turkish National Team this year, and next year I will have an assistant coach from the United States. In that I will have a lot of possibilities to learn something. That's what I'm trying to create in my staff.

Also for example, if I would have continued coaching the German National Team, I was already clear that I wanted to have in my staff a successful men's coach in this summer. That's why we were also thinking about you, because you are working in Germany, and was one of the first names. Then we didn't decide to continue with the German National Team, but also that was the idea, so always in this direction.

It's a very interesting theme. We've done 16 or 17 interviews now – something like that – with coaches from all over the world. Nearly all of them talk about learning and getting better and that you can never stop and you have to keep improving yourself and it's a really strong theme from all of these coaches.

I think if it's not like this, how can we teach our players to become better? I think it is normal we want our players to become better. I'm coaching Sheilla and she's a two-time Olympic champion and I want to make her better and she wants to become better. How can I be genuine in doing that if I think that I'm good enough and I don't have to become better?

I cannot teach something that I don't believe. I believe that everybody can become better because I believe that every one of my players can become better and I'm not a better coach than Sheilla is a player. If she can become better I also can become better. This is, I think, a very natural process, a very natural way to think.

I agree. To talk about some specifics now about the training and working with the team, how do you look at the different parts of the season? Do you work in different ways in the different phases? Focusing on the club season rather than the national team season.

Basically the way of working doesn't change. I try to have, as much as I can, two training sessions a day. One training session is individual work and physical work. It's pretty much one hour fitness and one hour of individual technique and another session that is team work. This way of working is actually the same from the first day to the last day. It is the same from the first day to the last day of national team.

I believe too much in this hour of individual work where there is basically one coach for every player in the gym. If maximum, I have five players and I have more than five coaches every time. This is the part that I really believe in so much.

Of course then, there is the-six on-six in the evening, but it's not in the evening because I'm also changing a lot. When it's further from competition, I'm now liking much more to have six-on-six in the morning, and the individual work and fitness at night. When it's closer to competition, I do the opposite. I cannot say your morning is individual, night is six-on-six because it's not true. That's why I just like to talk about two sessions.

This doesn't change much. Of course there is change in the amount of work. Maybe in the beginning of the season when we are far from an important competition, the volume of work changes a lot. The volume of work changes a lot depending on the time of the competition. That is clear. The further we are from the competition; the six-on-six training is three hours. The closer we are to the competition; the duration of training is around two hours 30 minutes.

It is our system so there is less focus on the opponent. The tactic is not so important because it's like I want to give a clear system about the way we want to play volleyball. When we are in the second part of the season when the system should be already something clear, then I go into more specifics about the tactics and opponents that we have to deal with every week, which of course becomes more important.

I know that a lot of my colleagues will judge me very badly about that, but I was always against the big programming. In Italy we have some very specific ways to cycle or maybe also in international, macrocycles, microcycles.

I'm pretty against [that] because of course I made my plan. I also try to give to the players when I can a monthly plan; when we train and free days and so on, but it's our job, and it's a daily job. I know what I need tomorrow exactly after I see what happened today. Because I can put in my mind "Yes, today we work side out, tomorrow we work block and defense" or "Today we work reception, tomorrow we work more defense or setting". Then if today I see something that was not enough or was so weak or maybe I saw another part, and tomorrow already I have changed my mind.

It's difficult for me to give you this answer because I don't make big plans. It's like I think being a coach is like being a doctor. You see every day what your team needs more and then you adjust your work around what the team needs — if they need more aspirin or they need more antibiotic or they need more juice. It's something that you just face day by day and you just face training by training.

You said that sometimes you do the six against six in the morning, sometimes in the afternoon. Is there a reason for one or the other?

Yeah, like always I took inspiration from Velasco. He started with this system. If Velasco starts something, I always try because I always believe it's something clever. I can tell you that I had great result because the main idea is about the focus. I mean it's obvious that people can focus better in the morning. It's already proven in any office that from 9:00 to 11:00 everybody is more productive than from 13:00 to 18:00. This is clear, so it's clear for myself individually and it's clear for every person.

That's why I like a lot the six-on-six in the morning. Because the six-on-six is actually the most concentrated part in the training of the player where they have to really pay attention [to] any details. I found it great to see some six-on-six training in the morning, I really saw big a difference from the six-on-six at night.

The level of attention never dropped too much and the focus of the player is from the beginning very high. At night I just give them a lot of repetition of technique, where of course there is always a little focus needed, but not as much as the six-on-six. The session is a lot of repetition and strength and conditioning with the trainer.

Then, as I always like to do, I also like to ask for feedback from the player, and we have great observation from our eyes, and we have great feedback from the players. I like to use this system now a lot, especially further from the competition. When we are near the competition, I don't really know if this is correct, but I like to train more at the same time we play matches.

This is the only little change, and that's why near the competition I prefer to train the six-on-six at night because it's more like the time where we play matches. Far from the competition I really like the idea of the team work in the morning and individual work in the evening.

I haven't heard this idea really before. American teams, the national teams work in the mornings, but this I think has also some historical reason. I'm not sure that it was for reasons of attention, but of course when you say it it's logical.

The Americans told me they are doing this because it's the only chance that they have. Because they have a huge gym without air conditioning and they cannot train at night. They told me, "We do one training a day." I prefer to have two trainings a day, but with this new reason. With this new idea I'm happy and the team is happy.

These are two good successes already.

When it comes to developing the concept of the team how do you go about this work? You said with the German team you did some work with a sports psychologist and mental trainer. What are your ideas for developing the team concept?

The team, at the end, is the result of our job, I believe. Then there can be some exception, where the coach does nothing to create a team, but in that way they are creating a team. This is the most logical, the most difficult part of our job. It's the most logical because if you don't create a team you won't win anything, and the most difficult because there is no formula to create a team.

Of course we can say the things that everybody knows. You have to have the same goal, you have to treat the person with respect, you have to be all the same, blah-blah-blah. This is something that is obvious. I can't tell you anything new.

The magic I think I like to see every year is the team becoming a team. Because no one season is the same as another. There are always one or two changes in the players, there are always one or two changes in the staff. There are always little or big changes, but in the end a team has to become a team to perform.

How you do that? I think the first very, very, very important part that I try to always put in my head everyday is that the least important player on the team is the one that has to have the most attention from me. This is one rule that I have in my job with the player and with the people in the gym.

The man in VakıfBank who is there only to clean the gym and put the net up, is the first one I say "Hi" to in the morning and the last I say "Bye, bye" at night. The language sometimes is complicated, but I try to give really a lot attention to him and it's because he's really the least important.

The same is with the players. The more I care about the younger players of the team, the number 12, 13, 14 in the team, the more the team will be united. Because this player they will be part of the team, they will feel their importance from the coach, and so they will give everything to the stars to perform well. We start to come together.

As we start to become, you know, me helping the young that they want to be stars. The stars, of course, belong to me because I'm the one that gives them the instruction. We are starting to become one team, together with the man that is putting up the net and cleaning the gym, and together with every member of the staff. This is important to me, and this is just one thing.

When you want to create something great, you just have to put everything together and everybody has to have the same importance. There are a thousand examples of this. The example that I use most is of the orchestra. There is one guy that is just using the triangle. He's playing this triangle once every 30 minutes, but he has to do that with the same passion that the main violin is playing the solo all night. This is the team. There is no other exception.

It's so important how the coach is in the gym. How much I can be fair with everybody. How much I can put my hand on the back of everybody, the concept I can tell you about the team. It's more something that I think is magic. That's the great part of the job, because it's something that you see that is developing and creating.

Actually, you don't know how it came. I mean you know, but you don't know, but in the end it came. Sometimes it came great, sometimes it came terrible. When it goes terrible, you feel guilty and you start to ask, "What was my mistake?" At the end, when it goes terrible, you realize that as a coach you made a lot of mistakes. Because you were not fair with some player, so this player took so much power, and then she put another player in a very bad situation.

The way I like to think is it's never the fault of the player. It is always my fault that I let this happen. Of course, it's not a democracy, because there is always somebody that has a different job, but it's this idea to be one that makes a big difference.

This I like to think of like magic because this magic is the result of our job. It's not the result of luck. It's not the result of some circumstances. Sometimes, for sure, something extraordinary can happen, but it is mostly the way we act with everybody. That's why it's so important that we can give attention to every little detail that there is in the gym.

In your career, you worked in different countries sometimes as a national team coach where you were the outsider, sometimes in a multicultural group. How do you go about working with different cultures and understanding and working with people from a range of different cultures?

One thing that I like a lot that happens sometimes is to know that a Turkish player meets a German player or a Bulgarian player or an American player or a Holland player or a Serbian player that has worked with me and they are saying all the same things. They are joking about me or telling stories about me, but nobody is surprised about what the other one is saying.

That means that I'm basically the same coach. It doesn't matter if I'm coaching in Turkey or in Holland or in Germany. I try to be myself everywhere I am. Then we come back to the idea I said at the beginning about being authentic, to be real. I don't try to adapt myself. I don't try to change myself. Because this is me and this is the way I like to coach you. We have to create the team together. That's why I like it when the players talk about me they don't find any surprises.

Then, of course, I have to adapt a little bit for little cultural differences. What I'm always telling everybody is I don't know if I was particularly lucky or if it is really like this, but inside the gym there is not a big difference to training a Turkish team, a German team, a Holland team, a Bulgarian team that wants to win.

If they want to win, they are the same. If they don't want to win, if they are not really motivated 100%, then of course there are differences. Of course there are countries that are always very disciplined. There are countries where if they don't really have a big goal they are less disciplined. That's okay. You can see also the way some countries drive cars, so it's in the culture. It's different.

When a team has a goal, and a clear goal, and they want to achieve something, I don't see in the gym any differences between a high level Turkish player or a high level Holland player or a high level German player or a high level Bulgarian. They all go in the gym with the same idea. We want to be better every day and we want to win every day. It's another magical thing that you know is really the same.

Of course, when I leave the gym, if in Turkey I don't look three times right and left, I am dead. When I leave the gym in Germany, I already know that I will be the worst driver in the whole country. In the end, this has nothing to do with our job. This is just a different way people are living – they are eating, they are talking, they are having fun.

In the gym I think there is only one language. There is the volleyball language and the top sport language that is the same in the world everywhere, so you want to improve every day as much as you can.

It's a really interesting observation. I think a lot of the times we talk about cultural differences, at least in sport, they are much smaller than we might imagine if we read the newspaper about how people are. Once they are in the gym, there is a lot more similarities than differences.

I totally agree, I totally agree. It's really like this. I mean outside the gym it's so... I mean if you now look at Turkey, Germany, you know what's going on, you cannot even think they can live together. Then you put Christiana Fürst training with Gözde and they are training in the same way. They have the same character.

They both want to be the best in the world. [Outside, their countries] can kill each other, but then these two they are exactly the same because I'm talking about two top players. These two top players, they act exactly the same.

A little bit more general things about the qualities of a coach. The coach has to do a lot of different things with terms of relationships and tactical knowledge and technical knowledge. What do you think are the most important parts of the work for the coach?

Communication and knowledge. I believe these are the two most important qualities. I'll just answer very quickly. Maybe if I think about the main things, I can give you a clever answer. The coach has to be able to communicate with every member of the gym. From the cleaner to players to the staff, and to understand people, and then to make the people believe in him, and give people a way to come together. You cannot do this without communication. This communication is the base of everything.

If you are a great and amazing communicator, or you are like the best psychologist philosopher in the world, but you cannot teach a player why he cannot attack a short diagonal angle, then you lose everything.

That's why I think it's about communication and knowledge, because then the player is okay. If you communicate with him, he'll say, "Oh, he is a great coach. I admire him. He gave me a great goal. He put the team together. He's great, amazing wow." Now we go in the gym. I take a block. "Coach, what can I do?" Then your answer is, "Come on, come on, you can do it." Then you will lose respect day by day, because when the player asks you, "What can I do, why did I get aced?" You will have to tell him what to do. You have to give them the answer. If you know why we cannot stop the player, you have to tell the team how you can stop this player.

If you don't have the knowledge, but you have great communication, its bullshit. If you have great knowledge, but you cannot communicate your knowledge, it becomes bullshit because they don't listen to you.

This combination, I really believe, is the key of everything. That's why I think every one of us, every one of us needs to try to be better at these two things. I want to learn a new drill. I want to study the team better to make my players better, to give my players a better answer. In the same way I want to become a person that has good relationships with everybody. I want to be better with the communication.

We hate as coaches, when there are moments where you don't want to speak with somebody. This is the thing that happens to everybody where you really think, "I cannot even watch him or I cannot even watch her. I don't want to talk to her." It happens to all of us and this is the moment when you have failed, because this is where you don't want to be. You always want to have good communication, a good talk with every player, and with every member of the staff.

These are really the two key words. Actually it was not so unclever an answer. Because I really believe these are the two key words.

I think the answer was a great answer and clever.

Yes I am thinking I will keep this for the future.

We are thinking about the work of the team during this season. Maybe like the iceberg, the match is the small part of the iceberg that everybody sees and the big part that's under the water that happens in the privacy of the gym. Which part is more important?

For what? To keep your job the most important is the match. This is clear. I mean in the end–

Okay, I'll change the question a little. In terms of being successful in winning the match, is it more important the work in the week or the substitutions and time outs that you do during a match?

Okay.

Your answer could be still correct because sometimes if you call the timeouts or make the substitutions it means you did a good job even if they had no effect.

Yeah true, true. I think that when I won my first Champions League… I mean I'm not a great social man. I don't even remember where I wrote something, but I know a lot of people, a lot of my friends said, or maybe I just said to a journalist "Now people are talking about me and that I am a great coach, but I am the same coach I was yesterday. The difference was that now my team won something that everybody saw. This doesn't change anything about the way I'm working and the way I'm teaching volleyball. I was teaching volleyball the same three years ago when I was losing and I'm teaching volleyball the same now that I win."

I believe that if a coach is a great coach, it's not the coach that has more medals, but it's the coach that improves players more. That means, also maybe his team plays the best that the team can play, but it's not the reality. The reality is showing that the best coaches are the ones that have more medals. It's always a difficult topic. I really believe that the job of the coach is to make the player better, and to make the team better. This is our job.

Of course I am very happy when I win a championship, but at the end I am much more happy if I arrive second and then I got three emails from my player and they are telling me, "Giovanni, pity that we lost, but thanks a lot because I cannot remember all the things I learned this year because I learned so much and I became a better player thanks to you." This email for me counts more than this medal for sure, but in the world we are living nobody cares about this mail. Everybody wants the medal.

In the same way, there are weeks that we are training badly, because maybe I am pissed with one player, or the club is bothering me, or I am not having a clear idea of what I have to do, and so the training is a mixture of nothing. Then comes the match, I'm losing 2-0 and then desperately, I change five players and I win 3-2 and I am a hero.

Then there is another week that we train more perfect than Bernardinho or Ze Roberto could match. Then we go in the match, we shit in our pants, I make two changes. They make a serving mistake and we lose 3-0. This is what happens. It's difficult to say what can be more important.

I just think that the match is the result of the work. The timeout and the training and the adjustments in the match are what you train for in the week. That's why it's great, because if in the match, I want to put one player in, it's because in that week this player has shown me something, because in that week I gave some attention to this player. Then because in this week, this player made something, that in that moment, in that match I said, "Okay come in." Then maybe she changed something, or the timeout. You know I cannot make a timeout in Japanese. I will make timeout telling basically the same thing that I use also in the week, because this is my language, because this is my way to speak about volleyball.

That timeout maybe one time can be amazing, successful. That is still the result of the work of the week. At the end, it is all part of how well you work in the week – How well you train in the week. How careful you are about all the details in the week. Then the match should be the result of that.

Yes, I tend to agree with that, but you hear sometimes some different things. One coach [Dutch coach Redbad Strikwerda] we spoke to said the match was more important because it has to be the match because this is where the players will lose the faith in the coach.

I heard Hugh McCutcheon also talk that he would like to be good at everything, but if he had a choice he would be better at teaching. It's like everything, good coaches who approach from a different angle.

Yeah, that is the good thing about this. Always there is no true answer and there is no one answer. I really believe so much in the work, so nothing in life comes without that. That's why I'm a big, big believer in how much you can produce from Monday to Saturday. Then the Sunday you just collect what you have earned and maybe you do great, but the other team is better than you. Then you just have to go back and work harder.

Maybe you can work as hard as you want, you can never reach the level of the other team because also they are working hard as well. This is facing reality and is another very, very critical part of our job, how well you handle this moment.

You talk about the work here. Maybe I already know the answer to this question, but what's your favorite part of coaching, the thing that you like doing the most?

Communication and teaching.

Of course teaching.

Also fighting, I like a lot.

Fighting with the –

No, by fighting I mean to compete. Competing I like a lot. I mean there is no one who trains without points – no one at all. This is all about competing at the end. Myself, I like to compete for everything, for everything with myself, with my friend, with my wife, with my colleagues. Competition is a really nice part. I mean the competition is the benzino [fuel] of everything. Because without matches, without competition, maybe we don't like this job as much as we like it.

Of course we like to teach, because we like to win. The better we teach, the better our players become, and the more chance we have to win in the end. This is maybe another part that I really love a lot, you know, this competing – with competing, with everything. The way I see life, it's always a competition. First of all against yourself, and then against the adversity that life can give you, and then against the other.

These three aspects, this is communication, the time with the team, and creating the team, I love it. The teaching part is what I am here for and the competition is the benzino of everything, the one that really gives you the gas to go.

The competition is the thing that keeps you motivated when working eleven and half months of the year for eight years in a row?

Yeah, together [with] to make the players better. I mean for sure I can coach a team for up to twelve months without a match, but at the end, it will be very, very complicated. It will become very complicated if you don't have competition. The competition is what also motivates the players to become better, to try to win and to try to become better. It's all connected.

In the end I think of our job like Lego. There is no other thing because at the end we want to win. At the end we are doing everything that we can to win. Make the players better is, for sure, an amazing part or the most important part of our job, but because at the end we want this player to win. This is why the competition has so much importance.

To go a little different direction now, I know because I know we've

spoken about this before. You were maybe one of the first coaches to use the tablet with the video in practice also.

Yeah.

This is a few years ago now, but what technology do you use in the practice and in matches to help you, and your staff, work with the players?

Actually, I'm very surprised between us because I don't see every coach using that. I don't understand. It's so easy and so useful because I mean maybe all the coaches are better than me to remember and analyze things. For me everything is so much clearer, when I see the delay in my video when the rally has finished. It is much clearer to understand what's going on and that is the most important part.

That's what I like so, so much to have. First of all, the thing that I like more is just to have this delayed video. Now I don't know if you already use that, but with the new Data Video [Data Volley 4] you don't only have the delay, but also you can see all the points before. Maybe something happening in 13-14 and of course then there is technical time out at 16-15. When the player come back you can very quick search 13-14 and show to the player what happened. This is amazing.

You are already using that [Data Volley 4 was not yet publicly available at the time of the interview]?

Yeah, yeah I'm already using that. It is amazing. It is so easy, so easy and so quick. I think it keeps the record of the last I think 10 points in video so you know okay 13-13 happen something, I signal then I go into time out, "Hey watch here. That's what we spoke about, look." You know and you can show it and this is incredible and easier for the player.

Even if you don't want to show it, it's good for you to see, and then you have all the statistics that are updated continuously about your team, about other teams. It's a great help, because at the end our decisions are made 50% from our feeling and 50% from numbers. This 50% from number is so good to analyze every time, and you want to be perfect about that.

That's why I also believe also much in using statistics during the training. Not every time, not every time because you have to give to the player in the training the freedom to make mistakes, to become better. If you are always using statistics, if you always keep score then you don't give some time for freedom to learn new things and to take some risks.

In some parts of the season, when you are really training for the competition, then it's so useful to also have statistics at trainings. It's so great to have a good video delay in the gym. This has to be good to be useful.

For example, here in Holland they have a system in Papendal [National Training Centre] with television on the wall that continuously records the training with 10 second delay, seven second delay. But from the court you cannot see the television. It's basically for nothing. Sometime the coach that is literally outside the court and near the television can see a little bit, but it's for nothing.

If you go to Japan they have this huge screen, a really huge screen, think like movie theatre, at the end of the gym. That is something really useful, that you finish the action and you know you are working on block and defense, then you see, "Oh, okay the coach is right. I'm not moving my right hand in the right position" or "The coach is right. I'm attacking line, taking the ball one meter far from me, inside of me so I have to wait" and blah-blah-blah.

If you can use this, it's really something very useful. It has to be a good system, if not it's just a waste of time.

Yes in Berlin we had a big projector and we had this on the wall in the training gym.

Yeah, also I did this in VakıfBank.

Yeah and at Jastrzębski Węgiel in Poland here we have the LED scoreboard.

It is good.

You talked a little bit about statistics. You have them in practice also. I also like the point, and this is something I learned from one of my players one time about giving penalties or minus points for mistakes. The player told me, "Yes, but if I have a penalty for a mistake then I won't try to find a solution. I will just not make a mistake."

True.

I said, "Okay, now I learned something."

Makes sense.

Yeah, my player was smart.

I have two more questions. One is from a different angle. A lot of these interviews and studies, we always talk about the positive things. I have the feeling that sometimes coaches, younger coaches or learning coaches think that the experts never make a mistake. Sometimes I have this feeling when I read about the other coaches. So I thought it might be interesting for people if you could explain maybe one mistake that you made that you were able to learn from.

I think I make mistakes every day. Every day I believe I make little mistakes in communication or probably little mistakes in organizing a drill. I don't know if I am too demanding with myself.

A few times I really say, "Okay, today everything was perfect, bravo." A lot of times I say, "Arghh, this thing can be better. Maybe here I can spend one more hour. I let this player not fall down one time [in defense]. This should not happen. I have to not do that tomorrow." I think my whole day is filled with little mistakes. That's the clear part. That's why I like to have good staff near me, because they can remember the mistake and tomorrow we try to be better.

Okay, there are also big mistakes. For example, I can tell you one recent mistake. It was at the beginning of the international season with Holland, and we played a quarter final in Baku [European Games 2015]. The team was not ready for the tournament and I was not ready to coach this team, because I didn't know the players too well. I just became so frustrated on losing this match against Azerbaijan that I closed my communication. I said, "Okay, is this the way you want to keep going, losing? Keep losing, but don't ask me anything because I cannot help you with anything." I left the team alone.

This was one big mistake, when I saw for myself after, I really regretted. Of course at the time you are hoping for a reaction of the team, but in that case it didn't come. That was one mistake, one big mistake.

Even in these playoffs, the finish of the season in Vakıfbank. I think

I didn't play the second match with the best team I can. Because one player that should make the difference was not performing well at all so I preferred to keep her out of the 12 and I think that was a mistake.

Sometimes my biggest mistake is to not have the clear idea every time; so to be two, three days before [an] important match and still have questions, "Better play this player, better play that player. Better play this player, better play that player." I would like to be much more sure sometimes, just not to keep questioning myself every time. When I think about my mistakes, they are mostly coming from this part.

To the last little parts. Are there some books that you've read, some literature that you could recommend to readers, to other coaches?

I am very bad on that. I am really very bad on that. I can be very cool and tell you a lot of nice names, but that is not the reality because I am really a very bad reader.

I can tell you a couple of amazing books from amazing writers that I have (read), but it's not the truth. I am not a great reader at all and if I spend this free time for something concerning my work, I have the idea that I really can never, never relax for one second. I'm not a great reader. I am not telling you that I read some book that inspires me because it is not true.

I watched some movies that inspire me, for sure, like 'Miracle' for example about [ice] hockey. Another great movie I watched about handball, a German winner of the handball gold medal, world championship. That was another great movie. ['Projekt Gold'] Of course, 'Any Given Sunday'.

I try to take everything little I can and then make it mine, but I'm really not good at spending time for myself, 'til I make it in this life. I think maybe when I have only one team I can spend the other five, six months to learn a lot also from books. Up till now I don't have this power to do that.

The very last question is, what advice would you have for young coaches or coaches developing or coaches starting the path that we are on?

Quit this job if you don't have an incredible passion, because it's not a job that you can do with normal passion. Actually, I don't know why in this conversation this word never came, but it's another key word for me. The previous question you asked me and I said communication, knowledge, and I should have passion, because this is the base of everything.

It's not a job you can do without an incredible passion. You can be good at maybe all jobs in this world, but volleyball coach you cannot even be average without passion. This is the base of everything.

If you don't have this amazing passion, quit the job. But if they have this passion, don't give up. If you are not presented with a good opportunity, if you are losing a couple of matches, don't give up if you have enough passion. Of course don't stop trying to learn everything.

What I advise always to the young coaches is to spend less time going to coaching clinics, but use this time to go see a real training from a coach. If you can, don't watch only one, but watch at least three days in a row. That's the advice I like to give to all of them.

I think those are two great pieces of advice

3

RUTH N. NELSON

American Ruth N. Nelson has done something rarely seen in coaching. The common path of coaches is to start in the youth ranks in Juniors or school volleyball, then progress to the college or professional level, and then maybe to work with national teams. Ruth sort of went in the other direction. She coached at the college, national team, and professional levels. Then she moved to youth volleyball.

Actually, she went even further than that. She's working with kids under 10 years old these days. Her Bring Your Own Parent (BYOP®) program takes on a group of players many coaches wouldn't even think about working with! Ebony Nwanebu, 2013 NCAA Freshman of the Year, was one of Ruth's first players in the program. In the interview you'll hear about why she's gone in that direction.

Backing things up, Ruth accumulated over 500 victories in 16 seasons as a college coach at George Williams College, the University of Houston, Louisiana State University and the University of Iowa. Three of her players from Houston played on the 1984 USA Women's National Team.

At the international level, Ruth assisted Arie Selinger with the USA national team, was a national team technical advisor, and head coached the Junior National Team, the A2 collegiate national team, and the World University Games team. She also coached the Dallas Belles team in the Major League Volleyball professional league, and ran volleyball for the Special Olympics.

In 2014, Ruth was inducted into the AVCA Hall of Fame. She is also on the USA Volleyball list of All-Time Great Coaches.

This interview was done by John in July, 2015. To suggest that Ruth has a lot to say about volleyball and coaching would be a massive understatement. She's got a massive and diverse background in the sport, and she's widely connected, so that makes total sense. You'll find this is the longest of the interviews in the book. Basically, it was a case of asking Ruth a question and letting her take it and run with it.

One of the great aspects of talking with Ruth is that she gives you insights into volleyball's history that can't be had in other places. It's one of the reasons we chose to include this interview in the book. There are things that were happening in coaching and in the sport decades ago that volleyball people simply have forgotten or lost in the depths of time. Ruth is a great reminder that there is a history to our sport – especially for those in the USA who see volleyball as effectively beginning with the Men's gold medal at the 1984 Olympics.

Can you walk through your volleyball coaching biography?

I went to undergraduate school at University of Northern Colorado and played five sports. There were no scholarships at the time because it was Association of Intercollegiate Athletics for Women [AIAW]. It was run by a women's organization, whereas now it's the NCAA. A lot of people in the NCAA don't even know what the AIAW is.

I played five sports and graduated, and went on to graduate school. Starting in graduate school at age 21, I was the head coach at George Williams College. At that time my adviser was Dr. James Coleman, who was one of the Olympic coaches, and has since passed away. He was not only my adviser but also he mentored Terry [Liskevych], Doug Beal, Mick Haley, Russ Rose – all of us at George Williams College. They played on a USVBA team [US Volleyball Association]. Not USA Volleyball, because the names always change, but it's the same organization.

I started coaching men's tennis and women's volleyball at my first year in graduate school, and finished my coaching degree with a master's in physical education. I also had a bachelor's degree in physical education, with an emphasis in psychology, bio-mechanics, anatomy, and exercise. We got degrees in coaching education at the time. You were educated in all sports. I taught everything except swimming and gymnastics.

I started my first career there, and spent two years at George Williams. Then from there I started being trained by Jim Coleman as a setter because I had played volleyball in college and actually was dating a guy on the national team. I'd really stopped in Chicago to see him.

Jim Coleman asked me, "Do you want to go to graduate school?"

I said, "I really don't know. I'm on my way back to the East Coast to teach tennis in a private tennis camp."

I ended up at graduate school there. I wanted to be an international setter. Of course, everybody always tells you what you can't do in your life. I'm pretty much motivated by what people say I can't do. If I decide I want to do it, I'm going to do it.

I made the national team that Summer of my first year of graduate school. I ran into a couple of players then on the national team – Mary Jo Peppler and Marilyn McReavy. They were out there then. I met them for the first time. Didn't really know them personally. I ended up really enjoying meeting them.

They needed a setter in Houston, Texas for their club team. At the time, you needed to get a transfer from your job, and I was working during the Summer with Northwestern Mutual Life Insurance as a sales recruiter. I got a job transfer to Houston. I moved down to Houston after two years at George Williams. I finished up my master's degree and started volunteering at the University of Houston right away, as well as playing on their EPU club team. At that time you had to be very careful of your amateur status. I couldn't receive any money. I was a volunteer.

I ended up staying eight years at the University of Houston during that time. I played on the national team. I also coached. I played on the national team with Flo Hyman. She also played for me at the University of Houston.

We were quite successful, obviously, at Houston. That's where Arie [Selinger] came in. He became the head coach, a full-time coach, and actually was paid by a friend of mine who was an oil well guy. Arie had graduated with a doctorate degree at the University of Illinois. I knew him kind of through Jim Coleman and Bertha Lucas when I was in graduate school. I chose to stay at the University of Houston when USA Volleyball decided to move the team to Colorado Springs, the first Olympic training center, in 1974 – even prior to the men having an Olympic training center in Ohio.

One of the most important things that I felt like is I wanted to continue my education. I quit playing in '74 and became Arie's assistant coach. Then it came down to, "Do I go with the national team as an assistant, or do I stay with the full-time position?" I was teaching and coaching at the University of Houston.

I chose to stay, but then I traveled with the national team all the time. It was in Colorado Springs during that period of time. Then from there I went to Louisiana State University and took that job. I really wanted to build a program. I'm a program builder. I always respected Andy Banachowski for as long as he was at UCLA, but that wasn't my style. I really enjoyed building the program.

I was there for four years. Then I went from there to the pros. It was the first professional women's volleyball league that they had. I coached the Dallas Belles. Shortly after that I went and took the head coaching job at the University of Iowa. I was there two years and decided it was time to get out of Division I because I felt like I didn't want to adapt what I consider my philosophies to the new generation kids. I went full-time with Special Olympics – not only as the Director of Volleyball, but also in sports marketing, corporate marketing on an international level. [She started with Special Olympics part-time as Director of Volleyball in 1981].

After spending time doing that, I jumped back to Dallas in '95 and started doing some training [with school kids]. I missed it. Over the last fifteen years, I've really spent an awful lot of time with the 12s. Then I've specialized in 10s. Now, I'm doing a lot. During that period of time, I started with kids like three and a half years old, four years old. I was curious to see what that age group could actually do, their attention span, and how could you really develop players over a period of time.

That leads me up until now. I doubled back three years ago coaching an A2 team [one of USA Volleyball's junior national teams, commonly called the Collegiate team]. The reason for that was I wanted to know specifically what was happening at that level, and did I have kids that I was training that could easily transition back into that. In 1984 I had three college players – Flo Hyman, Rita Crockett, and Rose Magers – who all started for the '84 Olympic team. I spent 12 to 14 years going back and forth with the national team, traveling as a technical adviser, coaching the World University Games team, and coaching the junior national team.

You look back on your career and you wonder, where is it that you are and where do you need to go? I think that I had a calling and the calling was that I love seeing kids develop to their potential – without reservation, no matter what their skill level is.

I think a lot of people are surprised that I can train five and six-year-olds because I'm used to dealing with Danielle Scott, five-time Olympian. She was in my junior program in Baton Rouge. You're talking about a lot of skilled athletes throughout my career. I felt like why shouldn't a ten-year-old have the opportunity to be coached by someone with my expertise? That's where I am now. That's why I've developed my program for 10-and-under kids to engage parents and kids together because we're finishing up the millennial generation and we're now going to the iY generation.

I'm seeing that the kids have gotten progressively... They're not allowed to fail in this country. I don't know much about any other countries. They're not allowed to fail. Therefore, what happens is when they get pushed to the wire, they want to leave. That's why you're seeing so much that's happening across the country with kids going to a college for one year.

The other day a kid said, "If I don't like it Ruth, I'll transfer somewhere else."

When we went to college, you didn't go to transfer. You went to graduate, and then get out in the real world. It's almost like learning to adapt to what's going on. I now have become specialized in an area where I'm doing exactly what I want to do and no one tells me what I have to do and what I don't have to do. How's that?

I'm sure there are a lot of people that would be envious of that.

I guess when you get older, you get to choose some of those things. Because I think I'm old enough now, I get to choose.

Before I get on to your specific coaching, I want to drill down a little bit on what you're doing. The program you're talking about is Bring Your Own Parent, correct?

Yes, it is.

Why don't you describe what that's all about?

Okay. Fifteen years ago, when I started to do more training, I was seeing the need for the younger groups to be able to be exposed to some basic fundamental skills training. I felt like in order to do that, I needed to look back on my nieces and nephews that were playing soccer thirty, thirty-five years ago. What had happened is the son or daughter wanted to play soccer. The best coaches at the time were the foreign coaches because they were the ones that were exposed to better soccer. It was interesting that Mom and Dad coached a team because their son or daughter wanted to participate in soccer [and there weren't enough foreign coaches].

I thought, this is going to happen in volleyball because you're going to run out of coaches. What happens when Mom and Dad really might not have the exposure in a sport like volleyball and they want their kids to improve in their skills? I started looking at it like, "How do I get the parent engaged?" Most of the parents want to go drop their kids off and come pick them up.

I said, "Hmm, that's not really what happens as far as what I'm concerned when you're talking through age five through ten years old."

They need to practice at home. Whether it's against the garage door or whether they're tossing the ball up and catch and setting it, or they're jump roping, or they're skipping. The parents need to be totally engaged in this, but it doesn't have to be more than maybe 10 or 15 minutes a day at home.

I played around with Volleykidz [and VolleyTotz]. I utilized that name and got an organization to actually trademark it in the early 2000s. I did a demonstration in 2003 at the AVCA Convention. The parents were all engaged. At this time I had a young player I started at three and a half, which was Ebony Nwanebu. She was a player that ended up at USC for two years and just transferred to the University of Texas. Her and her mother found me on the internet.

I said, "You know what? This is the way it's got to happen. You've got to get people engaged."

I said, "Okay, let's come up with a name."

I came up with up Bring Your Own Parent. The parent must be engaged in every session. You can't send your aunt, your uncle, your big sister, your brother. You've got to come as a parent. Husband and wife, no problem. They both are educated. If one is working, the other one will bring. If they can't come, their daughter can't come.

A lot of people have tried in the last five years to get me to change it, but I really believe that the 30 minute to 45 minute ride to training, that hour in training once a week, and that 30 to 45 minute drive home could be some of the most valuable time that I felt a parent could have with their kid. Because, as you well know, everybody I'm sure around the world is all busy doing things. In this country, Mom and Dad probably are working. In a lot of cases, parents are working one, or two, or three jobs. I felt like what I noticed with me growing up, we had more quality time, even at the dinner table. It's like kids, all they want to do is text. There's no form of communication anymore.

What I decided is that this could be something that I really think could be valuable for the future. I talked with some of my friends that have been around for forty something years. They go, "Ruth, we love the idea. It's the next generation." I agreed.

It takes people with expertise to really work around the program to try to make it to be the best it can be. I trademarked it. Now, I'm going to certify my first six instructors next month. I've done three demonstrations at the AVCA Convention. I've done three consecutive years in a row with Art of Coaching. People absolutely love it. You don't have to have the same background I have. You can be a parent that wants to be better at what their kid is learning.

I think probably one of the most important things for me in the development of instructors is finding the right people that really are around elementary schools kids – that really love it. The energy that you have to have is like... Andy Banachowski said to me, "Ruth, how do you deal with that age after you've dealt with Olympic athletes?"

I said, "I have sixty something nieces and nephews."

I hate to say it, but I love that age group. I've got five-year-olds that I'm teaching the Japanese floater serve to because they're not strong enough to hit overhand. They'll not be strong enough until they get to nine and ten years old. I think with my background, because I have had so much in physical education, and the psychology, and the bio-mechanics side, I do understand how you can motivate kids and parents to want to become the best they can be and to have fun doing it.

You just mentioned bio-mechanics. How much of that whole mode of learning specificity do you incorporate into your program?

We do an awful lot on hand-eye coordination with tennis balls. We throw footballs for upper arms strength. I try to relate some of the things that parents can do at home. We actually started this year for the first time for five and six-year-olds fifteen minutes of performance training. For the eight, nine, and ten-year-olds we do twenty minutes of performance training. A friend of mine is a performance specialist. We believe that what's happened is when we grew up we did hopscotch, we did jump roping, we did all the movement. We played more than one sport. All of a sudden, everybody is trying to emphasize people to be specialty in special sports and give up on everything.

The one thing that I have noticed is that all the kids that are in our program do at least one to three sports, or even cheerleading and dance. Cheerleading is such a big thing for girls, especially in Texas. I don't know what it's like with the rest [of the sports], but we do involve a lot of skipping, shuffling, step-hop, hand-eye coordination. We look at their movement skills. How do we become efficient on the court? How do we understand? I include math in it. If this is a three-meter line and that's the nine meters, what is it between half of this? We do a lot of it dealing with not just volleyball but life lessons and the anatomy of what your body can do and what it can't do at five years old.

Do I tell them this is their bicep, this is their tricep, and that you need to have strength in antagonistic muscles? Absolutely not. We do talk about, "Okay, see that? That's your knee. That right there, is that muscle big? Okay, that muscle and that muscle work together. Now you need to bend down. Now we need to keep our knees over our toes." I'll do more of that on the parent side so that the parents can function at home so that the kids are doing good movements that's not going to hurt them. We do a lot of jump rope. We do routines that help with their footwork.

Do we do ladders and stuff? We never even knew what a ladder was when I was growing up. What we'd learned and used for a ladder was we had badminton line, tennis line, basketball line, and volleyball line in our gymnasiums. We did footwork and movement patterns with them.

In the back of my mind, I'm looking at a five-year-old kid. I know a nine-year-old, unless you're a pretty good athlete, you probably are not going to consistently serve nine meters back from the net, over the net consistently. Why is it when a kid goes to a clinic somebody spends thirty minutes in telling them they got to serve from the end line, when you know as well as I do that potentially that's going to hurt their shoulder?

I think there are some adaptions that I do that I believe will help them be successful, and that will also teach them more about the game. Because to me, it's important to understand the game. Playing at five years old – unless you're in Brazil, or California, or Puerto Rico – the culture is not there for those kids to learn all these things. There are so many other things that kids can do.

Just winding back, because some people may not be aware of definition here. You mentioned performance training. What does that incorporate?

When I consider performance training, I'm talking about speed, quickness, and agility – not strength training. When we first started, it was strength training. I was my own strength training coach because we didn't have any strength training coaches [for women's sports] at any of the universities that I went to, except at Iowa.

You mentioned that kids in certain cultures get out and get a chance to play a lot of volleyball. How much play do your kids get in the gym when you have them?

What we do is we spend anywhere from seven to ten minutes at the end. Depending on whether they're the five and six-year-olds or they're the nine and ten-year-olds will determine how much of the pass-pass and attack that they do. However, I do have the parents catch the ball while the athletes have to actually pass it or hit the ball. As they get older, the parents still do that because the whole idea of the training is focused on the athlete, not the parents. However, I can tell you this. The parents that have the least amount of knowledge of volleyball are the ones that seemingly improve the most on their skills.

We do have some playing now. All the kids that started with me at five are now ten, eleven. Now, the parents actually participate with them where you have two parents and two players. The players have to hit against each other and the parent has to hit the ball or pass the ball. Once it becomes out of control where the athletes don't get a lot of passing or attacking, I have the parents go back to catching and setting, or catching on return of service.

Okay, like a parent-player doubles?

Yeah.

Have you seen Slamball? [A variation of youth volleyball played on a significantly lower net so the kids can hit aggressively]

Yes, I did. I have seen that. I saw that on the internet.

What do you think of that?

Everyone has said, "Ruth, why don't you do this or why don't you do this?"

I look back on how I learned to play tennis, because tennis was my primary sport. I did that all year round, whereas during the Fall you played volleyball, then you played basketball,then you played field hockey, and then you played softball. But you played tennis all year round. For me, I think any exposure to anything and any sports really helps you become a more well-rounded and knowledgeable because I can tell you this. Defense, the movement may be different in basketball and volleyball, but the idea of following mid-line to someone you're guarding, or a pass that comes to you, or a volley at the net, I can tell you that I think I was a better volleyball player because I had had so much exposure to all different sports.

I think that everybody gets their niche of what they're incorporating. It's like hacky sack. That was so big for a while. I see all the new things that are coming out, but I also believe that you need all those things. I think I'm more suited to this iY generation because I get bored very easily. Maybe that's why I enjoy developing programs. I went from George Williams to Houston to LSU to Iowa.

I do a lot of consulting now with DI and DII colleges. I can see that I'm much better now as a coach than I ever was before. Because I've learned to be more diplomatic. It doesn't matter what skill level you're at. I think all those things are great, but I think you've got to find your niche in what you believe in. I believe that I am best suited for 10-and-under. I told someone the other day that once I start training only five and six, it's not because the eight and nines are out of control. It's probably because the parents are getting too engaged and involved in everything.

What are the prospects of these parents turning into coaches in their own right somewhere down the line?

I think actually, they're the next generation coaches. A friend of mine, Doug Beal, who is the CEO of USA Volleyball ... I used to set with their men's team. On that team was Mick Haley and a bunch of the guys that are still out coaching. One of the things I said to Doug is, "They are the next generation, because you know what? They're knowledgeable. They're learning from the basic fundamental skills."

Take a look at some of the better junior coaches in the United States. They weren't volleyball players. They were football coaches. They were maybe not even a coach, just maybe someone who played.

I think what happens is, if you learn basic fundamental movements and skills, you become much more knowledgeable because you become what I consider a new sponge. A new sponge absorbs everything. If you're an old sponge, it has nothing to do with being old in age. It just means that you feel that you can't learn anymore. You're an old sponge. I consider myself a new sponge. I learn every day I'm in training. For me, if you asked what's one thing that probably bothers me most about junior volleyball in the United States, it's people think because they've been coaching for 10 or 15 years they know everything. They don't know what they don't know.

I think that when we grew up we wanted to learn from everybody. You surrounded yourself with the best in the world. You have to decide what you wanted to be.

When I was growing up, I wanted to be like Billie Jean King. She was the best. I got tennis lessons from Darlene Hard, four-time Wimbledon Champion. I think you have to decide what the best is and you have to decide what level you want to be at. Not everybody wanted to be at the same level I was at in volleyball or in tennis.

I think that once you quit learning, I don't know how you can be satisfied with what you're doing for people. You must learn every day.

I laugh when I work with five and six-year-olds. When I see them focus so hard on a skill that I have to get them to laugh. Dakota, she just turned five years old. She is jumping 12.3 inches utilizing a VERT. I work with her three minutes, once a week, on just jumping. Three minutes. Not three hours. Three minutes. I don't think you need to get these young kids to spend hours and hours and hours, because I've never believed that quantity is better than quality.

Related to the coaching stuff, I'm curious to get your opinion on this. One of the shortcomings I've long felt there is to the traditional coaching education/certification process is that it's set up for somebody who has the opportunity to be an assistant coach – to be mentored by another coach. The reality of the situation is more reflective of what you just mentioned in terms of juniors where people get thrown in. "We need to coach. You're a warm body. We're going to give you this team." Instead of having someone who's got the support of a senior coach that can take these certification materials and learn how to put it in context, they're just thrown all this stuff and not taught the framework until maybe the third level, CAP III or whatever an equivalent might be somewhere else. Have you been involved in any of that sort of stuff?

I actually was part of the first CAP program. I had an FIVB rating when we first started because I was working with Jim Coleman. Actually, I feel that it's very important to have a certification program. I really do. I can tell you, I was thrown in at age 21 to coach a college team where four players were older than I was.

I think that you're looking at two aspects. One is, there's an awful lot of dollar signs behind coaching junior volleyball these days in the US. I think there is a different thing that's driven people to do different things. We were driven to coach. Obviously, after 40 years I'm still doing it. It's never been about money. It's been about helping others and helping them into a sport.

However, at 21, I could have just said, "I'm coaching. I'm doing this, I'm doing that."

No, I surrounded myself. I was around Jim Coleman. I was around Bertha Lucas, who coached the Chicago Rebels. Her daughter played in the '68 Olympics. You have to decide how much you want to learn and how much you feel you already know, and how much you think you don't need to learn.

Somebody said the other day to me (their daughter is playing on a club team, and I have this happen a lot), "Ruth, this is what's happening on our club team. Do you agree with this or not agree?"

I said, "It's not about me agreeing or not agreeing. You can't expect the same thing from your club coaches you expect from me, because I have an education. I have six years of experience just from undergraduate and graduate school in the world of being a teacher, a coach, a trainer – understanding all these aspects."

What was my excuse for stopping to learn? I could have had an excuse. I think you have to find or figure out a way.

An example is I have mentors in my BYOP® program. All my mentors are high school and middle school players that I train. As part of training with me, they must mentor. There's no choice. Now, ten years ago, those kids of the millennium generation, they mentored because they thought that was a way to give back. Now, this generation, doesn't necessarily. They don't think of mentoring until you tell them and let them get involved, and they realize how important it is.

It's like one of my juniors in high school the other day. She was coaching my BYOP® team because we played in a little league three times, and then a little tournament. She came home and she told her mother. She goes, "Mom, I didn't realize how hard it is to coach."

You know what? If you have success in juniors and you win, I think the majority, and I'm not saying all, but the majority of junior coaches think they have nothing to learn because they're already winning. When we were learning, you had mentors around you that you were learning from.

You're asking me, "What's the solution?"

I don't consider myself a coach anymore. I'm a trainer. I don't want to be a coach because everybody does one year of coaching juniors and they're a coach. I was trained as a coach. Now, I feel I'm a trainer because I train people all the time. I still learn.

How do you get the younger generation to believe they need to learn? You know what? I think it's the responsibility of a director of a club. If the director of the club is not supervising, what happens is...

Somebody says the other day, "You know what? We're going to have five teams at fourteens."

I said, "Do you have five coaches?"

"No, but we can get some parents to coach."

No, you can't just get parents to coach unless they're educated.

It goes back to what you just said to me. Yes, I believe that those parents that start with me at age five with their kids, they are the next generation coaches for maybe ten, eleven, and twelve. Do I feel that they'll go on and be successful? I'll tell you this, they'll at least understand that where they started and where they are now is because of they've been wanting to learn and to learn more. You know what happens? If their kid is now 11 and playing club, they have been around me since three and a half. Do you know how educated those parents are after being around me all those years?

They're asking the question, "Ruth, why don't coaches that coach youth not want to get better."

I don't think it's just about getting CAP I, II, and III [The primary USA Volleyball coaching levels at this writing]. I think it's what you just said. You've got to be mentored by somebody.

You want me to tell you something? There aren't very many people that want to mentor. I have ten coaches that I mentor. Three of them are high school and the rest are college. Who wants to mentor people? It takes so much energy and effort.

I was part of the AVCA mentorship program for a couple of years. I really think that it's very valuable. I think it adds to someone that really wants to be mentored.

Let's say that you've got a chance to coach a junior team. You know what the average pay in Dallas for head coaching is? It's between $750 and $1,500 a month to coach a junior team.

Wow.

The average kid that plays in a competitive program is spending $3,500 to $6,000 a year. That's $24,000 in four years. The average kid now in Dallas is in club six to seven years. Figure that out.

Yeah.

My question is, if I'm going to be a coach, if someone's offering me $750 and I played in college, what is going to help me understand that I need to learn more?

Do you know how much money I made in the twelve years that I traveled with the US women's team? Zero.

I had somebody the other day, says, "Ruth, I heard you're looking for someone to hit balls," because I really don't want to hit balls anymore. I'm way too old. I don't want my arm to hurt every day.

They said, "Normally, what I charge people is $20 an hour."

I said, "Excuse me! You want me to pay $20 an hour so you can hit balls for me? I'll teach all the kids how to hit balls." I about died.

In reality, I tried someone and they couldn't even run a drill. I thought to myself, "You're going to charge me so I can train you." What's wrong with this picture?

Right.

Let me tell you what I really believe. I believe that the Art of Coaching is one of the best things that's ever happened to this country. It's interesting because Andy, Terry, and I used to do the same thing in the early '70s. We used to travel. It was paid for by [sponsors like] PRO-Keds. Everybody did all kinds of these clinics. I'm going to tell you that you get three guys – Russ, who used to be in my badminton class in undergraduate school at George Williams, Terry, who was one of our coaches and also played, and John Dunning – and you get them in the room and you hear John Dunning talk about swing blocking. Russ gets up and says, "We don't swing block. We block, but we swing block in practice so we can beat John's team."

You don't find that kind of atmosphere. I am so pleased. This is over three years now that I am seeing three hundred and fifty high school coaches coming and listening to these guys who really love the sport and have passion. Now, you can say whatever you want – that there's money that's made, and whatever. The point is this there are high school coaches that really do want to learn. The most invigorating thing for me now is to see you've got high school coaches who will come to this, but the majority of junior coaches don't come.

Why is that?

Because we know in high school they don't pay you more than about $3,000 to $5,000, and you're teaching. Maybe the person that's teaching and coaching in high school has a different perspective on why they're there. Even though some of the high schools they pay a little bit more, but they're still not paying that much. I love what they do because it gives you a sense that it's okay not to do the same as somebody else. That's why it's interesting.

When I first started back training in 2000 in Dallas I was consulting with three club programs. They said, "Ruth, we're going to teach 5-1 throughout the whole thing."

I said, "5-1?"

They go, "Have you not run a 5-1?"

I said, "I ran a 5-1 at Iowa only because I had one setter that was experienced. At Houston, Flo Hyman set for me. I ran a 6-4. I ran a 6-6. I ran a left side attack. I ran a right side attack. I put your left foot in front. We swing blocked."

It's the same stuff they're doing now. There's nothing that's changed about the sport except the scoring.

Somebody says, "The players jump higher and they hit harder."

No. More basketball players are playing volleyball. Does Cuba hit any harder than they hit twenty years ago? No. There just are more people playing the sport. In the early '70s I was the first coach to really, really recruit the minority athletes. Are there that many more on our national team? No, there's three or four.

To me, I love what I do and I'm going to keep doing what I do. If I get to a point that I don't love it anymore, I'm not going to do it. I can imagine those little ones need somebody who'll love it as much as I do. If I can I want to inspire more mentors in high school to come back and coach, which I'm seeing now. A lot of those kids that were in college have graduated.

I started training a team in 2000. I didn't coach the team because I didn't want to deal with parents. I trained the team four days a week, one hour of volleyball was six players and the other six were doing performance training. On Tuesday, the same thing. On Wednesday, we did an hour of performance training together and we did an hour of volleyball together. On Thursday, it was split again. We utilized, the weekend tournaments is how we got to play together and we worked hard.

During that time in 2000, everybody was mad at me and said, "Ruth, now we're all going to have to start doing performance training because you're doing it four days a week."

I said, "I did it because I felt like every player on that team needed to become stronger, quicker, faster, more agile, more flexible."

All of those kids went on to college. They weren't all on athletic scholarships. All of them graduated. They now are out in the real world. They're giving back and they're still coaching juniors. They are doctors, exercise physiologists. There's advertising people.

You know what? They must have enjoyed what they learned during that process. I think if you can figure a way where a person develops a love and a passion for a sport, they're never going to stop. I believe that's Terry, that's Russ, that's Doug, Mick, all those people that have been around the sport when it was really a lot of fun. I think it's hard.

Someone said, "Ruth, don't you feel that there's a lot more pressure at DI than when you coached?"

I go, "Are you kidding me? I got fired at LSU."

I left coaching in '91 as the highest paid coach in the country – $43,000 in Iowa. Two years later, the coach was making $150,000 at Iowa.

Wow!

The sport obviously has changed, but I still love the sport and I still will mentor. I still believe that I can learn and I'm learning every day. If I can do it, why can't others do it?

Related to what you were talking about doing the performance work... There was a story in the AVCA magazine a couple of months ago. I'm forgetting the author's name, but he was a former Division I coach who was coaching 12- and-under in Texas. Do you remember it?

Yup.

He talked about how he basically trained those kids the way he would train his college team and talked about how proud he was of the running combinations and quick attacks, and things like that. The question that immediately came to my mind was, why is that team running – I don't remember if it was a 6-2 or a 5-1 or whatever – a quite specialized offense, from a couple of perspectives. A) Do you really need to? B) I know there's a push among at least some of the national federations. I think USA Volleyball is one of them. I know Volleyball England is another. They're trying to go completely against specialization at that age group. You play 6-6 or maybe you play a 6-3 or something like that.

Mm-hmm (affirmative).

What's your feeling of that differential in approach?

I can say this. I wish that no one would specialize until the kids are 14 or 15. The reason why is who are we to know what's going to go on with that kid?

Here's an example. I've got a kid that's 11 years old and for two years she's played club. Because of her size, she now has been put into the DS/libero aspect. I think they become one-dimensional. I don't think they really recognize what the game is all about. If you don't understand what the game is all about and all the different positions and all the different skills, why would you really love the sport in this country? I can't speak for any other country.

To me, one of the best trainers in this country in junior level is Rose Magers-Powell. She's at Huntsville, Alabama. She was a starter on the 1984 Olympic team. She set for me three years at Houston and set for me a year at LSU, and went on to the national team. Flo was a setter for me at Houston.

Everybody asked, "Why are you using her as setter?"

I said "She [Flo] said after that, 'Ruth, I never had the feel for what the game was like until you allowed me to set.'"

Now, I didn't really like to set. I liked to hit better. My point is why is it that you would want to specialize someone at a young age in the first place? That's my question to somebody.

Somebody says they're going to get better.

They're not going to really understand the game. All these five, six, nine, tens, they all come and they're going to learn everything from me. Granted, when Ebony was four and a half years old, her mother laughed at me when I said, "Ebony is going to be a national team player. She's going to be an Olympic player and she's going to be 6"5'."

You look at someone's parents. You guess, and the point is she can play left, middle, and right. However, what's happening in these kids getting to club is they automatically specialize someone because why? Are they teachers that really believe in teaching the kids skills or do they just believe that they need to run drills?

An example from when I was at I.A.D. , which is a 12-court facility [in the Dallas area] I think is one of the finest in the world. I was there as the Director of Volleyball for two years. I started doing some data. Guess what? Stress fracture, L5-S1. Stress fracture leg. Guess what? Middles only can hit off one foot. Guess what happens? Left side players, all they're doing is what? Hitting, hitting, hitting. They're not passing.

To me, if you're going to specialize someone in a sport, and now you're going to specialize them within a specific category within a sport, maybe they might be better at that. But you know what? Don't you want to really enjoy the sport?

To answer your question, I think you're really hurting the kids if you are specializing them before fourteen.

I actually had a correspondence with the author of that article. The impression I got was he feels a certain amount of pressure to win. That for whatever reason, people think that 12-and-under team with that club, or in that region, or whatever needs to be winning or otherwise it's going to be considered a failure. You obviously have some connection with the club volleyball and in Texas. What's the mentality these days?

I think you've got two things. I think there's winning at all cost that's happening, and then there's money. You look at an average club that has 20 or more teams. You're talking $1.7 million budget, or more.

Now, does it take a lot to stand up and say, "Look, this isn't about what college I put a kid in," because you know what? If you look at the data, how many kids get scholarships in reality? There aren't very many. You know what? If you've got 90% of the kids that play in high school and they don't even go on to college sports, why are we specializing kids to make them, only have to take one sport?

John, if you look at this, why is a parent feeling the way they feel? It's because they sit in the stands and they hear the other parents are saying these things. You need to help empower the parents about where you find out about the education side.

It's like somebody said the other day, "Ruth, my daughter is thinking about playing up on an 18s team and she's only 17. The club said she shouldn't do it because she's not going to get looked at for recruiting."

I said, "It's about how you market your daughter. It's not about a team that wins at nationals, because there are so many other tournaments prior to that. You have to educate the college coach about where your kid is playing."

They go, "Do you really believe that?"

I said, "Yeah, I believe that."

Because in 2000 when I was training that team, we had 100 coaches watching us in Las Vegas. We didn't have any players that went to USC, UCLA. We had players that graduated from Belmont, Barry University, Cornell, Columbia.

To answer your question, I've seen teams go and win the open division. Those kids have one or two offers. The question is, are they matching their academics with where they want to go first? Then second of all, does that school need someone of their ability?

A friend of mine who played with me on the national team coaches at UMass, Boston (Terry Condon, a 3-time all-American at UCLA. She and I played together in the 1972 national team). She said to me, "Ruth, we're a DIII school. This is what I tell the parents. The most important thing is this. You've obviously planned for your daughter for the future. Whether she gets any type of academic aid at any school she goes to, you are planning for the future."

I think the problem is parents think... You know what? I think there's two parts. The education on the parent's side, and the club's side.

Do you remember the whole Tonya Harding thing that happened in figure skating? Remember that whole thing that happened and the blame? [Harding was implicated in a scheme to knock her main rival, Nancy Kerrigan, out of Olympic contention in 1994].

By and large it is this. Are we as a general public looking at the number of medals that we get at the Olympics? Yeah, obviously. Then where does that filter through. NGBs [National Governing Bodies]. Then where does that filter through?

I can tell you that there only used to be one junior national team when I coached the team in 1984. I had the '84 kids that became the '88 kids. Now, guess how many junior teams there are? Fifteen of them and maybe even more. They are traveling all over under the name of USA. My question is, is it truly about the development of the sport or is it about money?

Fifteen, yeah, that's a lot.

It may not be. They're not titled US Junior National Team, but they're a high performance team. I think that's important because you know what? Let's get real. How many players have I coached since 1970 – over 40 years – that actually went on to be superior at the Olympic level?

Remember my background. My background is Jim Coleman, Bertha, Mary Jo, Marilyn, Arie, [Kazunori] Yoneda, [Shigeo] Yamada, [Hirofumi] Daimatsu. Being exposed to all those people in the world. And Flo, because she was on the national team with me and I happened to be in that. Rita [Crockett], Rose, Sherryl [Moore], Danielle, and Ebony if she wants to. Maybe Mary-Kate Marshall, who's at Oregon State. My point to you is how many players do you think? [The answer is 4 who made the 1984 US Olympic team, 3 of whom were starters.]

Now, if you want to get involved in the rules, why do we have two liberos in club? Why are we trying to incorporate the rules at the Olympic level, or national level, or NGB level at the high school level? Why?

I can tell you, one of the best experiences in my career was 15 years with Eunice Kennedy Shriver with Special Olympics. I came in as their first full-time Director of Volleyball. The reason I chose to do that in 1981, is because she said, "Ruth, you can have your sport the way in which you want it." There's no sport in Special Olympics that's a priority sport like in the rest of the US. You're either Olympic sport or you're not Olympic sport.

I believed that that was a very, very critical part of my life as far as coaching was concerned because I coached two teams and trained two teams before the 1985 games at Baton Rouge, Louisiana. One of the things that I learned is that anybody, no matter what your ability level is, can love the sport and have a passion for it. Maybe what's happening is people have gotten so caught up with making money that they've forgotten the reason why they got involved.

Going back to something you touched on a little bit in terms of coaches as teachers. Mick and I were actually talking about this a little. The observation he made was that a lot of your generation of coaches, and probably generations that followed on a little bit, were primarily trained to be coaches. They were physical education majors and then did master's degrees in coaching and that sort of thing, whereas these days coaches tend to be less about just being teachers – educators – and more about being technicians. Is that something fair? Is that something you've observed?

There's no doubt that the education is not there to be a physical educator except in high school. A lot of times there you're finding people that still are in physical education even though there is not a lot that's being done in physical education classes because of the fact it's the way the education system has gone.

Now, my question to you is the tactical part. There's so much access to some stuff on the internet. I think what happens is nowadays everybody is so really what you said earlier. That is, all they care about is winning, because, "If I don't win, they're going to get another coach. If I don't win, the club is not going to get the best players. If we don't win and get scholarships, then the other kids are going to go other places.

What is the reason for even having a club? In Dallas, over 150 clubs. Guess what? You can pick and choose where you want to play. You can pick and choose if you want to go to college and play. It has nothing to do with what club you played for. It has to do with the learning aspect.

Let's go back and say, okay, are they the technical side or the tactical side? I think to me, everybody judges success differently. If you asked me, "What is success?" I would look at the development of players, whereas someone else might look at success and say, "So and so has won five national championships at the DII level. They're successful."

I look at the development side. I think that's because of my background. We were taught to develop and analyze skills and videotape.

Here's an example. I do a lot of Skype training. I do jump training. I have my own program in the pool that I started in 1972. Dr. Mary Abdall did her master's thesis on it to show the success of how jumping in the pool relates to less injuries, improvement jumping, and so forth. Then I've been involved in the MVP which is a machine that was actually utilized by astronauts. I knew the engineer and we used that. It's almost like my background in education, and the mind is always trying to learn more. I think that you rub off on people. Just think of how many people Dr. Jim Coleman rubbed off on. Look at that group of people.

I would say if you asked me one thing, "What is the important thing that really has not happened in this country, in the US?" It is nobody cares about talking about the history. I knew who Daimatsu was when I was 21 years old because Jim Coleman told me who Daimatsu was. He told me what they did. Did I agree with them training eight hours, six, seven, eight days a week? I still have one of the original training films. It doesn't matter whether you agree with the way they did something. It's you were exposed to everything. The more you get exposed to, the better you understand what success is. Success to me is not about winning.

I saw Dakota the other day at five years old turn around and look at the scoreboard. I looked at her and I said, "Do not look at that scoreboard. You get your pass. Get your feet around. Get the ball up and get excited when you get that pass up." That's about an education. It's about how you feel about your sport.

How do you do that?

I think people that go on to coaching are feeling that way about the sport. They feel that you can be successful. You can run a 5-1. You can run a 6-2. Who cares?

Everybody laughed at me in 1970 in World University Games team when I ran a left side attack. I ran a left side attack. Somebody wrote something about it, I don't know eight years ago. They go, "We just decided to do this." No, I did it in the '70s. We all tried this stuff. We tried swing blocking. We tried 3-person serve receive.

Bottom line is this. How much time do you have to teach kids what you need to teach them? That will probably dictate what you're going to end up teaching them. I had a 10-year-old the other day, and I had a college kid that came back that was working on passing. I saw that 10-year-old was really upset about something. They were sitting over in the side waiting for the session to happen. I went over to her. I said, "I know you're upset right now. You know what? Guess what? She needs help on her passing." This was a sophomore in college. I said, "Could you come out and help her?"

She goes, "Coach, her arms need to be further away from her chest."

A 10-year-old can tell a college kid because they see what happens – the end result. Why don't we teach kids to analyze their skills? I teach a five-year-old how to analyze their skills. I teach the little ones how to analyze their parents. They go up and their parents put their hands up and the kids show them what they need to do with their hands. "Why do you need to have your hands like that, Dakota?"

"I don't want to jam my fingers."

Then in my mind, I'm thinking, you don't want to jam your fingers because you're not going to like the sport. There's a reason for putting your thumbs in a certain position. I think it depends on how much you tell people what they need to analyze.

It's like somebody says, "My coach is telling me that I'm not hitting the ball hard."

I said, "Okay. What did they suggest you do?"

They said, "Just swing harder."

I said, "Was it your back swing, your forward swing, your arm swing or your follow through?"

They go, "I don't know."

I said, "Ask your club coach that."

Then, if they come back and they say, "This is what they said, just hit harder," then I know as a trainer that I've got a free ride of saying whatever I want.

If the kid comes back and says, "My back swing is way too slow," then guess what? I'll help that kid's back swing get better.

You know what happens with this generation?

Everybody is so interested in criticizing what everybody else is doing – whether it's right or wrong – that they've forgotten that there's a kid that's 12 years old, 13, 14, 15, that's being told by two different adults what they're doing wrong. Now, the kid's looking and saying, "Do I believe my club coach? Do I believe my trainer? Do I believe my high school coach? Because my club coach is telling me that my high school coach doesn't know what they're talking about."

You go in a restaurant and what happens? Your food is late. What comes out? The waiter comes out and says, "Hey. Look, I'm really sorry about your food's late, but the cook is the problem."

That never used to happen. That customer service person would come out and say, "I'm really sorry that we've had a delay. We'll get you your food. We're going to offer you a free dessert. We're really sorry."

What's happened? People first are not accountable. Second of all, they think that they are owed this. Third is they can't stand it when people make them be accountable. This generation.

You say, "Ruth, what's going on? Why are these?"

I say, "It's my fault. It's my fault. Guess what? I'll make up to you."

What is it that you cannot admit that it's your fault? I think it's part of learning. I got fired from LSU. Am I proud of it? I can tell you this. I sure learned a lesson. I think everybody should be fired once because you know what? You'll re-evaluate yourself. You'll change if you really truly believe that it's everybody involved. It's not just you. It wasn't just the administration. It wasn't the players. It wasn't just one thing. Everybody is involved in it. Everybody is willing to blame everybody but themselves.

I'll tell you who had the most influence on me after I got fired from LSU. I said I would never go back and coach ever again. Mick called me. He says, "Ruth, I know you're saying you're not going to ever get back in coaching, but you need to remember that there is a lot that can be learned through every process that you go through."

I said, "No, I'm not ever going to coach again."

I ended up being flown to Dallas to be interviewed for my professional team, the Dallas Belles. My general manager was Gary Carroll. He helped develop the Canadian Football League with John Ralston. They met me at the airport.

The first question that John Ralston asked me is, "Why did you get fired at LSU?"

It was like, here's the A.D. at LSU. There were fifteen people who got fired that year. He said in the media, "Ruth needs to go coach the Olympic team. She's best suited for there."

I thought in my mind, "Okay now, what is it and why did I get fired?" It wasn't just because of administration. It wasn't just me. It was everything about everything that you need to learn in this process.

I said to him, "I think there's probably some things that I could have changed. I think that I've learned from that situation, and I really do want to be better about coaching. I want to be the best I can be. I think that as long as I'm open to making changes in coaching, I'm going to be better."

He says, "You're hired."

I go, "What?"

My general manager Gary Carroll changed my approach. That's when I went back to college coaching, because of him. He said, "Ruth, all the training happens in practice. When the game comes, it's show time."

Do you know I became a cheerleader after that? I loved every second when I went to Iowa. When I went back people didn't want to hire me because I was the first one to get fired. I wasn't even the first choice at the University of Iowa. I told this to a kid the other day. I said, "It's not bad to be the second choice." At the time, boy! It was like I wasn't quite ready to say I was the second choice because I knew I had more experience than the other person. I can tell you I became a cheerleader. To this day, I'm a cheerleader.

You know what? All the players that played for me that now have been around me, and they see me doing things, they go, "Ruth,...."

And I go, "You don't need to say it. I wish I would have changed earlier in my career."

John, think about how many people can stand up and talk about things that happened to them in their lives that are terrible? It was the best thing that happened to me. I sure read *Who Moved My Cheese* many times because I don't like to change.

What were you like before you became a cheerleader? What was Ruth's on-court demeanor?

Very disciplined. All you needed to do is look at me to know if I was happy or no. You didn't need to yell, and didn't need to curse. You just knew how I felt if you looked at me.

I really love the sport. It is what we are.

Think about this. Everyone always says, "You are the way you've been trained." When I was on the national team I had Moo Park as my first coach. Jim Coleman was very laid back. He's the one that first started... They didn't call it first tempo at the time. Arie really started talking about tempo with set. Jim Coleman was running a 71, a 91, a 31. I learned all that when I was setting with him. He used to train me every single day because I wanted to be a setter.

What was it then? How did I change? Because I thought you had to be tough. You know what? Because I was so young and I was always around the kids that were only a few years younger than me, that I felt like that's what I needed to do.

Somebody asked me the other day, "Coach, what do you think? How are you as far as stuff now as you were when you were in college?"

I said, "I'm 10% of what I was in college."

They go, "Seriously?" because I am very structured, but I really have a good sense of humor. I just wish that I would have made those changes.

I can tell you this. The 10-and-under kids benefit from my change. Maybe I would have never been at this level had I not had such ... Who would have thought? Again, we go back to football. Tom Landry, Gary Carroll, John Ralston – all successful football people – probably influenced me more besides Jim Coleman than anybody else in my career. It doesn't have to be someone who's in your sport.

Do I consider myself motivational? Yes. Do I think that I can motivate a team? Yes. How did we beat Illinois when they were ranked #1 in the country in an hour and fifteen minutes, 3-0 at their own facility – full house and everything? Because it's all about motivation. It's all about training. If you know you've trained everybody to prepare themselves to be successful, you'll be successful.

I think it's my psychology background. Thank God I had psychology – almost a double major in psychology – because I think that affects not only parents these days but kids.

Let me ask you something about pro volleyball since you coached it at the time when it existed. Can professional volleyball in the US become successful? Become a viable ongoing sport?

Let's just say this. If you asked me, "Ruth, what has changed since 1970?" Everybody always says Title IX. I don't think it's Title IX because I don't think that's changed that much. Yes, there's scholarships, but the fact is this. Until you get more media – male and female – that their daughters play the sport and they go watch them, will it ever really be televised as much?

Now, let's go to the next part which you're asking me the question. Professional volleyball. Now you've got to remember where I've been in Texas, in the south, which male sports dominate, and it's a man's world. However, I can tell you that a lot of mentors you realize are male. That sport is dominated by male coaches now.

My question is how do I feel that the sport has changed and what's been an instrumental in making the change? As much as I hate to say it, it's Karch Kiraly. The reason why is because I think he cares about the success that he has as a coach that he's going to make sure that women's volleyball gets notoriety.

I can tell you this. Arie changed the way women's volleyball was played in this country, and many times around the world. Was he endorsed or embraced here in this country? Probably not.

He probably is more respected now because they saw what he did and how successful he was considering the fact that you had Debbie Green [setter] playing front court, sometimes in the middle when you're playing against Cuba, and Flo moved to the right side. Rose moved outside and was still successful. Flo played all the way around and every player played all the way around.

Why do we have to specialize now when in 1984 they didn't specialize that much? Yes, in setters, yes. In reality, everyone played all the way around. Debbie Landreth [now Brown] played all the way around

Everybody says the game's changed so much. I look at what's happened with women's volleyball. What is it? Karch has brought notoriety. Is it because USA Volleyball has supported him? Okay, let's say this. Would the US men's program hire a male coach that has two years of experience? You answer that question.

Not likely.

No, no, they never have. In reality, the only female coach we've ever had was Lang Ping. It's not because no one's interested. I think what happens is you're talking about a country that's very much dominated by leadership in male. [Carly] Firiona, who was with Hewlett-Packard, now they're talking about her and how they fired her because she wasn't being successful. Did they fire every man that's not successful? No.

My point to you is I believe Karch has been one of the most influential things in our sport. The other person is Kerri Walsh. Kerri Walsh didn't spend very much time indoors. Yet, guess what? The media loves beach volleyball, women. You know what? In fact our sport is becoming more popular in this country.

I haven't forgotten about what you asked me about the pros, because I think it's part of this. You must have more leadership by women in order for the sport to grow into what you're talking about as far as the pro league. Or you must have people that aren't involved in volleyball run this sport, like Gary Carroll and John Ralston. They were not volleyball people. They were marketing and football coaches that saw that the media saw women in sports and what they wore and the way they displayed.

I'll never forget when we did the first draft. You know one of the biggest conversations was, "What are we wearing as coaches?"

You should wear what you're supposed to wear and you're a role model for women in sports. Nowadays, I'm sorry to say that I saw some people at JOs [Junior National Championships, sometimes still referred to by the old name, Junior Olympics] that they were wearing tank tops with tattoos showing. What but our sport? Would you ever see that in basketball at the top level? No.

My question is, are we making it a sport that is a leisure sport? Are we making it a professional sport?

Gary Carroll and John Ralston said, "Look, when we travel this is what, everybody should be doing. This is a sport that we want people to respect. We want them to say, 'That's women's professional volleyball.'"

I can tell you, I loved that about those guys.

You're not in the collegiate ranks anymore but you might have

some thoughts. To my mind, it's getting to the point where the so-called Power 5 conferences are almost de facto professional volleyball. Where do you see that going?

You know what? Let's take in the '70s. Everybody in the whole world thought we're professional because we gave college scholarships in 1974 with Title IX. Are we any different in the sense of complete commercialization? Maybe volleyball in the Power 5 will help get TV contracts which will allow DII, and all the other DI schools, and DIII schools, and NAIA schools for volleyball to be popular.

I can tell you this. I know for a fact two years ago the Big Ten – because I was in the Big Ten and I know the person who was on the committee for the development of the Big Ten television contract – said that women's volleyball packs a lot of stadiums in the Big Ten. Many times the stadiums are not packed when women's basketball plays. In reality, you and I know it's all based on money.

Are the rich going to get richer? Yes. Yes, they are.

How can the sport still continue to develop knowing that?

First of all, we know where all the best athletes are going to go. Guess what? They can't continue to increase the roster unless they're going to have a JV program too. You've got twenty kids that are now on rosters. I can't even hardly believe that DI schools have 18-20 kids.

Will that change that much? I think it will change a lot. Is it any different than any of the other male sports that are in those conferences? Do I hate to see it do that? Yes and no.

You know what? John, it's almost like someone asked me the other day, "Ruth, how do you decide where to spend your energy?"

I said, "I have a list." I have an A and a B."

I tell this to all the athletes. "I want you to list on A everything you love about volleyball. On B, I want you to list the things that you don't like. I'm going to give you fifteen minutes a day that you can complain about it. After you complain about it for fifteen minutes, I don't care who it's to – your friends, your parents, whatever – you can't complain anymore. "

I state that I'm going to spend time on the things that matter to me –

that I can have an effect on. Guess what? On the Bs, I really don't have many things left over there, whereas before I used to have a lot of Bs.

Circling back because you've touched on this already. Women in coaching is a continuous debate, or at least talking point. Since I started coaching Division I, I know every year, there was at least one more article about, "How come there aren't as many women in coaching volleyball?", "How come there aren't enough women at the top level?", "How can we keep more women in?", "How can we get more women involved?" What do you think is the core issue here and how, if at all, can we improve the situation?

First of all, I think it's almost like we have to come to a consensus. Is it important to have women in coaching? Because that maybe is one of the things that, when we grew up, the majority were women coaching.

You've got to remember, we all had physical education degrees, like Marilyn (master's degree physical education). Mary Jo. Linda Dollar. I can go down the list of female coaches.

Now, everybody wants to say, "Yeah, because women want to have a family. They want to have kids, and they just..."

No, that's not necessarily true. I look at Vivian Stringer. She was at Iowa, coaching women's basketball. Her husband took care of the kids. She was coaching.

I don't think it's all about family. I think it's a question of women that love sports. This is my gut feeling. I think you're going to find more women in this generation that's going to be graduating college going on. I think you're going to find more of those women coming back to coaching college. I think it will change. The reason why is because I think those that do go in...

Here's an example. Danielle Scott. Why is she not recognized in this country? She's the only 5-time Olympian. There's three in the world. Brazil, Russia, and her. I think she's the prime candidate to go back and coach at the collegiate level, but she's not finished playing yet.

I can tell you this. Where Flo was making $25,000, you've got players that are making $2 million now. The question is what do they do after they can't play any longer? Do they still love the sport, or do they love the sport because they're making all that money?

You take Rose. I bring up Rose a lot because she's a very good business person. She's the only Olympic player that I know that has paid for and owns her own facility in Huntsville, Alabama, and is coaching now, finally, at the DI level. She was at the NAIA level for 17 years. I would put her up against anybody as far as a trainer is concerned.

She was also coached by Arie. She was coached by myself. She was in Japan for ten years. She was at Martin Methodist. You can go down the list. The question is, do I see her as a potential down the road getting more involved in the sport? Yes. I also think she's influencing a lot more of the youth which we're considering women in sports.

But I still think John, you still have to go back and you've got to have people at the decision-making level that are women. USA volleyball has never had a woman in charge ever, except one. I think she filled in, Becky Howard. Becky and I used to play on the same team when I was growing up in Colorado. She was absolutely wonderful.

Then you say, "Okay, why isn't there?"

I can't really answer that. I'm hoping. You know the one person that made the biggest difference in women's sports of anybody else that I know of in this country is Donna Lopiano – Dr. Donna Lopiano. Her background was softball and volleyball. She became the women's A.D. at Texas over men and women. She changed the world for athletics there. They respected a woman that could raise money.

You know what happens? There aren't very many women that really want to be in those positions, I don't think. If somebody asked me, "Would I change the way I do things now? Would I still be at that level?" Yes.

If you asked me who was the best boss I ever had it would be Eunice Kennedy Shriver. She could have been the best President probably we ever had. There was too much death in her family.

How do you get more women involved? I think what happens is there's got to be a network of women that really support each other. I don't believe that there's a lot of that now. I think it's like we said. I really had a lot of role models that were male and I really appreciate all the male role models.

Also, there are some things about, "Hey! Women in sports." You treat them different than men.

I coached men's volleyball. I coached men's tennis. Do I feel that on every single coaching staff there should be males and females? If you've got a male head coach you better have assistant coach who's female – or associate head coach. If you've got a female head coach, I think it is good to have an assistant man that wants to be better because they want to learn more about how to coach women in sports. I think there's a lot of demographic stuff that happen in women's volleyball and girls' junior volleyball that a guy is not exposed to. Why is it that there are more guys that are coaching junior volleyball than there are girls?

Are there?

Yeah. I look around at the Dallas-Fort Worth area and I go, "Wow!" It's a business.

That would be the question that I ask because the money invariably tends to get tied into this debate because people argue that it was when the money started coming in to volleyball, and especially in Division I, that the proportion of women head coaches started to shrink. We could tie that into club coaches in a hotbed like Dallas, or maybe other places as well in the country. What would you say to that?

I think that there's a way in which, most athletic programs are run by males. I think there's two or three women in the country that are running men's and women's departments. I don't think there are very many women that really want that kind of role. I think there are some women that really do enjoy sports at the highest level. First of all, administrative-wise. That means that a volleyball coach...

Let's just take an example of a female volleyball coach is going to report to one of two people. One is the SWA [Senior Women's Administrator] – which is really a woman that's been in charge of the women's department, because now you've got to have women involved – or the male.

If you were to ask me which one would I rather report to? I'd rather report to the male. Why is that? Because I think that anybody who's been brought up around sports really can talk sports.

Guys approach it differently. It's almost like you don't know. Nobody knows what you know until you tell them what you don't know. A guy may go in and interview. He's going to say, "I'm coming in. We're going to win the national championship. We're going to recruit this player and this, and this."

I don't think women come in and do that. I don't think women are taught to do that. I think they take a different approach to things.

That's why if you asked me who do I think is one of the best coaching staffs in the country, I'm going to tell you John and Laurie Corbelli [Texas A&M. Laurie is the head coach, with John as the assistant]. John was with us with the national team for almost nine years. Laurie was at Texas Lutheran when I was coaching. The combination of a husband/ wife team... Oh, my goodness! In volleyball I think that it's positive, because especially for that diverse group.

To answer your question, I think that women as a whole approach male A.D.s very differently than a male does. I think also the reverse is I think a male A.D. approaches women coaches differently than they do a male coach.

I think there's a lot more. You know what? It's always been said since I started in the coaching ranks, it's the Good Ol' Boys system. Guys are helping each other. There aren't very many women that help each other. There really aren't. Is it because you're outnumbered now? Because it used to be all the women helped each other.

I can tell you I knew Pat Summitt [highly respected women's college basketball coach] when I was coaching Houston. I knew Joan Joyce when I was at Houston. You knew all the women coaches all over because of the organization.

Let's now address the NCAA. Has there ever been a woman in charge of the NCAA? No.

Now, we're talking about a second organization. You had the AIAW, which was completely run by women, change to the NCAA, which is completely run by men. Now, all of a sudden, the NCAA is controlling the women's organization. Do you think it's a priority? No. I don't think it's a priority. I think it's like anything else.

My best relationships were with the football coach and the basketball coach at the university, men's basketball coach at each of the universities that I was at.

Hayden Fry [football coach at Iowa]. I trained some of Hayden's football players. Arnsparger at LSU. He'd come and say, "Okay Ruth. I can't believe you're running the offense. You have more plays than we have on the football team."

Yeoman [Houston] says, "Ruth, you deserve a trainer because your girls work hard."

It's almost like, I think you almost have to prove that you deserve something, whereas I think when a guy gets something, I don't think they have to prove as much. That's my opinion.

Looking from the outside. I never had a problem. Like Cedric Dempsey... He was the A.D. at Houston. I absolutely loved that guy – absolutely loved him.

Now, there's some that I've not really cared too much for. I can say that I think that you have to produce. Now, someone says, "The pressure wasn't on Ruth to produce."

I say, "No, we had pressure. We didn't have any staff."

I didn't have one assistant coach at Houston for eight years. I did it all and I taught. In my 16 years, I taught, supervised student teachers, and coached. At Houston and George Williams, I coached two sports.

When someone says, "Yeah, you didn't have the pressure."

Yes we did. It was internal pressure. My internal pressure was probably more than any pressure any athletic department would put on me. I think it depends on how you're brought up.

To answer your question about women in sports, I have a feeling that time will change. I don't know if it will be in my lifetime. I will continue to mentor female coaches on why it's important for them to be involved in women's sports, because I think it's critical.

The mentorship thing.

Yes.

It's good to circle back to that, because there was an article I read which had nothing to do with sports. It was strictly business-related. It had to do with mentorship differences between the genders, and how the mentors approached mentoring men versus mentoring women.

I'm remembering correctly, the subject of the article was a male senior manager. He at some point realized that in mentoring men he was mentoring them on a technical level. What skills do you need to develop to advance your career? When he was mentoring women – he obviously only realized this after the fact – what he found himself doing more was mentoring them on building self-confidence. It was more of the psychological and less of the technical. While it was valuable to them obviously, they were still coming up short because they weren't getting the technical mentoring that the men were getting. Is that something that you've seen?

I think the best boss I ever had was Eunice Kennedy Shriver, and the reason why is she was to the point. She told me exactly what I needed to get done. "I'm going to leave you to it because you're an expert at what you do." I think that a lot of female administrators that I've had in the past, they weren't the decision maker.

It's like anything else. Me personally, if you ask me who do I want to deal with, I want to deal with the person who makes the decision. Don't give me three people that have to go up the chain. I want to know the person, and I want to know exactly what you're expecting of me.

Let's look at female coaches now that are now coming into their first year of coaching. What exposure are they given to success? Success to them means winning. We were brought up completely differently. Success [to us] meant that you had kids that are graduating from college. Everybody already has in their mind that they're winning or they're losing. It's almost like how you approach success in winning or losing.

I'll never forget Dr. Cecile Reynaud said something to me at a CAP clinic. Marilyn and I were doing a refresher course. She [Cecile] goes, "Ruth, you coach more 13s and 14s than I do. Tell me what you would do when you sub."

I said, "This generation you don't ever sub anybody out for mistakes, because you now have completely lost them emotionally."

In men's tennis, once you're proven and you're the head coach, and they respect you, it's like you tell them, "I want you to serve volley and I want the shot to go to their backhand deep." You say that to a guy and a guy does it. You say it to Sally, "Sally, I need you to jump." She goes, "I'm jumping."

I go, "No, you're not jumping. Okay, now what I'll do is I'll put a VERT on you."

She jumps thirteen inch, and she goes, "I guess I'm not."

It's almost like it doesn't matter if you're a male or a female coaching a female team. It's almost like girls are so emotional about everything. I think it's gotten worse, because if you never failed in something, how do you adapt to anything else?

Right.

I don't think there's enough failure going on.

It's interesting that you talk about that because Anson Dorrance, the North Carolina women's soccer coach, wrote in one of his books years ago that the way he looked at the difference between coaching men and women was with a female team or a female group of athletes, all you needed to say was, "We need to do this," or "We aren't doing this," and every single one of those women is going to think that it's her fault. If it's a male team, you actually need to show them, "You, specifically you Joey, see on this video right here, you're not doing this right." Otherwise, none of the guys are going to believe it's their fault.

Now, I have a question. I had two years ago a 13-year-old boy I was training. Every session that he was in, he cried, because I was asking him to do stuff.

Now, that [what Dorrance said] might have been true 10 years ago. I'm not sure that guys are... They are different now. I'm not so sure that they like failure now either. I only say that because I'm not training a bunch of guys.

Are guys really different at certain level? Let's say high school.

We all know they're going to be different at the international level because the expectations are different.

My question is are female athletes and male athletes really that much separated now because of the iY generation? Because guess what? I know you do approach guys differently. I coached a men's volleyball team at Houston. I can tell you that I love coaching men, because the fact is, it's just like what you said. I do believe there's a different approach that you have to take.

You know what's sad is, why do you need a different approach?

Someone called me and asked me, "Ruth, tell me, how is it that you are so good at recruiting minority athletes?"

I said, "It's no different than if you were to recruit a player from another country."

They go, "What do you mean by that?"

I go, "It's a culture difference."

They go, "I never looked at it that way."

It is. It's no different than if I'm going to recruit a kid from Oak Cliff and Southlake, two different demographics, two different socioeconomics. My point is that I do believe that you have to approach everybody completely different now.

You know what's really sad is? I think for me, my feeling is I can be picky on who I train now. I wish that it were that easy for everybody else. I'm so happy I am where I am today, because I believe that I got a chance to coach when it was the most fun time in coaching. The athletes loved what they were doing. They loved the sport.

Now I want to be able to have an influence on those female coaches that want to be mentored. I do have a male coach that drives in three and a half hours every Sunday that trains with me, that wants to be better.

I've always had male coaches too that I mentor. By and large, I'll mentor anyone that believes that they can learn still.

Those that think they can't learn? They shouldn't probably be around me on the same court.

You mentioned the mentoring. Before you talked about doing consulting work with Division I programs. When you do that, what sort of things do you focus on?

First of all, I look at this. In every successful program there's always been somebody before you that made you successful. You didn't come in and just be in the Final Four. No program. I look at Kentucky. Marilyn, was there. I look at Florida, Marilyn was there. I look at Sul Ross. Marilyn McReavy again. The only reason is because that's history.

My point is that I think mentoring people is very critical in the development stages of giving your expertise from which you've been exposed to because someone says, "Ruth, let's put you next to somebody who has 40 years of experience."

They said, "What would you say? Is that coach better than you?"

I said, "It doesn't have anything to do with who's better. Look to see what exposure each of us has had."

If someone's only coached at DII level for 40 years in the US, there's no way that they were exposed to what I was exposed to. It doesn't matter that they didn't choose to do that. My point is that if you're not exposed to lots of different ways to approach things, how can you even be the best you can be no matter what level you're at? Even at junior high level or even at high school. I mentor a lot of high school coaches too.

I may go in, and I may sit, and I may watch the training. I'm not a person who comes in and says, "What you're doing is wrong." I'm not someone who comes in and says, "I don't like the offense you're running." I don't come in and say, "I don't like the way you do this." I believe I'm non-threatening. I'm very supportive of that coach, no matter what level it's at.

I do believe with the exposure that I've had in so many aspects besides my education and experiences that I've had, that I can be very objective.

I don't believe I'm subjective. I believe I'm very objective based on my experience.

I may say, "You know what? I think the most important thing is really developing a culture within your staff."

If you are sponsored by X company, then every single person that's on that staff has to wear X product. You can't have someone saying, "I got up late today and I just put on something else." You know what? That's culture. I think that everything filters from the top-down, just like I do it in a junior program. If the club director does not say that you need to quit wearing jeans when you're coaching, then guess what? Everybody is going to wear what they want, correct?

Right.

I think it's easy for me to come in and get that team excited about their coach, and respecting their coach, and rejuvenating a group of kids, because you know what? I've made so many mistakes in my entire life and my career that I think that I can look back and say, "Okay now, what are the things, Ruth, that are very important?"

If you asked me, what are the most important things I think in a staff? Loyalty, loyalty, loyalty. Everything else you can teach someone. It's very difficult to teach loyalty.

Right.

Why is it that people have to be recognized at what they do as an assistant coach, or a third assistant, or this? I walked in and I was Arie's assistant. I did exactly what he wanted me to do. I ran the drill exactly what he wanted. He told me he wanted to emphasize certain things and I did that. Why is it nowadays that you have an assistant come in and they're going to tell you everything they think that you're doing wrong? Where did they get all that experience? Why aren't they there to learn?

I'm sure that you've listened to my speech for the AVCA [Hall of Fame] induction. It was addressed to everybody. Everybody should be respecting. Everybody should learn from anybody. I tell a junior kid, "You need to learn something for every experience that you're in. This club coach, that assistant coach, this club experience. You've got to learn something that you know exactly what it is that you've learned. You can't be complaining about everything. When you become a head coach and you are on the line to be fired or not, then you get to make those decisions."

Then again, I think there's too much specialization in coaching staffs. Think of this. You've got someone who's coaching the libero. You've got someone who's coaching the defense. Look at some of these DI programs. Then you've got a kid that's trying to figure out, "I'm trying to do this, but does it mesh with this? Does it work with this?

I think the ideal leader is the person who gets people at their strengths that they have, for instance, "What do I lack?" What could someone actually say they lack in?

It's almost recognizing where you are in your life and career and profession, and really become better at the things you're not strong at. Don't spend a lot of time getting at that. Why not surround yourself with the best people? Don't you think that that's what leaders are? They find the people that are good at things. I also think that a good leader also learns to mesh people in with what they're doing.

When I'm mentoring a DI coach – or a DII, or DIII, or in NAIA, or high school – I think it's very important to help that person understand how do I get better? I don't get better just by coaching. I get better by expanding my piece of the puzzle.

I tell a kid in high school, "This is such a small piece of your puzzle of your whole life that when you look back in college you're going to look back and you're going to see that puzzle was a lot bigger than that one piece that you were bothered by."

It's finding a niche that you really believe that you're good at. People always ask that question to me. "How did you know that this is what you wanted to do?"

"I did it and it was fun. I did it and it was so rewarding."

Have you ever been around a kid that the kid says, "Coach, there's no way I'm going to touch the rim," and they're touching 10.5 now?

One kid the other day said to me, "Ruth, I did not believe that I could do this."

I said, "That's my responsibility to make sure that you get there first so that you recognize how much better you could have been."

She goes, "I didn't recognize it soon enough."

I said, "No, if it's August 1st and it's your first year in college, then it's probably late. It isn't late because this is August 1st and it's your junior year in high school."

People don't believe in themselves, John. I think that's the problem. They say they do but they really don't believe in themselves – in what they can do and what they can't do.

I think I was talking with somebody about this recently. Our role as coaches, as much as we're there to provide technical feedback, the tactical feedback, or whatever, we're also there to show them that they're actually developing – that they're on a path to getting better because we can see it. They're so close to it, they have a hard time seeing it.

You know it's funny. When I first started my BYOP program, I had all the players. We took pictures. Then I had someone design the cartoon characters based on those pictures of those kids. Then they got to come up with what they wanted on the back swag. They got to come up with all the slogans. They get to come up with all the cheers. One of the best cheers that a five-year-old came up with is it says, "Pink and black, don't talk back." Because we were talking about respecting your parents.

A five-year-old.

Yeah.

Cheers, that they really want to engage and they want to have a sense that they're part of it. I think women in sports. I think that's one of the hardest things because they really feel part of it, because every time you turn on the TV, you're watching a male sport. It's no different than when we were brought up. We really had nothing. Men's sports had everything. How are we still loving what we do? Because we have an appreciation to have had nothing. Our first set of shorts – and at the time you remember they were... I don't even know if you remember this, they're called bun-huggers [briefs].

Yeah.

At LSU, guess what? The secretary cut our shorts off from the store – the bookstore. We got them and sewed them up, and we had a pair of bun-huggers. I paid for the full set of Adidas shoes from our first LSU team. If you don't understand the history, you have no respect.

Let me give just two quotes that I really believe in, "Old school ideas make it happen and become new school methods."

The other day I said to someone – I put it on Facebook – I said, "I am so happy I'm old school." It's almost like, if you can't be proud...

And I always say this too, "Without knowing and respecting the history, there is no future."

Someone said that people won't talk about the history. I said, "Because they weren't part of the history."

They want to make you think that what is now is the history and it's not. Daimatsu was the history in the 1964 Olympic Games with the first volleyball involved. The guy was absolutely ... like I said, I have the tape of the way they trained. You know what? That probably made the history of what the sport is today. The culture around a sport.

Someone asked me one day, "Ruth, why don't you do what everybody else is doing, but just do it better?"

I said, "Because I don't agree with what everybody else does."

Because I think what I'm doing is better already.

No, I never said that. You've talked to me a long time and you should know I wouldn't be saying that.

Internal dialogue.

Yeah. If you're not really having fun...

Here's an example. Stephanie Schleuder really developed the Minnesota program. She and I were in the Big Ten. We were coaching. We had four or five people scorekeeping. We're in Hawkeye Arena, which is just this unbelievable place. We had to play the best kind of defense because we had an average block of 13 inches. I had the average ACT of 27. We had to play good defense because we were the worst blocking team. We had to run down balls and all this. I'd look down at Steph. We had the best dialogue. Our jobs still were on the line. We could still get fired. I'd go, "Steph, don't you need to sub?" I'd do my little S like sub. She would just crack up. We had fun, but we were competitive.

It's become so cut-throat that it's... You didn't demean someone to beat them. You beat them. You beat them because you outplayed them on that day. It didn't mean that you were a better team overall. It meant that day you were better than they were and you beat them.

Now it's like... I don't like to see it with people arguing across, and the parents yelling from the stands and saying the score is wrong.

We were playing in this league. I saw a parent doing that. I called the time out, and went and talked to parents. I said, "I don't want you doing anything with the referee. I don't want you even looking at the referee. I want you to cheer when we do three hits and your daughter gets the ball up in the air, whether it was over the net or not. That's more than what she did before. That's what you need to get excited about. That's what I'm excited about."

Somebody says, "Ruth, how do you really educate the parents?" I said, "One person at a time."

Let me ask you something based on your earlier description of yourself as a program builder. If you were to take over a Division I program now, what would your priorities be?

First of all, I would like to have a program for one year because I'd like $300,000 a year. I'd probably come back, and I would develop minority programs and youth programs for free.

Seriously, I think first of all, I do match very well, like I told you, with the iY generation because I do get very bored. You will never see me do one drill more than probably five to seven minutes, at the most. I think that this generation loves that because they get so bored. I think you can make things challenging, and fun, and creative. I think that I would look at things like I've always done, and that is making it entertaining, because to me the sport is so exciting.

I think to get everybody to really work closely together, that is an unbelievable feat in itself with this generation – the iY generation.

How to get the community involved?

I'm always a big believer that you can get people excited about the sport. It's like Coach Arnsparger, the football coach. He came over just to watch because we were running plays. You can get other people involved in the sport. I think the hardest thing is that I think you get so hung up on two issues. I still think it's happening now. That is, how much more women's basketball gets than you do? Or second is, how much you think you should be getting in support that you're not getting?

You can't ever really begin to look at that. You have to figure out, "How do I get more of those people to support what I'm doing?" Because what I'm doing is really exciting and fun. I think what happens is people forget that this really is fun.

Would I in reality want a DI job? Absolutely not, because you have to be what Pat Head Summitt said about four years ago. She said, "I spend 80% more of my time doing team dynamics than I do anything else."

I can say I was never a team dynamics coach. My team dynamics was, "Okay, we're at LSU, and guess what? You know how to canoe, correct? Yes. Okay, that's your partner. I want to see you down at the bottom of the river when we get there."

That was my team building.

Now, I'm extremely good at team building when I go in and I mentor, because I'm good about, "Okay now, this is how you do it. This is attitude. 'A' stands for what? 'T' stands for this. 'I' stands for this. What does this mean to everybody? I want you to stand up and tell me what you think is important about the 'E' and 'equal'." I'm good at that stuff now. Maybe because I'm realizing that I should have been doing more of it, but then maybe I didn't need to do more of it because the kids weren't different then. Maybe I would have been so much more successful had I done that.

I think to me, the most fun is helping someone recognize at whatever level they're at – at DI, DII – it's all the same because they all believe that what they're doing they want to be successful. I love seeing that person see how they've developed over whether it's three days, or four days, or five days, or seven days that I might be around in a different situation – or maybe I'm Skyping the team before they're playing and doing something motivational.

Somebody says, "Ruth, how do you feel that you can do this?"

I go, "Because I love what I do."

I have energy. I've never not had energy. Now, do I get tired when I come home with five and six-year-olds? Oh my God! It's like I have to come home and say, "I can't even believe how much I wanted to laugh out loud because they did something or said something really funny."

One of them looked at me the other day and said, "Coach Ruth, do you practice at home?"

I had to sit and think to myself, in my mind. Do I practice what I'm going to say to them? Yes, I do because they crack me up, because I do know they get excited about things. To me, it's more getting the parents excited about what their kid does. They will laugh and see that their kid just got a pass, and a pass and an attack.

The other day, three five-year-olds, the parents said to me, "Ruth, we would have never thought our kids could do this." That's the problem, because people don't believe that they can do it.

Yeah, it drives me crazy. I hate it when I go into a gym, or talk to a coach... I used to do this with high school coaches. I would ask them, "How come you're not running a quick attack?"

"We don't pass well enough."

"Do you see the problem with this right now? You're not giving them a reason to pass any better."

Interesting to me. You know what one of my players said to me the other day. She's a high school kid, a junior. She says, "You know what Ruth? I'm really getting better at passing."

I said, "Yeah, that's what you're supposed to do."

She says, "We never practice passing ever in practice."

I said, "What do you mean passing?"

They go, "No, like a free ball. Like when somebody hits a down ball. They don't jump or maybe they hit from the back court."

I said, "That's probably why you can't run your offense. If you can't pass the free ball, how can you run an offense?"

Because we run more stuff on free balls than we do on service reception, because now everybody does it.

You know what I did? I taught an eighth grader the other day in seven minutes how to jump float serve. An eighth grader. The kid has never jump floated.

Now, I taught an eleven-year-old how to do it in five minutes because they had no habits. The eighth grader had seen other people. Do you know what that tells me? That kid was so attentive to learn. I think the problem is I do believe the iY generation kids want to learn. I also think you need to help them so that they understand the reason why they're hitting the left side line across the net is because they're dropping this shoulder down and they're swinging there because they're coming over the top of their head. Have them go throw a football? You can't throw a football over the top of your head.

You could try.

Yeah. That's right. Obviously they're not a quarterback, huh?

I think I've exhausted basically my questions. Is there anything that we haven't talked about you'd like to bring up?

I would just say this. Love what you do, do what you love for as long as you love it.

I believe no matter what level you're coaching at, you've got to see that you're having an impact on whatever level it is. Do not ever, ever worry about whether someone is going to come and thank you, because if I waited for a thank you, I would have quit my first year of coaching. You do it because it's for the right reason. You don't do it so that you can get a raise. You don't do it so that you can be the next high performance coach. You don't do it and say, "I need to coach at the college level because there's more status there."

You've got to look at where you are and realize how much of an impact that you are making. I can tell you that I am making a bigger impact at this age group than I ever was at any other level. It's probably much more meaningful to me because you see the joy of a five or a six-year-old who then becomes a ten-year-old – that they are better suited because I've taught them how to play and all the skills, and to understand the game. "The most important thing is that you can now serve from the left side. You can serve from the right side. It's not about serving from the left side so they can run the left back. It's about serving from the left side because the angle is different."

I think you can teach the kids offensive and defensive things. We have what we call line defense. We have line receive. We have line free ball. They're all the same, because the first time we ever played we had 27 out of rotation calls because I had them come to the huddle and shout a cheer and they forgot where they were. Get excited about something because it doesn't matter what level you're at, because if you can show that you're enthusiastic about what you do and you train them to become the best they can be, they will always still enjoy the sport. And don't allow them to feel they can't do it.

4

JEFFERSON WILLIAMS

Transplant Jefferson Williams has amassed a ridiculous amount of silverware while coaching in his adopted country, England. His men's club teams have won 20 national championships and 15 cup titles. The women's teams he's coached have grabbed another 12 national titles and 11 cups. That adds up to 58 major championships, which is hard to beat.

Jeff has also been involved in the England and Team GB programs in a number of different roles over the years. This includes leading the English Men's National Team from 1987 to 2003. All this he manged while holding down a day job! He is considered a mentor to many of the current generation of U.K. coaches.

This interview was conducted by John in July, 2015. It is one to which many readers can probably relate because Jeff is basically a part-time coach and always has been. As such, he's faced many of the same challenges a lot of coaches face.

Share with us how you got into coaching and where it's taken you.

I was born in Jamaica. I immigrated to Canada and I discovered volleyball at high school on the South Side of Montreal. First played in '75 not realizing that volleyball would be a big event in the 1976 Olympics. I saw it then for the first time really live – well not live, but I saw what the game was about. I was impressed with the Polish team and a guy called Skorek. I then took it up seriously from 1977 in the Canadian Junior National Team, and played for a club called Hochelaga in Montreal. We went on to win the Provincial championships, as well as the Canadian Junior Championships.

In the Summer of 1977 I played in a tournament in Hawaii with the Junior National Team, against the likes of Dusty Dvorak, Steve Salmons, and Karch Kiraly [future USA National Team players]. We went on to win NORCECA in 1978 in Mexico, and then I got a scholarship to Rutgers Newark.

Up to then I had no interest in coaching, really. It was pretty much just playing, but then I discovered that during the Summer some of my teammates went to a volleyball camp up in Port Jervis, New York – the World Volleyball Training Center based at the YMCA Huguenot Volleyball Camp. I applied for it, went up, and have been hooked on coaching since. A Japanese head coach and a guy called Scott Mose [head women's coach at Rutgers] ran the camp for many years. I saw the way they did things and started being influenced by them.

I started going back to the camp and picked up a lot of tips on coaching. After I graduated university, I went off to Sweden. I linked up with a guy, Ralph Hippolyte, who was coaching at the University of Pennsylvania. He was a visionary, and he opened my eyes to some of the possibilities. A lot of the things that he used to coach us at the volleyball camp exposed me to a different way of thinking about the game. To this day he's still my mentor, and a lot of the things that he taught us back then are very, very relevant. They are very relevant today.

I joined him in Sweden in 1982 after I graduated. He was coaching a volleyball team in a small town called Nyköping about an hour or so from Stockholm, and I joined him there for a season. Then he went off to France [to coach the Women's National Team] and I coached the women's team in the club the year after – and Ismo Peltoarvo then took over the men's team after Ralph went.

From there, my coaching developed. I spent 2 years in Nyköping then went to join a team in Uppsala – a team called Ultuna, who are no longer in existence, I don't think. I coached them for a year, not very successfully. I suppose I wasn't ready for that level of coaching, so it didn't go that well. Someone else took over the team, but I continued to play for the team for a couple of more seasons.

I was still doing the camps in the Summer. It was there that I met and married an English girl a few years later, which brought to me to London in 1986 and I've been here since. During that time, when I first came to London, I settled in and played for the Malory Volleyball Club. and from there, I coached England Women's Cadets. I think it was like an under-16 team.

Six months later, in 1987, I took over the England senior men's team. I was with them from I guess '87 through to 2003. I took on the Malory team during that period from about 1991. I've been head coach of the Malory men's and women's teams since.

I went on to assist Ralph Hippolyte with the GB men's team between 1990 and '97. I was the interim head coach for the women's GB Olympic team from 2006. I coached them for a year before Lorne Sawula took over. Now I continue to coach the Malory teams, but do less of the national team stuff and a lot more around coaching education – tutoring coaches and working with coach development.

Yeah, that's the resume of my coaching to date.

You were a player-coach you mentioned in there. How long did that go on?

Well, in Sweden I was a player-coach for one season, and as I said that was not quite disastrous, but it didn't go as well as I would like it to have gone. With Malory I was probably player coach from 1991-92 through to the day I retired, although I'm not fully retired yet, but I haven't really played for the past three seasons. For the first couple of years I played and coached, then I had an assistant who worked with me for about six seasons before he took over his own team, a guy called Ian Le Grand. He went on to coach the GB women's sitting volleyball team. I suppose I was his mentor whilst Ralph was my mentor, and I've continued to work with some of the younger coaches as well. I coached Audrey Cooper, who was the GB women's coach who took them to the Olympics. I was her coach for about 16 years at Malory, and worked with her and her teammate Amanda Glover as the attempted to qualify for the beach volleyball at Sydney 2000.

Talk about the challenges of being a player-coach because I'd venture to say that a lot of people who talk to us probably won't have been in that position before.

Yeah, I'm not sure I've really thought about it. In effect, it probably is difficult because it's easy enough in training sessions where again it's more about preparing the team and trying to see how you integrate yourself into the team. I took a back seat so even though I was a player-coach, I was in effect a coach first and player second. So I became more of a super-sub. I suppose that my role was to change games when they weren't going so well. I knew I could. The level we were playing at here in England, I knew I could come in and change a game.

I did that for many years, especially after Ian left the team. Whilst Ian was there, on match day I was more a player and during training sessions... I ran the training sessions to prepare the team, but on match day I handed over the coaching to him, so again he pretty much had control of what went on the court. It was part of his development and it allowed me then to concentrate more on the playing side.

When he left, obviously, yeah, I went back into the role where I was more a coach than a player. It's quite challenging because, in effect, as a coach you're managing the relationships on court and you can probably take a backwards step since it's one dimensional. On the court you're probably first a player and off the court you're a coach. There on the court you have to hand things over almost to the captain, but I was still a leader. So in a lot of ways, yeah, there's additional pressure in knowing that you have to be responsible for your own performance, but at the same time being responsible making decisions for people on the court that in effect might be doing a bit better than you, but you've seen something that they need to change.

It didn't always go well. I know in the beginning we had some players that were big egos. It wasn't that easy to manage them. They took themselves out of the picture. Then it became a bit easier when you had the guys that came into the team that were national team players and understood a bit more about performance and the reality that, yeah, sometimes things just happen a certain way because it's for the good of the team and not necessarily to build individual ego. It became easier once people knew what the situation was, what they bought into. The fact for me was it was about the team and it wasn't so much the individual. Yeah, and experience.

Let me ask this, because you've got a perspective of things both in terms of having been part of the system but also being an immigrant to UK volleyball. How has the sport developed in the time that you've been in the country?

Wow! Well, look at it this way. When I first came over, I probably – I wouldn't say stole – I borrowed quite a few things from Sweden. When I was in Sweden, that's the time probably the best group of players that they had were coming through the system. That was the group that went on to go to the '88 Olympics as well as to the finals of the European Championships in '89, I think it was, where they lost to Italy in the finals in Stockholm. I knew that team was influenced a lot by Anders Kristiansson and what he did. Two or three of the players were in my team at Nyköping, which was coached by Ismo, who was also part of that coaching set up at the high school in Stockholm.

They had a lot of the influence directly otherwise from Hippolyte and all of a sudden got some feedback and some knowledge of what Kristiansson was doing. The offense that a lot of the English teams play now, including the national teams and a lot of the club teams, I brought with me from Sweden. When I came to the U.K. back in '86, the national team was at the stage where they were still playing high ball through the middle and didn't have a lot of understanding about structuring offense around quicker sets. There were some decent athletes, but the volleyball they were playing was outdated. With the Malory team we started to change things.

In a lot of ways we were able to attract some of the better players because we were a bit more adventurous. People saw that we very quickly became successful because our technique was so much better than what the other teams were doing. In my first season, when I joined Malory, they were mid-table. That first season we surprisingly – not for us, but for everybody else – we won the cup. I joined them about almost a third of the way into the season and we managed to finish fifth. The next season we managed to poach the best young setter in the country, a guy called Richard Dobell. He came down from the Midlands to join us, and another guy from up in Bradford, a guy called Steward Dunn, joined us. Those were two of the best young players around, and the history of Malory just took off from there.

We went on to win a lot more than we lost. The technique that I brought to the U.K. kick started things. Ralph then came in the back end of 1990, start of '91. He came and he even more so influenced or took what we were doing another few steps. When Ralph came, the guys had a good understanding of modern volleyball, and with his vision he was able to move things rapidly, rapidly forward.

If I'm honest, if you look at most of the coaches that are in their performance pathways – the likes of Simon Loftus; I know Joel Banks who is currently coaching over in Belgium, the Belgium juniors; Audrey Cooper to a certain extent; Ian Le Grand; Keith Trenam – we've all been influenced by Hippolyte and what he brought with him in the '90s. That's what we're still surviving on I suppose. He left a vision and a knowledge base that we were able to capitalize on. To be honest, we had success with a lot of the things that he was trying to do in a very short period of time with not much resources. His vision was second to none and a lot of what he taught is just now becoming clear.

I'll tell you back in 1991, sorry, 1981 at the volleyball camp that I mentioned – at the YMCA Volleyball camp – he had us run something he called a Star Wars Offense. He said, "This is where I think the game is going to go." He had us play the 5-1 system with five attackers mostly set up. You could see where things might work. We were running it successfully. At least we thought it looked okay. Three years later, in the '84 Olympics, Brazil beat up the US with the jump serves and the back court attack and then from there, things just went boom.

He had this vision that even the timing of the offense that people are using now, these are things that he said this is where we're going to be going. True to form, that's where it is. I didn't, at the time, as a player, really understand. I wasn't a coach then, but it was eye-opening. I just thought, "Well, okay, yeah, yeah, I can see," but I didn't really believe.

When he came in 1990, he had even more ideas as to where we wanted to go. He had results that were very, very unexpected because we had good athletes and a good knowledge base. We didn't have a lot of time or resources. We were training once a month for a 2-day weekend, plus the stuff that the guys were doing in their clubs, and we managed to beat France, Romania, Australia back then. It was a very successful team I think in British and in English volleyball.

Unfortunately there's no senior national team at the moment. Maybe, maybe they'll come back. [England returned to senior international competition in 2016]

Well, yeah, my understanding is that we are about to start an under 23, which is a shame because you would have thought coming out of 2012 we should have plans in place. That's why I can say without any doubt that the period of the '90s where we had the first GB team left a legacy far beyond anything that the 2012 Olympics program left, despite the fact that they had, I don't know, seven times the resources. That means a lot more time, a lot more. Still there's debate of whether they [the 2012 squad] had better athletes. I suppose some people might dispute it and tell me that I don't know what I'm talking about, but given that I've been through both programs, I can and I will still say that we got a lot more out of the '90s GB program than we did out of this Olympic program. The legacy without a doubt is from the '90s.

The impression that I've gotten, especially at the upper levels, is that volleyball in this country is more an immigrant sport than a local sport.

It's understandable. It's probably changing. Or is it changing?

I think because our proximity to Europe, and the fact that London is a world capital, and a lot of people want to come to London, inevitably some of these people will have a volleyball knowledge and they will want to continue to play the game whilst they are here. Again, that's always been the case, but the other problem is that volleyball is still very much a minority sport here. Consequently, our better athletes are not going to go into the sport. The women will inevitably go towards netball, then basketball or something else, but we don't get the best athletes. At least historically we haven't. I'm not sure that's changed. I'm not sure how that's going to change anytime soon.

You're right. The immigrants come in and because of better experience, better knowledge of the game, etc., they find clubs and inevitably they are a better level than some of our local-grown players. To be honest, it can be depressing. Look at the likes of Polonia, who are based in London. Looking at them last year, I think they probably had one or two British players.

Northumbria, because they are offering scholarships, are able to pick up some of the better English players, but a few years ago the majority of their players were actually Americans. There are not many teams that don't have a majority of foreign players. One of the things I used to pride myself on was that Malory was predominantly British-grown players, but even that's changed over the last few years. We have a youth academy, if you want to call it that, and while in there the players will come through, and they'll now go to university. In the past we used to benefit from players moving away from their local areas to come to London, going to university, and because Malory was an attractive option, again, because of descent organization, decent coaching, and people knew that they could benefit, get better from being a part of that. But that's changed. Clubs that are based around institutions [universities] are now getting players that we used to get.

So yes, you're correct. There's still a majority of influx from Europe.

When I was coaching the Devon Lady's I only had one English player.

Again, not surprising, especially down that way. It's just not surprising at all. Even though I know that Denise Austin at the Beach Volleyball Academy, they won the under-18 competition last year, so they are managing to get some athletes into their program while they drop down Plymouth and further down. I'm surprised there's volleyball down there because they are so cut off from everyone else.

The isolated lower cluster.

Well, they are. They are very isolated. I don't envy them the travel, to be honest. The way the [National] league is structured, they don't have to go too far north, but if they ever have to go to Northumbria then I suppose they would ... I'm not sure they would survive because it's bad enough going from London to Newcastle. That's Plymouth to Newcastle. That's a long trip and costly. [Note: Below the top level – the Supers 8s – the National League has a geographic split.]

It's true even with the University. The men and women both played in the southern premier league this year and one of the toughest trips was having to go to Sussex, which on the map is not that far.

Minor roads though, isn't it?

Yeah, it was a horrible trip. Actually what was even worse was the women had to go to Edinburgh for a playoff.

That's definitely a flight right?

No.

No?

They didn't fly. They took a coach.

Oh dear.

Starting at 2:00 AM. Played a match at somewhere around noon and came straight back.

Wow. I wouldn't like to do that at all.

Anyway, just going back, you talked about Japanese coaches when you were doing ...

The camps, yeah.

With the camps, right. How much has that factored into the way you coach over the years? Can you specifically say, "Oh yeah, this was definitely a Japanese influence?"

It's probably a small influence. I wouldn't say it has been a lot, to be honest, because I don't know if they still do that. The Japanese used to... The individualized drills and things weren't as linked as they should do, so if they were service you'd serve, you'd serve, you'd serve, then training the combos, you dig, you dig, you dig. Whereas I was probably more influenced by the Americans that say you get better transfer if things are linked as closer – I don't even call them drills, the exercises – the closer they are to the game situation, the more transfer. You can see where some of the Japanese philosophy is important. The case for me is how you mix that.

There is still some influences, but probably it depends also I think on the level that I'm coaching. If you're coaching younger players, I think it might switch. I won't say 50-50. Maybe a little bit 60-40 as far as doing a lot more with the individual skills so we can get that ingrained. Whereas you get to players who are used to playing and who understand a bit more about the game, skills have been acquired and it's a need to test that or to put in the situation. Then the individual stuff becomes less important for me. With the teams I coach now – especially when I was with the women's developmental squad – a lot of it was more small amounts of individual skills but more so working at it in a game situation.

I like the American philosophy that says the best way to teach passing is to pass and hit, the best way to teach hitting is to pass and hit, etc., etc. Then you can breakdown and look at the skills that you are highlighting and focus on that. But I like the flow that it's linked to the game situation. A lot of me now is working towards that. I have discussions with other colleagues, and we argue and argue and argue. But yeah. I'm more towards the game-like, so the more game-like it is the better.

I want to get back into the philosophy development but let me ask you this. What's your day job, so to speak?

I work for a housing association where I'm the director of a small association catering to young single homeless from the Caribbean background primarily. We also manage some general need stuff that is open to anyone in the public who's homeless or requires housing.

Okay, so basically, you're not a full-time coach?

No. Volleyball is my hobby.

How much time do you put into volleyball and what's your volleyball schedule like?

Well, if I can go by last season, let me see. Monday, Tuesday, Thursday, Friday I would have training on ... Monday was just the Super 8 men. Tuesday it was the academy, then the Super 8 women. Thursday, academy then Super 8 men. Friday, Super 8 women. Saturday matches, and Sunday and Wednesday were normally my days off. When I was involved with the national team then obviously once a month when we had national team camps I would be away from Friday to Sunday. Now that I'm also part of the coach education team, it depends on if they call me up to help deliver a coaching course during the summer. That may take up a few weekends, but in general the summer is my recovery time opportunity to reengage with my family.

It sounds like each team has two training sessions a week, about two hours a piece?

Yeah. That's two, six, however that works. The matches are normally back-to-back when we are at home. When we're away, sometimes back-to-back if the men and the women... Over here they tend to link. Like Wessex has men and women play on the same day along with Malory and Newcastle. When they don't, many other teams play on a Sunday which would then mean that match on a Saturday, match on Sunday. Yeah, that would be 12 hours coaching. Then the matches, which could be on a Saturday. It could be anywhere from I'm away from 12:30 through to 6:00, that's when were home. When we're way, it depends on where we're going.

Let me get back to how your philosophy developed. You talked about getting more into the "game teaches the game" sort of approach. How has your overall thoughts, or coaching style, or however you want to describe it, evolved over the years?

Oh dear. That's a tricky one. It's difficult when I talk about philosophy because I never really try to pin down my philosophy.

It doesn't have to be that formal. Just your approach. How you dealt with the players. How you strategize, or plan training, or whatever.

I'm the type of coach, I like freedom and I always resist a heavy-handed approach. Because of that, I tend to be quite... I'm laid back, but at the same time I like the boundaries. I set boundaries and within those boundaries, I'm as flexible as possible, but when somebody steps outside the boundary then something happens to me and I can get very angry. Within those boundaries, I like players to be free to express themselves in whatever role it is that they play in. Understanding of course that yes, whilst the individual is important and we all want to see people grow, get better at what they do, ultimately for me the team is important – is more important. The team winning for me is more important than that you're having a fantastic game. It's not all players, but there's some players that will be happy that I played well but the team lost and to me, that's a selfish side of it. I'm a very giving person, so I like people around me that are that way.

The people do that in different cases. I had a guy that played for me many, many years ago, a guy called Joe Mildred who was... How could I describe Joe? People just said he was selfish, but he wasn't. He behaved in a certain way. There are certain things that he didn't understand the importance of it. I remember once he came in. We were playing a very important match, and everybody is warming up and doing this thing, and he's sitting on the bench with a newspaper. All he said was, "Well, tell me when you're ready to play."

I thought, "Oh dear, how do I handle this?" And I thought, You know what? Just leave it. Yeah, just leave it. Let him do what he wants to do."

The other players would give me a go, "Why are you letting this guy do this? Why are you letting this guy do this?"

I said, "Well, let's see what happens."

He comes into the game, warms up, comes into the game, dominates the game, helps us to win. We had a chat with the guy and said, "You know what? This is how he is. As far as he's concerned, he's warm. He gets himself ready to play a certain way."

Yes, we can say this is a team stuff, you're going to do this. Bang! Bang! Bang! Bang! And it takes him out of the zone that he wants to be in when it comes time to play.

This actually happened a while before because he was also one of the national team players. Actually at national team level, I thought I needed to be a little bit more firm with the players. And so what he got away with at club, he tried to get away with at the national team and I wouldn't allow him to do that. I actually kicked him out of the national team. I thought he'd probably leave the club after that, but he didn't. He still came back to the club, and strangely enough his behavior at club was different from the behavior in national team, possibly because I allowed it a little bit more at the club. But national team it was a little bit different.

In effect, I probably coach different teams different ways. I look at the individual and I try to see how best to accomplish and manage them as opposed to managing and trying to manage people the same way. I've been accused of playing favorites to people and being harder on some of them than the others, but as I said, I like to think it's because I have figured out how best to treat an individual player.

This wouldn't be the players complaining. This would be other people looking in and saying, how come such and such.

I try to explain and they don't understand, so I said, "Okay. It's okay."

As long as the players understand and they buy into what we're trying to do and understand that this is a part of the team and what their role is, and as I said, the boundaries. The boundaries are set, and if you behave within those boundaries then there's flexibility to get away with some things. Well, not get way with some things, but to express yourself or do what is best for you.

We talked about your volleyball influences culturally. Let's flip it around. You're from Jamaica originally. You lived in Canada. You spent time in Sweden. You have been in the U.K. for a long time. Are there any of those cultures that you find dominant in your coaching style? Not necessarily in terms of how that country plays the game, but just in you?

I suppose for me it's a unit discipline. My culture in Jamaica, it was very disciplinarian. You respected the elders. You don't talk back. You understand that you're a young person and this is what it is. There are certain things you don't do, so the boundaries are there, and what's set. I've obviously continued that throughout my stay whilst I was living in the family home. Once I got out, then obviously that discipline still remained. Yes, I had freedom, but I also knew that there are certain things that ... I knew what right and wrong was.

For me, in a lot of ways, I'm probably a very good team player because I understand the objectives that... Well, I like to win. I like to win, and when I win I very quickly forget about it. When I lose, it stays with me for a very long time until I get an opportunity to set something right. I don't like to lose, so consequently I'm very, very, competitive. And I'm a fighter, so I like my teams to have spirit, but most of all to understand that we are a unit. When it's time to play, then we need to bind in that. Yeah, there's nothing wrong with being critical sometimes, but as long as we understand what we're trying to achieve, fine.

That's something I learned from the American side of things, especially in college where it was very competitive. You were on a scholarship. Yes, they are paying for your education, but to do that you still have to deliver. You still have to get your grades, you have to deliver on the volleyball court, and be competitive because you want be a part of that first six. You want to be playing every match, so that teaches you to compete.

When you didn't play... I was lucky enough that I played most more often than I sat. I had a lesson when I was with the Canadian junior team and something that's sat with me for a long time. I was a young player.

As I said, I started playing in '75 and in '78 I went in to be a starter as an outside hitter on the junior team. When we went to the NORCECA championships in Mexico – a place called Durango in '78, I think it was – there were two guys that were in the senor team that they brought back into the junior team to strengthen the team for the championships. One of the guys was an outside hitter, a guy called Paul Gratel, and he came in as an outside hitter. I'm the one that lost my place because of him. I thought at the time it hurt, but I realized also that the fact that he was in the national team – a starter in the national team – made perfect sense. It still hurt, nonetheless, and I thought to myself, "Okay, I need to compete against this guy." I was ready to compete. Then I got a finger busted, and that was me out of the tournament.

I probably wouldn't have won the place back, but that taught me then that you know what? Nothing in life is forever, and you're only at that particular situation. Somebody else out there could come along, and you have to be ready to compete, and you have to be able to do your best, otherwise somebody else would take it. That taught me a lesson.

Going into college, I realized that if I wanted to play a lot, I was going to have to show what I could do on the court. I also learned that it's important to train hard and practice.

That definitely influenced ... It influences my coaching to a certain degree, because I try to tell players – especially here in clubs in England where everybody has to pay to play, and sometimes it's difficult to get across to somebody – just because you're paying the same amount as that person, it doesn't guarantee that you're going to get the same playing time as that person. What you need to understand is that in a situation where we're trying to win, the coach is going to do what he or she needs to do to win.

It doesn't mean I don't like you. It just means that for this particular situation maybe somebody else is better. Your job is to get as good as the person and in the position that you want to get to, and my job as a coach is to help to do that. I'm not going to reward you. I will reward you at times if the situation allows, but don't expect that just because you're part of the club or part of the team that it guarantees you're playing. It's a message that's very difficult to get across sometimes.

I think I lost my train of thought a little bit there.

No worries.

The last thing you said about the playing time and the philosophy, Ismo [Peltoarvo] actually talked a little bit about that with regards to Sweden and how sometimes the problem you have is not sharing playing town around enough. It's not from the players who aren't playing. It's from everybody else. Like, "Susie hasn't played enough. We should get her on the court." This is definitely not a philosophy that really comes up in the States all that much.

That's what I'm saying. That's where I suppose my mentality comes from because there is an expectation that I will train hard, I will do my best, and if I'm good enough, Coach will play me. If Coach doesn't play me, then what it means is I've got to go work harder and to impress Coach. When I get an opportunity to play, then obviously I will show Coach that I should be on the court. Again, that mentality is what drives me to a certain degree and I fail to ... I can't sympathize with people who don't understand that. Quite often, it's very difficult. That's one of the things that probably annoys me most.

"Coach, why am I not playing anymore?"

Don't ask me that question because again, you know my philosophy, okay. I do this. I'm about the team. I help to develop you. You contribute to what the team does. If you don't see that – and sometimes it's difficult – but that's the way I'd like to be all the time. Not easy.

In the national team, I can afford to do that because then this is a selection. It's the performance in the environment. This is what the expectations are. If you don't like it, you can go. Okay, in the club it's a little bit different. Nonetheless, it's still the mentality that drives. I just have to tone it down a little bit sometimes. Not totally, but a little bit.

That reminds me of something that I struggled with at the club level in England. The conflict between participation and competition. I know in my particular case, during the time I was with Devon we had certain players who would train with us but who were not really part of the competitive squad. They paid their dues, week to week or however often it happened, and the club allowed them to come in and train. I know Devon wasn't the only club like

that. I know other clubs do this as well. From a coaching perspective, it's difficult.

It is. It's not easy, but it's manageable. As I said, it's a case of balance. It's balancing the club finances, what the club needs to do to stay afloat, and what you as a coach need to do to benefit the athletes that you have, because for some people it's social, while for others it's about the competition. The two things are at different ends of the spectrum. Yes, you can be social and still want to win, but you're not prepared to do that extra bit that you need when it comes time to compete and to win. It's different and it's how you balance that.

I have a difficulty. I have coached social volleyball, but I go in with the mindset knowing this is what it is, and if this is a social club then you know this is what it is. I'll give them enough. When it comes to the competitive teams, I try not to mix with people who then come in. If you're not a part of the club or if you're from a different team in the club, there is an expectation.

I have this belief that any player, any team, needs to be able to understand how to play at three different levels. You need to know how to play when you're better than a team and you know you're going to win. You need to understand how you play and what you need to do when the other team is just as good as you are and you need to know, "How do I win?" Then there is the other level where you know that the team you're playing against is better than you are, and you're going to get beaten up, but you have to understand how to take the hit and still come back. I think it's important as a part of any development that you understand these three levels.

It's not easy to get that across to people sometimes, but that is a part of my philosophy and beliefs.

Let me ask you this, because it is something else that comes up not just in England, but I think in a lot of places when you're dealing with club volleyball – especially below the top level or two. Attendance. How do you deal with situations where you're just not getting consistent full attendance in practice?

Oh dear, oh dear, oh dear.

It's a problem, that one. I have that problem at the Malory club at the moment. In the past it didn't used to be that way because again, people knew that ... It's easy when the difference between players is not that far. When you have two or three guys, or three or four guys, that are battling for two positions – or a couple of guys battling for one position – they know, "You know what? Maybe this session I miss is going to be the difference between me playing, or being in the first six and not being in the first six." So they are motivated to attend.

I find that you have more of a problem when people are very secure in their position – "I know that I am better than such, and I'm so much better that if there is a match that we need to win that Coach is going to play me anyway."

That is the difficult one to manage. The only way around it is from the outset to put down the ground rules and people understand perfectly well that this is what it's going to be. "I expect you to make X amount of training sessions. Okay, if you're sick, if you're injured, no problem. You can come and you can still do something."

Here it's difficult to get that buy-in, but where I played, especially in college, that's the norm. There are no reasons to miss training. There is no reason to miss training at all, unless you're on your deathbed, and even then you still want to go with a blankie and wrap yourself up and watch, because you don't know what you'll be missing.

Here, the reason people ... "I can't make it tonight because I just missed my bus." "I have the flu." "My nose is running." "I'm hungry." Just any little thing. Then, come match time, they rock up with their kit and they expect ... When they don't play then they sulk.

It's a tricky balance. It's a tricky balance. I've had this season where people missed matches because they wanted to go play beach volleyball in December. I'm thinking, "Really?" I think, "You know what? Not a problem. I'll remember it. It's okay. You can go do what you want to do."

They've counted, and they think, "Well, you got eight players, so if me and her are missing, that's okay. You don't need ten because somebody is going to have to sit on the bench anyway."

"Okay, thanks for making that decision for me. No problem. Okay. Go on."

Then they wonder why you don't talk to them for a few weeks. Yeah, that's the girls most, the guys don't do that.

Since you introduced the idea of gender differences ...

Well, I shouldn't generalize, but this last season I can definitely say that that happened. Maybe it was just female beach tournament and not the guys. Then again, most of the guys in the Super 8s team just tend not to play beach anyway.

Let's carry the basic idea of that discussion. Do you approach training the men any different than you do the women, or how you handle them on a player management perspective or anything along those lines?

I've been asked this before. I don't really think I do, you know. My philosophy doesn't change as far as the way I like to run my offense, the way I work my block-defense. Some technical adjustments maybe, but as far as whether I'm harder on men or harder on women, I don't think so. I think I just look at the individual players and try to gauge things that way. There would be some female players that I've worked with that I've probably been a lot harder on than some male players because their mindsets are different, their expectations are different, and you can just... As a coach it's your job to know how far you can push somebody so they don't go beyond their limit and they don't just disappear on you.

As far as the mental side and physically what I demand on the volleyball court, there is not a lot of difference in techniques, skills, etc. It's just small difference which if I'm honest I probably don't pay a lot of attention to. I don't have time to go into finer details. With the amount of time that we have, it's a case of trying to relate, as much as possible, the fundamentals and any technical adjustments that I need to make within what you're trying to do. There are not a lot of differences as far as my coaching style between men and women.

Talk about how you progress yourself through a season. Competition starts is October, season will wrap up in Aprilish, depending.

Depending, yeah.

Then you've got the cup competition that runs alongside them.

With the Super 8s teams there's a playoff at the end. With the lower level teams there isn't a play off unless you happen to be in a relegation/promotion battle. Do you structure your season at all with certain breakpoints in mind, or certain peak periods in mind that you're targeting?

To be honest, in the environment that I work, it's probably difficult to do that because we hardly do any physical, because time doesn't allow. In the preseason we'll do some plyometrics. I expect the guys to do any physical stuff on the side, to be honest. We have a guy that worked with us our last couple of seasons that structured a program for us. We probably start preseason late August because some of the guys will play on the beach during the off-season, and we give them a week or so to come back indoors. The main thing this season was actually to start again back end of August. There's a tournament we've been to in Sweden in Borås. We wanted to go back this season but we didn't have the players available to do that.

Then in September we'll start kicking our intensity up as far as our preparation games are concerned. We start the season at the back-end of October, and then it's just building the team and the team staff.

When Malory was very successful, it was very easy for us because we could always ... We always had a base of players that had a good understanding of where we were going so we never really dropped off from one season to the other. It was never a case of trying to integrate four, five players. It was a case of trying to integrate one or two, so it was very easy to continue where we left off. It was almost more about how physically fit people were, and not having to build structures, talk about our offense and how we're going to do this and defensively, how ... It was very quick for us to get back into our stride.

The team has changed quite a bit, so a lot of this we have to go back to build from scratch. The first few weeks of the season will be trying to build the team. Ultimately, the season starts too early, but it comes down to finances and people being available in August as to whether or not we could start in August. We're late starting and it normally... Having said that, last season we actually started very well. I don't know whether or not we had a number of guys who, even though they were new to the team, they were not new to the systems because they were playing similar systems with clubs that made it a little bit easier for them to integrate.

It's just weekly as we go forward into the season looking at we're playing and whether or not we're going to do anything differently, then working to build our team unit and trying to do something to match prepare and influence what they do on game day. I think last season, because of the way the matches were structured, there were some times when we went a couple of weeks without a match. In those weeks we would try and do a little bit more physical stuff – get a guy in to do some more physical stuff with the guys – then still have our opportunity for ball work and to build.

It's governed really by the time we have, and where we are in the season and where the matches fall. I suppose if we are going to talk about peaking and all that, it would be a case that we need to look more at the physical side which is not something we do that much to be honest.

In terms of your bench players, do you make a conscious effort of trying to get them in at least a little bit in a match? Or do you have a philosophy of trying to work players in periodically as starters from a developmental perspective?

Yeah, it depends. In the past, when we were very dominant, I would very seldom play our strongest six because I would always try to mix. Just trying to keep a balance in the team so the team isn't weakened. You may play with four starters and two bench players. I probably might struggle any further than that. Nowadays, where we are, every match is important and we could lose more than we win. You're trying to concentrate and win, and then it becomes a case who you are playing – see how you like the match-up with the best six that you can in a given situation, and then manage the game as you would when you're playing against somebody who is likely to either beat you or lose to you.

In that case, subs are normally made to impact the game and based on the situation, as opposed to giving someone a chance. If the opportunity is there – let's say we know someone is a good server and can hit the target with that serve – yeah, you might put that person in. If he or she gets a couple of opportunities to serve and defend, then you know what? They have contributed. It's as I imagine the game is going to be played out. I make decision based on the best personnel. Yeah, if the opportunity arises for me to give my other players an opportunity, then I will do that, but not at the expense of losing the match.

The two training sessions that you have each week, how do you approach planning them?

Looking at the Super 8 men, the Monday session will probably be devoted let's say 20 minutes to half an hour to our physical stuff just to make sure we have some kind of base to take us through. Ultimately, we will probably just do some ball control stuff – digging, setting, spiking. There is attacking over the net or setting up some kind of defensive situation where it will be game-like but within the influence on linkage – offensive linkage.

Then, if we decided that we're going to focus a lot on tying down our offense, we will build it into service receive so we still continue to link and set it up into a competitive situation. On Thursday we tend to flip it and think about our block-defense – how that's going to work out – and work on the linkages between block and defense our, transition from defense, and then put it all together. Put the first six, or the perceived first six, into offensive situation and then challenge them in block-defense whilst we work specifically against the team that we're going to play. It's as much as possible game-like while still trying to develop a little bit of a skill and the linkages between, especially our setter and our hitters.

You do an A team versus B team split in your second training.

To a certain degree. It depends. In the days gone by it used to be easier because there would not have been a lot of difference between the As and the Bs. But now, where there is likely to be a big difference, there are times when I would probably mix it. Let's say I want a bigger attacker against what I perceive to be my setter front court, or maybe my opposite going against my outside hitter just to challenge.

It's a different level, different contact, more intensity etc., etc. I'll mix it depending, but when I decide to go offense then yes. I'll make sure that the people on the court are in the positions they are likely to be in so we build those relationships, and then I run my substitution pattern so again we also get a chance to tie those down. When it comes to block-defense, then yes I'll juggle things around to focus a lot more on the net more so than what happens behind the block.

What are you like on match day? What is your demeanor on the side line?

Well, that's changed over the years. I suppose in the '90s, early 2000s, when we were fairly dominant, people used to say I was so laid back, I was horizontal. Those days when you used to sit down, and we were unable to stand up, I was the stroller on the chair – almost sitting on my back. Nowadays, when you are able to stand up and move around and abuse referees more often...

I suppose it varies. There are times when if I'm coaching women, I'll tend to be a little more encouraging and I'll get into the thing and applaud and encourage, etc., etc. – try to be very positive. The guys I suppose I'm harder with. I stay more in the game. Yes, I encourage, but I'm not a cheerleader then. I yell occasionally but then they know that when I yell it's because they've done something stupid.

Apart from that, I still tend to be fairly calm, unless the referees upset me, in which case I go to another level. Then I need my assistant coaches to calm me down, or my captain to come and tell me to behave. I'm not as laid back as I used to be, but I'm also not over the top. I'm not ... I try not to change my demeanor too much.

It's interesting because I think most coaches would say they get more laid back as their career progresses, not the other way around.

It's the winning or the losing I think. There are some matches where you come in where for whatever reason there is a lot of friction between you and either the opposition coach or the team itself, and passion is running high, and things change a little bit. If the players on the court are fired up and passionate about what they are doing, the more they get that way, the more laid-back I am – the more relaxed I am.

It's when they are on court and they don't want to go – they seem like they're sleepwalking – then something flips and I just ... Then it becomes different, so I think pick up the emotions and I try to fire them up and probably get a little bit more... Not negative, but a little bit more vocal. When they do well, winning or losing doesn't matter, because I can see. I can see they are putting in their shift. The more they work, and the easier it is for me, the more relaxed I am – even if we're not doing that well.

When you're putting together your starting rotation, do you think match up at all, or do you just try to put out your best rotation?

It's always match ups, but most coaches tend to go with the same thing. I will try and research score sheets and see what people do in a situation and try to get the match-ups that I think are best for me – hoping, of course, that they don't change, because if they then change then you're right back to where you started from. A lot of coaches will do the same thing but I do look at setting up to be against the middles especially. I try to get my middle blockers against the right middles, or the right opposites, whether I want to try to stop somebody, or try to dominate somebody. Yeah, I do look at match ups.

How much do you use stats and or video in your coaching?

To be honest, probably not that much. It's not that we don't. We have the facilities to do it but it comes down to time. I think somebody would have to ... If it's a match that – let's say the season has just started and somebody has new personnel that I don't know anything about – I will try to get a hold of something to have a look at them and see whether or not there is anything that I can gain from there.

Coach's philosophy here doesn't change, so you almost know what most coaches are going to do from season to season. A lot of it is more players moving teams. But you know what players do anyway, so you figure that if they do something with team A, chances are they go to team B, who's philosophy is this, they're going to do the same thing.

It's the new players coming in that you don't know anything about that you'd rather think, "Well, I need to have some kind of idea how I'm going to counter this player." Yeah, in that situation, then obviously I will try to do my best to do some scouting and to match prepare. I'll do some scouting just to get some information that might be helpful.

What about in training, do you use any video or anything like that in training?

I have for some of the younger kids to ... Actually, not just for the younger kids. With technology nowadays, I have occasionally taken my phone or my iPad out and quickly videotaped something to show somebody something. Again, yes, but not as much as I could possibly do. Again, it comes down to time.

You talked about this a little bit in terms of saying you know the

coaches and their styles. There is quite a bit of coaching stability at the Super 8s level, and maybe even lower down, isn't there?

Yeah. There is. You look at the likes of Sheffield. Trenam, he's been there for a while, Northumbria, Dave Goodchild has been there for a number of seasons. Polonia it's Vangelis, whether he's there or not. Wessex I think Vangelis has been there. Jonathan Luko. Dan Hunter a season. Who else? Obviously Malory has been there. Lynx has been some changes, on the men's side that is. On the men's side there's a good four or five coaches that are still in post and have and have been for a number of years.

Is the level of expectation – the pressure and all that stuff – very different than it would be in a professional league? Not that Sweden is a very high, demanding league, but there is a lot of turnover from what I understand, never mind other leagues.

Well it is. It's as much pressure as you put on. I suppose if you have sponsors and you're paying people, then you have certain expectations, but it doesn't mean that because we don't have the money or aren't paying somebody that the pressure needs to be any less. I suppose it's the pressure that you put on yourself to win or to lose. That doesn't change. That doesn't change at all.

It's probably down to the individual. I could be just as passionate and wanting to win for nothing at all other than just for winning and what that brings as much as somebody who is getting 100,000 pounds a year. It's just your expectations of yourself and the people that you're working with. Yeah, it would be nice to have the other things that goes with it, but it's down to you to make it mean something.

Let me shift over to the work that you do on a coaching development perspective. You also get a chance to see developing coaches, younger coaches, newer coaches. What do you see as the biggest thing that they need to learn, or the skills they need to develop you when you're working with them?

It's surprising, because I think that even though a few of our older coaches are the ones that have been influenced by the Hippolyte generation, and their understanding the game is quite good, even at that level there are not a lot of people here that understand how to teach the fundamentals, or the technical innovations that may come from understanding the fundamentals.

Yeah, you can throw a ball on the court and people can dig, set and hit, but the intricacies as to... We all know the game flows a certain way, but why do we do certain things the way we do it? What's the rationale behind it? How do I develop it from putting the little building blocks in place. Let's say for instance at the university, I would see somebody come in for a quick. There is a movement here. How is it all linked? We see the likes of Brazil, and we see a still shot where in a specific situations players are doing exactly this and you think, "How is it all linked together?" What's the timing systems, and how do you develop the players to do that?

That knowledge is there, but I don't think it's disseminated downwards as much as it should be. Even our educators don't have that knowledge. I've worked with a number of tutors before, and it's sometimes what they teach or what they are passing on, knowledge-wise you think... The ones I have worked with, we've had discussions, and mostly we agree that what I'm saying makes sense. But then a lot of them that I haven't worked with, or haven't really seen is where there is concern. There is a syllabus, yes, but the information that goes into the syllabus and is passed on is different. You could go to a Level 3 course run by Tutor X and a Level 3 course run by Tutor Y and you come out of it with different things. It's not as unified as it should be.

That's something we're hopefully working to correct. I like to see other coaches in the performance pathways, and will start working towards the same thing. I had a technical role across the [national team] squads where I would visit training sessions and input and see what people were doing and feed back to them and tried to influence things where I didn't quite agree with the fundamental principles, etc. That was five, six years ago. I'm not sure.

We need somebody to still continue to do that and I'm not sure if that's happening. I'd like to think that if it's not happening, then it will. I know we have these coaches that are supposed to start mentoring the development coaches. Whether they are the right people, I don't know, but hopefully that's something that will happen.

One of the things that I did like about the Level 3 course was that there was at least two points of external input. You did the four

days or five days of the on-site course, and then you went away and you do the continuing professional development seminars. The other part of it – when I took it, I don't know if it's changed in the most recent version – you had to do a journal of at least 10 entries. For most coaches in England that's potentially a big part of a season. Then you had to be assessed. Somebody had to actually watch you coach for a session, and sit down with you afterwards and talk you though their observations, which isn't always the case with a lot of other certifications that I've seen. At least from that perspective, I like that.

The one issue though – and I haven't gone through it because they wavered me into a Level 2 when I first came over – is because the first two levels are UKCC [U.K. Coaching Certificate], and not Volleyball England, there's an element where they are not volleyball-specific – as might be the case, say, in US volleyball where you're doing CAP. Do you think that's a part of the struggles getting the lower-level coaches to think in terms of volleyball application and how to train the skills?

I think it is without a doubt, because I know for a fact that even though I don't deliver on Level 1's, I know that a lot of what they do is about how to coach. So there is very little input as far as skill acquisition, or rather the skills themselves. I don't know if they tell you how to acquire them, but they definitely don't have any fundamental stuff at Level 1, hardly anything at all.

At Level 2… I just did one the other day. I came away from it thinking something needs to give because again, a lot of the stuff that used to be on the old Level 2 we're not even touching because we're still doing a lot of … You're giving people opportunities to micro-coach and they are doing that because they picked up some of those skills on Level 1, but the "what to do" is still not there.

By Level 3, I won't say it's too late, but if the Level 2 coaches are already working as a head coach then yes, they know how to go and instruct the sessions and make sure that things have been done in the right… Well things are being done, but not necessarily right things.

The UKCC situation is good, but it needs to have an opportunity for more volleyball-specific stuff. I'm not sure how they do that. Maybe the idea would be between Level 1 and Level 2 there is a workshop that you need to attend to acquire knowledge of the fundamentals of the game and how to teach and how to develop those, so by the time you get to Level 2 you can start imputing or impacting that into 6-against-6. At Level 2 a lot of it is run 3-against-3, 4-against-4 and moving towards 6-against-6. There's something missing and if it continues this way then we might be developing coaches that don't have the volleyball knowledge base to teach the staff.

Having said that, a lot of our performance coaches probably don't have that either. I said I think I'm one of the better teachers around as far as the fundamentals. I know Keith Trenam is because I've worked with him for long enough. I wouldn't want to swear about others because I don't know.

For those that aren't really familiar, the idea of the Level 1, Level 2, Level 3 is that when you're Level 1, you're qualified to run part of a session.

Yes, assist – be supervised.

Level 2 you should be able to run a session by yourself.

Yes, you should.

Level 3 you should be able to coach a team through a season yourself.

Yeah.

I've talked to others about this, and one of the gripes I have about certification processes in some of the education systems is they reflect the ideal, but are not very reflective of the reality.

That's true, yeah.

Especially at the lower levels, which is where you think you'd really want the people who understand what they should be doing, those are the ones that get thrown in, "We need a warm body. You go coach this team."

That is true and I know that I have had discussions, but definitely I know for a fact that in some countries, they do put coaches where they are best suited. I think everyone wants to coach 6-against-6, and everyone wants to be coaching at the level where you have your performance team, but some people have the knowledge better suited at the stage where players – especially young players – are developing the skills, because I think it's important. The sooner you learn – the sooner they can learn how to do things the right way – the better, because trying to break bad habits once they have been ingrained becomes a nightmare. I think quite often we do miss a trick in that way.

Do you have a recommended reading list?

I'm not sure I do actually. There's a brain typing book that I've read from a guy called John P. Niednagel, it's called *Your Key to Sports Success*. It just talks about brain typing and how it influences your performance, and I know Ralph has taken this step further now. There's something he calls action types. It's something that I'm interested in, but haven't pursued as much as I should. I know Hippolyte has actually written a couple of book himself, one about management and another one about setting, I can't remember what it is. I've read them. Haven't seen them for a while, but I have them somewhere in my library. [Note: The Hippolyte book on management is titled *Strategies of Team Management Through Volleyball*. He also joined forces with Bob Bertucci on *Championship Volleyball Drills: Individual Skill Training*]

There's some autobiographies that I've read. Michael Jordan. There is a tennis player. I can't remember some of them. I haven't done a lot of reading in the last decade or so I suppose, but in the time when I was really trying to develop my coaching I looked at some of the American basketball coaches. Bobby Knight. And obviously Al Scates at UCLA was coaching when I was playing, so I've seen some of the things that they've done.

I'm probably not the best reader. I prefer to see things, so I will go and I will research the teams that are doing well. Italy, when they were at the top, I used to sit down and watch them for hours. Brazil I still sit down and watch them for hours. And Poland I pay attention to. I'm more a visual person I suppose.

Do you get out and visit other coaches and clubs and teams?

I was very happy I was able to visit the pre-Olympic final preparation for Brazil. A friend of mine who is a Brazilian managed to get me an invitation into the Brazil training session just before the finals. Just to see how they prepared...

It was good to know that they don't do anything different from the way that we've done it in the past. Unfortunately they had quite a few injuries, so I didn't get to see a full squad in operation, but you just saw some individual stuff they did, and how they tried to just look at how they were going to play – making sure that there was an understanding developing the camaraderie, the atmosphere, and the training session. That was Rezende [Bernardinho]. He's probably the last one I've seen.

Obviously, when I was in Sweden I would watch some of Kristiannson's training sessions. Tatsuya Adachi when he was around in France. Nothing recent. I suppose I would be looking at coaches who I respect their knowledge base and what they are doing within the game. I know that if I was now to have an opportunity, a women's team that I would like to look at would be the American women, the Brazilian women. Obviously, the American men, Brazilian men and the Polish men.

I'd literally like to spend two weeks with Brazil whilst they are preparing for the start of the World League. They get their players back in from the various club teams and they are preparing. I would like to see how they do that and how they re-integrate players into their team. But it costs money, and I suppose they [the federation] probably don't see me as somebody who's at the stage of developing to help their pathway athletes, so maybe they won't put money into me anymore, which I think is a shame. I'll probably just wither away, and then fade away, as they say.

No, I'm still open to learning. I was over in Sweden a few years ago because I have a son over there. And Simon [Loftus] was coaching over there. I went with my son to training and just observed what the other coaches were doing. I had opportunities to pop across to see Ismo, but I never got a chance to do that.

All right. We can wrap up with one final question. What general advice do you give to developing coaches?

Advice would be, knowledge is out there. Don't be afraid if you don't understand something now. As a young coach, you may think you know a lot, but you probably don't. Keep an open mind and don't be afraid to ask questions if there's something that you don't understand. And don't be afraid to share knowledge because again, the knowledge we have has probably been passed down from other people. Don't be afraid to be innovative. If somebody thinks what you're doing is not right, if you think it is, and you have a logic to doing what you're doing, then don't be afraid to be different.

Have a vision and follow it.

5

TERI CLEMENS

We all know examples of athletes whose careers were cut short in their prime because of illness or injury, but it's not something you hear happening in coaching. Unfortunately, that's exactly what happened to Teri Clemens. The after effects of a childhood incident ended her career after just 14 years coaching at NCAA Division III Washington University.

What Teri achieved in her limited time as a college coach, however, still stands up as one of the most amazing spans of any coach. Her teams won 7 national championships. In U.S. women's collegiate volleyball, only Russ Rose of Penn State has as many titles, and it has taken him far longer to reach that number. At one point Teri's teams won six straight titles, which not even Rose has managed. Not surprisingly, she was chosen AVCA NCAA Division III National Coach of the Year three times.

Teri recorded over 500 victories in her career. That's well below the win totals of coaching legends like Rose, Dave Shoji, and Andy Banachowski, but no one matches her 0.873 win percentage. That's tops among all NCAA coaches, regardless of division. Oh, and Teri also won three straight state titles while coaching high school volleyball in Missouri before taking over at Washington University.

Along the way, Teri authored the book *Get With It Girls! Life is Competition*. She was inducted into the AVCA Hall of Fame in 2004.

John conducted this interview in February 2016. It's hard to express emotion and energy in print, but the audio of the interview makes it obvious the sheer amount of energy Teri must have brought to her coaching. There's little doubt that had her body not caused her retirement she would still be coaching today and still doing great things with her teams.

The first thing we normally talk about in these interviews is your volleyball/coaching biography, so if you just want to walk through that.

Well I started off at a private girls' academy and I taught six years at Incarnate World here in St. Louis. In those six years, we developed a program that was very popular at the school. There was 475 students and we would have 125 try out for the volleyball team.

Wow!

It was quite a celebrity status to be able to play over there, very popular sport. We sold out the gym for every match, we won the last three state titles that I was there, and we did a lot of firsts. We were the first to hit quick attacks in St. Louis and it was very much of a surprise to opponents. We were the first ones to run tandems, and even to wear long-sleeve uniforms at the time. We introduced a lot of things because I just like to be a little edgy in my coaching, and so it was a lot of fun to just keep trying new things. Part of that was because I attended a lot of clinics nationally, so I would bring it back to the area. I felt like we were kind of innovative and I did a lot of stealing from others at that time as far as how-to's.

Then the position opened at Washington University.

I don't think they were looking for a high school coach at the time, but I was ready to go to the collegiate level and really desired to. They had done a search, but apparently had not found who they wanted and re-opened it. I was at the national tournament in Chicago and was talking to someone about, "Yeah I would like to go to the collegiate level."

They said, "Well I applied for that job at Washington University, but did not get the position."

I didn't know about the position so I thought I'd go for it. I went back to St. Louis and I called the Athletic Director and said, "I'm your coach." He brought me over the following day and interviewed me. I was there for nine hours interviewing with various people and the rest is history. I stayed for 14 years.

I read that you played in high school, but you didn't play in college. Is that correct?

Right, I went to Truman State University in Missouri, but on a softball and tennis scholarship and field hockey. I played three sports.

Wow.

I always intended to be a volleyball coach, though. It never changed. I was a setter in high school and breathed the sport, so to speak, and knew that regardless of what sports I played... I was kind of one of those natural athletes who could pick up sports, but that didn't matter. I was going to be a volleyball coach from day one, which really helped me because I went to every clinic I could find, even while I was a collegiate student.

That's interesting. I mean there's obviously a lot of coaches who have experience in multiple sports, but it's funny that in college you didn't actually play the sport that you were going to be going to coach. Was it just simply you got the scholarship opportunity, then you did other sports and not volleyball?

No. It's honestly because I wanted to play those sports and I wanted to coach volleyball. I wanted to play other sports and I still did throughout my life.

You wanted a little diversification.

I guess so.

Obviously you had a pretty good run while you were at Washington.

Yeah.

Now Washington University is a very academically oriented school. I coached at Brown so I know a little bit about trying to recruit that

sort of athlete. Is volleyball an easier sell to get good quality players at a high academic level than maybe other sports?

Well I don't know that it's different from other sports, except in the fact that:

#1 – From a Division III program in general, most aren't looking to be a professional athlete.

#2 -If you go to a major academic institution, you're probably not looking to be a professional athlete.

#3 -Opportunities are more limited in our sport, to be a professional athlete at least in the United States.

Because of that, I was able to recruit any students who met the criteria academically at Washington University. I wasn't afraid of talking to or labeling Division I, II, or III. I would venture to say 94 percent of the student-athletes on our team could play DI, DII, or DIII. They chose to play, and I really tried to not label it as a division, but rather the class of the program. You could be Class 1, 2, 3, or worse, but you could play Division I, II, or III. I recruited top-notch athletes who wanted a top-notch academic environment.

In your view, where would you rank your teams, when you were winning the national championship, versus Division II or Division I?

Gosh, I wouldn't even want to guess at that, but I do know that we played all Division I in the Spring, almost 100 percent Division I matches, and we held our own very well.

You talked about how you spent a lot of time going to clinics and camps and things like that to really learn your craft, even before you were coaching. Who were your main influences during that period?

I was very much influenced at the time by Chuck Erbe, Marilyn McReavy, by Cecile Reynaud and Stephanie Schlueder. I went to a lot of their type programs. Chuck Erbe was always doing clinics nationally and so I remember attending a lot of his. I think one of the best things – and I think I got this a lot from Stephanie Schlueder who was at Minnesota – is it's important to attend clinics, but it's important to adapt from those programs. In other words, you can be creative and innovative. I like to think I'm a little of both. Creative in that I develop my own style, but innovative in maybe I can take their style and adapt it to my own needs. I think you can do one or the other and be successful, but if you have both, it's really going to be a great advantage.

You coached entirely side out, correct?

Yes.

Just out of curiosity, and I don't know how much you've stayed up with things these days, do you think you would coach any differently now under a rally scoring than you would have then?

I like to think not. My game was always very aggressive, risk taker type of an atmosphere and I think you have to do that in rally scoring. I think that I would tend to be very similar. I like to think I wouldn't play a safe game ever.

I ask that because – and this came up with Bill Neville and with somebody else as well recently – the impression was that at least for the early years after they went to rally score, a lot of teams and coaches did get conservative because if you made a mistake, you lost the point. Whereas under side out, if you're serving, you could afford to be really risky.

It's true and I think we've seen a change in that. It got really conservative for awhile and I remember talking to coaches about this. I think my answer to that was especially in serving. You take especially a 14, 15, 16 year-old, they do not want to miss that serve when it cost a point. Now we're talking everything on the line, but we taught a method. We used this all through our career and I think it really works well in serving at all levels. An A, a B, and a C serve. It kind of takes the pressure off of a player if you teach them that they have an A, B, or C serve and make them confident in each.

An A serve, I'm going to aim for the middle of the court and I'm going to get the ball in. You should make your A serve 99 percent of the time. We would make them just repetitively serve A serves. When you got good at that, then you serve B serve. Now you're going to serve possibly three zones on the court, splitting the court vertically into thirds. I can have control over serving a more competitive, more pace on the ball serve, in the three different zones and do a lot of repetitions in that and get successful. Then C is my go for it serve. I can serve with a lot of authority, anywhere I want, and a bigger risk taking serve. We do that with a lot of repetitions, so if I called out to a player, "I want you to serve a C6," they know I'm going for it and I'd like to be in zone 6.

We got very competitive with that. We knew that we would only serve an A serve, well not very much at our level. But if I was coaching high school for example, or young club teams, I would only serve an A serve after a timeout at the start of a game, after a long delay – opportunities where I'm starting over. A lot of young beginners, I think it's good to serve an A serve, then a B serve, then a C serve, then start over because we all know what happens when you start cranking your C serves. You get farther and farther on the court or harder and harder until you put a hole through the back wall or the ball ends up in the bleachers. I think going A, B, C is a really good pattern for a lot of people.

Now at our level, we tried to go B, B, C, and once in awhile throw in a A and we got on patterns where we'd let them just rip on C's. I think controlling that gives you still an opportunity to be very aggressive with your serve, but you're not completely yanking the ball out of their hands.

Just out of curiosity, what was your method in training of working the B's and C's?

Well we would do a lot of competitions in everything we did, first of all. I don't give punishments. I like to make the reward intrinsic, so because I'm so competitive, I tended to recruit competitive people. I think a lot of us do, but I also taught competition by providing opportunities for success and so for example, if we were working our B's, they all know what the B is, so I would say, "You serve your group of three versus this group of three. The first person serves Zone 1, the second person serves Zone 2, third person serve Zone 3. You've got to do that for two minutes, and you're competing against another group."

If I was working on just C's, I might give you an opportunity to see how many in a row you can serve with no penalty for misses. That type of thing, so that I encourage them to go for it. If you encourage an athlete to go for it and then you punish them for going for it, or for not succeeding, you're not going to get anywhere with it. You've got to let them rip.

Just winding back, since we didn't actually touch on this, basically

it was health reasons that caused you to retire. I'm guessing only 14 years in at Washington, you were pretty much in your prime at that point and would've ideally kept coaching for years and years, and maybe even still today.

I'd like to think so. I'm really a coach all the way through. I can talk coaching all day long still. Having to retire was the most difficult thing I did. I made the decision with my head, but it broke my heart. That's really the truth. I had such bad breathing problems that I was missing volleyball events and major events. I missed the national championship one time. I was missing so many events in my last five years of coaching. Washington University worked beautifully with me in trying to help me to recover and we had one of the best hospitals in the world right there at Barnes and I just couldn't get through it. I was intubated, on a respirator, over 12 times within six years.

Wow.

I was pretty sick during that time. Long story short, when I was four years old I drank turpentine. My brother told me it was juice. It scarred my lungs badly and I had a lot of pneumonia and through that, I guess athletics really helped to push through it and finally it just all started coming back. I developed it in the lungs and throughout my body. I've been doing much better lately so I don't know, maybe I should go back to the coaching world.

Well that was what I was going to ask you. I mean, obviously you got the passion for it still. How strong has been the pull to maybe get back in?

The pull is extremely strong. However, I'm reminded on a daily basis that the reason I'm doing so well is because I'm not working 20-hour days and I'm able to focus on my health on a daily basis and take care of myself much better than I did as a coach.

Of course.

You know, when I was sick, I had six young kids too.

Have you ever thought about coaching club or something like that, where the demands are slightly, or significantly less?

I don't think I would ever make my demands less. That's the problem.

That's where it all stems from. I think that no matter when I coached, where I coached, or what kind of team I coached, I think that I like to win and I think that the type of development program that I put in the program would be too much for me.

I can appreciate that. I know the feeling. I was out of coaching for several year and then when I got back in, I was sucked all the way back in. There wasn't any halfway.

Yeah, then you get it. There is no halfway.

Let's talk a little bit about the practicalities or the specifics of your coaching style at the time. How would you describe the coaching philosophy you had? Obviously you said really competitive, but was there anything specific that you would say, "This is my style?"

Yeah, it all stems from a quote that our coach gave us when I was in high school. My whole philosophy stems from this and I think I determined right then that this was going to be the philosophy of my life on and off the court. It came from my high school volleyball coach and that's the reason that I was going to be a volleyball coach. The quote is, "In this world of give and take, there are few who are willing to give what it takes."

Number one, I knew that I could challenge myself to give what it takes and number two, it's kind of interesting because from the perspective of a coach and the perspective of a student-athlete, give and take is what it's all about. If I want to be the best coach that I can be, I'm going to take everything that I can from others, learn, listen, ask questions. If I'm going to give to others, I'm going to pass that on and share the knowledge that I have and do that freely.

If you look at the same thing from the term of a student-athlete, they need to listen, they need to ask questions, they need to continue to pursue how to be a better athlete, how to be a better student-athlete, how to be a better competitor, and how to learn both technique and strategies. They also need to give. They need to give to the younger players, they need to give to their studies, they need to give back to the coaches the respect, and to their teammates the respect. They need to give in the fact that they're playing the role that they've been assigned and the roles on and off the court that they are best at.

In terms of how you went about training... Let's start at the beginning of the season when you got the kids in preseason. I'm guessing you have them for maybe a week or so before school starts and you're running double days. How did you structure that? What were you doing in the morning, versus what you were doing in the afternoon, or in the evening?

Like a lot of coaches, we tried to make it like a camp atmosphere and provide a lot of different aspects. Let me start at the end of the day because we always finished with a swimming pool workout. We would usually do our jump training in the water to ease things because they had already been pounding the court all day. We did our jump training in the water, we did our stretching in the water, and not only did it help take the stress off, but it also helped flexibility and take away some of the soreness for the next day. I think that would be a good thing for a lot of teams to look into at least. As far as the training goes, we'd have one session in the morning on technique and one session in the afternoon on team play and working on strategies offensively and defensively. But in the mornings that does not mean that we didn't offer competitive opportunities, because from Day 1 we offered competitive opportunities.

I think that it differentiated us from a lot of programs – especially early in my career – in that everything I put on the floor was game-like. Everything I put in had a scoring system to it, and there was never just, "Okay I want you to pass 100 balls back and forth. I want you to serve 100 balls over the net and then pass it to a setter, who catches it and goes to the end of the line." I don't like those slow, boring drills. I like a lot of repetition, but I like them to be game-like. I like there to be a scoring system to them and we did that from Day 1. Having said that, I think the most important thing is the number of touches. Playing doubles and triples is going to give you a lot more touches than playing 6-on-6.

At the beginning, I think, at some levels, the high school level, you could probably train a team on triples games. I think that you find out a lot of things. You find out movement, leadership, competitiveness, hustle. Certainly technique and abilities shine through in triples. When I had 125 kids trying out for a position of 15, we played a lot of a triples and it's always been a favorite of mine early in the season because you get a lot of contacts on the ball.

Then mainly systems and 6 v 6 in the afternoon?

Yes. I'd say by Day 2 or 3 we're already getting into 6-on-6 and small drills. We're working very specifically. If I'm putting in an offensive play, we'll be running 6-on-6, but working specifically on that play. I think that's what a lot of coaches need to really do when they enter a drill is have a specific outcome. We're not just playing 6-on-6. We're not just playing, throwing out wash drills to see who wins. It's not about winning. It's about the development of a specific outcome that you're looking for.

If I want to work on a slide and isolating an opposing hitter, I want to throw my other two players – maybe the left side and middle – I want to throw them away from the slide so that I can isolate that hitter. We're working on just that, so one side I keep feeding balls in and let them play 6-on-6, but working on just that play and keeping score still. But they get a whole lot of opportunities to run that play. Then I introduce another play and we do a lot of that in the afternoon. Slowly introducing these plays and doing a major number of repetitions on those.

Master that one thing and then move on?

Right, but I think the difference is that I like to master the skills and the individual plays within a 6-on-6 environment. That's what our afternoons were really about. In the mornings you master the individual skills, but in the afternoons, you master those within a program. It still needs repetitions within the competitions, and that's what I think some of us forget to do.

I read that during the season you tended to try to avoid scheduling mid-week matches. Is that right?

Always. I did not play mid-week and I know some conferences, there's no options for you, but remember I'm in a major academic institution and it would be so stressful. In my first year or two when we had to, they were already scheduled, I saw the stress level just increase so enormously that I thought, "We just don't need to do this." We started playing on just Friday, Saturday and Sunday and I noticed a huge difference.

The other thing that I wasn't afraid to do was to give Monday off. I gave Monday off a lot. Any time we traveled, I gave Monday off and a lot of teams, a lot of coaches would be very surprised to hear that I did that. Or that I went very short on a Tuesday morning, because we practiced at

6 AM on Tuesday morning. However, we've got to remember that rest is an important factor of the season.

It really helped us a lot.

Compared to other coaches then, you had the benefit of being able to develop a plan over the course of a week, instead of having to practice, match, practice, match, practice, match over the course of the week so you're always thinking about the next opponent instead of maybe perhaps working more on some of your own stuff.

Well it's good and it's bad. The good thing is we had the week to practice. The bad thing is that we had to prepare for more than one teams because we were playing on the weekend.

Did you actually focus on the teams that you were going to play, as in try to replicate what they were doing or try to focus on certain plays that you were doing in anticipation of going against them?

Both. I think you need both. You want to run your own offense and defense very well, but you also want to be aware of who you're facing and what their tendencies are and so sure, we did both. We did video work, but time was a major factor at Washington U for the students and we [the coaches] would do the video work. We did not make players watch video, although once in a while I'd call a setter in.

You gave them the scouting report, but you didn't actually have them watch the video?

Exactly. Only a setter once in awhile.

Did you do a lot of A/B scrimmage, A team versus B team, or did you mix the squad?

A versus B. I don't think there's any advantage to not playing your team together, but what I did do is add assistant coaches who were very strong, male players, added them to the B team. I think your goal has to be to get on that A team and you have to give them opportunities to play together. I'm not a proponent at all of mixing up. Maybe early season until you have established what your mainstays are going to be, but I think that you strive to be with the elite group.

Two related questions. How big a squad did you normally have?

I'd have anywhere from 14 to 18.

I imagine that created some challenges in keeping that many players happy, especially if you're including the assistant coaches in your scrimmages. That leaves a lot of players on the sideline.

No, I never had players on the sideline. One thing that I think is really a good thing to do... Say I'm playing a 6-on-6 or running a 6-on-6 drill, have Susie switch with Mary and run three times and then have the other player come in and run three times. I think that's what we need to do and so before the scrimmage takes place, or the drill that you're running, say, "Mary, you and Susie will switch every three plays. Joanie, you and Martha will switch every three plays. Doug, you and John will switch every three plays."

Have it set ahead of time, especially in a small gym form like mine where you don't have several assistants. Have it set up ahead of time so that you can actually focus on what the outcome of the drill is, versus on your substitutions all the time. If you don't do that in advance, you don't know who's subbing or who you've subbed for and you might leave a player out of the entire drill. We never left anybody out of a drill and you only sat out for two or three plays at a time so they were always right in the drill because of that.

How did you change, if at all, how you did training over the course of the season – from when you started at the beginning of the year to when you're getting ready for the NCAA tournament?

Well first I'll say what I like to keep the same and that is I like a lot of repetitions all the time. But I'm not doing repetitions on basic skills. That was only at the very beginning possibly, and a lot of that in the off-season. As the season progresses, my practices get shorter first of all because they need more rest and more recovery time each day. In order to have them peak at the right time, you have to give them recovery time after practices and after matches. Practices get shorter, but the focus becomes very deliberate. We're practicing much more specifically. Especially when you get into post-season, you're looking at your opponent much more deliberately and their tendencies and fine-tuning rather than conditioning and learning.

How long were your sessions normally?

Early season we'd go three, three and a half hours easily for each session. Near the end of the season, they're about a hour and a half.

Just out of curiosity, would you change any of that these days under rally score? Because obviously back in side out days there was an endurance/conditioning element that maybe there isn't quite as much of any more.

I think I always trained for a high-speed – a lot of quick movement within our drills all season long. I never did any endurance training ever during season, so I'm not sure I would change anything. Looking back, I mean I don't know this, but looking back I'd say we did a pretty good job of peaking at the right time.

In terms of the subs, what was your philosophy on using substitutions during the match? Were you the type of coach who liked to get players in, or were you primarily focused on the starters, and if the starters aren't getting the job done, then make a tactical sub?

Wow, that's a tough question because I like to get subs in, but looking back, I did not sub a lot. I tend to think of the match as a test and the gym as my laboratory. So if I look at my practices as getting prepared for the test and then my best take the test. Everyone's goal is to be in the test and so I like to, obviously, keep others prepared and give them opportunities, but I might not have subbed as much as I should have. Let's put it that way. I might change that if I did it over again. I like to put away teams and it's probably not always necessary.

I assume that for most of your time in Washington, you guys were the dominant team. You must've played matches where it was going to be lopsided. You're saying you basically kept your starting six and didn't bring in the seventh player, or the eighth player, or whatever all that much.

No, I probably played nine, ten deep on a regular basis, but in evaluating, we were so dominant, why didn't I play more in games two, three? Why didn't I go to 10 through 15 more? See, now you get it. It's like as I age, I question myself more on that.

Yeah, well I think it's inevitable for all of us. If you're at all introspective, you can't avoid it. "I could've done or maybe I should've

done this." The problem is we don't know if the answer we had at the time was the wrong one or the right one.

Right, and that's if we don't ask those questions and constantly evaluate ourselves.

Yep, right. We're not going to get any better.

Thanks for letting me out of that one, John.

You talked about having male staff in there to help out, to make the B team more competitive ... Obviously having former players or current players would be a key component to this, but what was your coaching staff selection and development philosophy like?

Well when I first got to Washington University, I didn't have an assistant at all and then they told me I could have a part-time assistant. At first that person was already on campus – the intramural director. He was a great player himself and he at the time went to the Athletic Director and said, "I want to be an assistant coach." He hadn't coached.

The Athletic Director said, "What are you looking at?"

He said, "Either women's baseball or volleyball."

There was going to be somebody hired in each of those, so the Athletic Director asked him, "Which one?"

This was my second year and he said, "I guess I'd go volleyball because they're going to win it all," and so that was really ... very complimentary I think. But he was so interested in being there and such a task master and so perfect for the position. He stayed for my entire career.

Wow. You only basically had one proper assistant coach?

I had a volunteer assistant who was, if you can believe this, the head of the emergency department at Barnes Hospital here in St. Louis. He actually came over every day for practice.

Wow.

He didn't travel with us very much.

Right.

Just Joe and I traveled, but we were known as quite the team because we'd stayed together for so long.

Yeah, well that's definitely unusual.

It is.

All right, well on I guess you could say a related subject, what was your approach to selecting team captains and what sort of responsibilities did you give them?

I think my approach is a little different from most in that I think the expertise of the coach has to be part of the process. I like the players to have their input, so this is how I did it. I would let the players vote on two people each that they thought would be great leaders and we'd go over the qualities that we thought that they should possess – my input and the players' input on what qualities they should possess. They each voted for two people. Then my assistant and I chose the captain or captains so it was either one, two, or three depending on what we as coaches thought we should have.

The players liked it a lot because it was not a popularity contest. They had input and coaches had input and we thought it was a pretty good system. It worked for us.

And what sort of responsibilities did you put on them?

Captains are responsible #1, for communicating to coaches if there's anything the coaches might not know and need to know, etc. Also to be a sounding board for other players if they want to talk about playing time or off court issues or any kind of issues. I think captains have a good responsibility because they have to know when to talk to coaches, when to just help the player. But we were always very open and with all the players. I found that seniors were just as responsible as captains – whether the captains were seniors or not – for the leadership of the team.

Spring training. You mentioned you played Division I teams when you got out and got competition. What was your schedule like in the Spring? What were you allowed to do?

Well it changed every year. Doesn't it always?

We never knew what the rules were going to be until that year and they would tell us how many competitions we can have. Because I'm out of the loop, I don't know what they're doing right now, but I think it's less. I remember some years we were allowed to have four-competition weekends and some three and some five.

We would usually go to a one-day tournament on a Saturday for that many weeks. We'd practice just two or three days a week and did weight training and conditioning. At the one-day tournament there would be usually like five to eight teams and we would just play a round robin-type thing. Sometimes just two sets against each team there, but usually it was all Division I and Washington University.

Let's talk about recruiting. You mentioned that you wanted to recruit competitive women for the program, obviously. If you're looking for that characteristic, when you're watching a player or when you're talking to them, what is the indication to you that this is the type of competitive kid you want

I like to a lot of times introduce myself as the most competitive person I know. "Can you compete with me?" Then I'd hear the response to that right away.

Some people, some young players will take that and say, "You're on," and that's a definite interest. That peaks me right away.

Some will shy away from it and say, "Probably not. You've got a lot more experience than me. I probably can't compete with you."

Their response to that tells me a lot, but do they like practice? Do they like hours in the gym? Are they a gym rat? What if you played a game with your siblings? Do you guys get competitive in that?

It's just a general competitiveness, not necessarily just volleyball because I'm going to provide the opportunities for them to succeed. I'm going to provide the opportunities for them to compete. I want them to like those opportunities, not necessarily to have to win, but I want them to like the opportunities to compete and that's what I'm trying to find out when I'm recruiting.

Any other characteristics you were looking for?

Yeah, I think one of the most important characteristics I look for is unusual. I want to know if you're attached to your family. I want to know if there's a commitment to your family because, and I know there's extenuating circumstances, but in general, if you're close to your family, you have the ability to get close to a team. We always had extremely close-knit teams. Ask them whether they're close to their team or ask them whether they're close to their friends, there's not many 18 year-olds who are going to tell you they're not. There's not too many 16 year-olds who are going to say they're not. Of course you're committed to your friends. I want to know if you're committed to your family because that's where more trial and error and tribulations go on. I want to know if you are there for your family. If you're close to them, typically you'd bond pretty well with the team.

I imagine that having those sorts of competitive personalities sometimes can make things a little bit challenging bringing them together on a team. Though obviously if you're recruiting this family element, that helps to smooth things out. What sorts of things did you do in terms of team development or team bonding or chemistry creation with your teams say at the beginning of the year – or over the course of the season for that matter?

I think you could explain a lot of things at the beginning and keep the doors of communication open. At the beginning of the season, I like to really have a good session on what my expectations are of myself and what my expectations are of the players. Let them know that I'm competitive and I like to win, but I'm more concerned with the development and what happens at practice every day because I like practices. I like the development aspect of the game. They will like the matches, but I want to help them to like practices and enjoy practices. That's really my responsibility, so I owe them that expertise. I owe them an enthusiastic and positive approach and that positivity in my responses to them. I'm going to do my best to do that, and I hope that they will challenge themselves to maintain a positive aspect.

I also ask them – and I think this was really big on our team – in all interviews, in all communication with others, be it in the dormitories, be it in your classrooms, when you talk about a teammate, when you talk about the team, always talk about the positive things. There's going to be some negative things. There's going to be, "Susie faced me yesterday and I didn't want to have lunch with her," but talk about only positive things. When they did interviews, the team came off very positive and when you get in that habit of talking positive and saying and noticing positive things, it becomes a lifestyle. That's what I like to see in our team. The competitiveness comes from the opportunities we give them for success. The camaraderie comes from sharing those opportunities, so we talk a lot about that.

Okay. Maybe this applies a little bit more to when you were coaching high school than perhaps when you were coaching in college, but for those players who might not have been as competitive as some of the others, what did you do to try to bring them along in that respect?

Well I think our responsibility as coaches is to provide competitive opportunities and that's why I said that starting on day #1, we keep score on everything. One thing that helps a lot is to keep scores short-term. If I'm only playing short games to five, there's a whole lot more chances to win than there is if I'm playing a game to 25 all the time. I tried to provide not only opportunities for success, but many mini-opportunities for success in a short period of time. Susie, Jane, Mary all get to win because you're probably not going to win 100 percent of the time, so giving them lots of opportunities for success makes them much more competitive and it's contagious. My competitiveness is contagious and getting the opportunities to compete becomes contagious.

When it comes to match day, and you're on the sidelines, what were you like coaching in the heat of the battle so to speak? What was your kind of psyche. What sort of behavior were you exhibiting?

I'm a wound-up, excited practice coach. I'm a very calm demeanor on the sideline and that's because of the outlook I have for the match. I see it as a test. If I am all wound-up during a test, they might not perform their best. I enjoy the matches. I can only do so much. Come on. All these volleyball coaches who think they can change the course of everything in 30-second timeouts, it's not going to happen. So I'm very calm. I like to laugh when something funny happens and I like to enjoy myself and I want them to enjoy the opportunity. It's a test to see what we get to practice on Monday. That's really how I looked at it all the way through my career and it helped me to keep calm.

Now having said that, I kept a pen in my hand my entire coaching career. All 22 years, I kept a pen in my hand during every match and that pen was my reminder that it is to be a test, not anything but that. I threw my pen once in awhile, but I really tried to hold on to it throughout the course of my coaching career.

Well I suppose throwing a pen is better than throwing your clipboard or a folder.

Isn't that the truth? I really was not a very... I had one yellow card in my entire career. That's it, one.

And what was that for?

I was in New York and at the time it was a very different officiated game on the East Coast than it was where we were. Okay, let's say on that day it was. I can't remember specifically what it was, but it amounted to I'd had my limit of a particular call and I jumped up and I got it quickly.

I made sure he knew it was my first and only yellow card of my career. He didn't care a lot, but it was.

You were a sitting coach, not a standing coach?

Yes.

Very calm. I think I'd helped my team to perform. From the week, I always had the demeanor that we're prepared, we're ready. I always believed it and if we are prepared and ready, why do I need to be a maniac on the sideline? That doesn't mean I didn't respond once in awhile because sometimes that's how I got my point across – by saying, "That is not how we do it." Then I'd sit calmly again.

I'd be one to tell a joke in the huddle or to calm them down in different ways, but no I'm not a real feisty bench coach. When I wanted to make a point, it made a point if I stayed sitting down, right?

In terms of once you got into the NCAA's, or once you were getting into the real teeth of the championship fight, was there anything that you liked to do in particular in terms of your preparation with the team, to maybe keep them more focused or keep them on a more even keel, or whatever?

You might know this story, but when I was interviewing at Washington

U, the athletic director John Shale said, "Teri, how many years do you think it would take you to win a national championship?"

I said, I thought for a second and said, "Five years," and he looked very surprised.

He said, "You know, there's never been a national championship at Washington University in 104 years."

I said, "Five years then."

And he said, "Why five?"

I said, "My first season and then four years to bring in my recruits and that's the year we'll win it."

He said, "Well then let's make that an expectation."

We won it, our first championship, in my fifth year.

There you go, very good. The question is when you were in the championship context, when you were in the tournament, or getting ready for that final match or whatever, was there anything in particular that you liked to do with the team to get them focused, to get them prepared?

In every championship match, all seven years ... Actually nine years. When we didn't win, I did it too. I always prepared a performance for the team. Sometimes it was singing a song, sometimes it was changing the word to a song, sometimes it was ... One time I did the Knute Rockne speech up on a bench like he did in the locker room. I memorized the whole speech and used every arm motion that he did, everything. I always had a performance for the team in the locker room the day of the championship, always.

Was that just to kind of keep them loose?

Yeah, to keep them light. After a number of years, they would look as forward to that production as they would to the match, so it was kind of nice not to have them focused on the match for 24 hours before it. Quite honestly, I was pretty nervous about the performance every year, but I spent a lot of time on it and I always made sure that I was as prepared for that as I expected them to be prepared for the match.

You're obviously not involved right now, but if you were looking at the competition these days, how much harder do you think it would be to be a consistent title contender, a national championship contender?

Wow that's a really tough question. I'm not sure that I can answer that. I think it would be harder because there's more players. I don't necessarily think they're more competitive. I don't necessarily think they're better trained. I don't think they're worse trained either, but I think that the game itself being rally scoring makes for a interesting change in that probably.

When they were at 30-point games [the initial rule for NCAA women] and were talking about shifting it to only 25, I remember the discussion about a potential benefit that you might get more upsets. Probably not over the course of a match perhaps, but at least in a game scenario.

Right, and I think that's what I'm thinking about when I say that I don't know if you could have the same dynasty that you once had because I think there are more chances for upsets. Boy, I should get back in coaching and see if that's true! That got me thinking, but my gut instinct is that it would be harder to carry a dynasty.

Okay, well I was just curious if you thought that the field is deeper now, but you said there are more players so that kind of implies ...

I do think the field's deeper. I do think there's a lot more ... When I was coaching, it was hard to tamper with the top 20 at our level. It was very hard to break in, but now it's hard to break into the top 64, you know? It's like a lot more players, it's a lot deeper.

In terms of your coaching, I read in an article that you like to create new drills and even up to the last day of training, you were still fiddling around and having the players do new things. Is that a key facet of your overall philosophy?

Most people who know our program well might say that that's the difference is the way we ran our practice. I love to create drills. I don't like to save drills because I like it to be new and inviting every day. In fact, I had trouble a couple of years ago when I wrote a drill book even remembering some of my drills because I refused to save them on paper. It would make me create and I might do it better the second time.

I used to always develop drills and I would start off practice with, "Wait until you see what I have today!"

Probably 50 percent of them were very excited that there was a new drill and the rest wanted their favorites. I think it's really important to keep it new and fresh constantly. But always in designing a drill, know what you're specifically looking for, know what the outcome of the drill, know what the competitive angle is going to be, know very specifically what you as a coach are going to watch during the drill. Don't start just watching the play and getting into the rally back and forth. Very specifically watch what your intentions for the drill are. Know how you're going to incorporate the number of people in the game and keep everybody busy and know what the scoring system is for the drill. If you keep all of those things in mind, it's not very difficult to make a drill, to adapt it to the needs of your program. But you can also read the book.

That was something Bill Neville brought up. A lot of coaches, especially in the early stages of the career, they just take a drill out of a book, or one they saw in clinics, and plugged it right into their practice without really thinking about the context. You obviously went through that phase of going to all these clinics and watching all these coaches and you must've seen hundreds of drills being demonstrated or shown in books or whatever. Were you from an early stage adapting your own drills right away, or did you go through that phase of, "This is a cool new drill, I'm going to try it with my team?"

Honestly, I think that I kind of always had a creative edge. Even in high school, I'd be like, "I bet we could make this better if we did this," in my own mind. Not that I said it to my coach, but I always kind of had that wanting to create.

I always think when I talk to other coaches, you don't have to be creative. You don't have to be able to make drills. You just have to be able to be innovative and adapt other drills to your needs and not just take the drill that you get at a clinic and automatically run through the drill and think that, "Wow, he seemed to think this was a better drill than I do." Maybe it's because you weren't adapting it quite to the needs of your program.

We all have a different number of people in the gym when we're running a practice, and we all have different methods of retrieving balls. Shagging is a big part of every drill. Having established plans on how you're going to do that within a drill is important because if you want to run a fast-paced drill, you've got to have a fast-paced method of getting the balls back into play. Let's face it, some are practicing with six balls and some are practicing with 150 balls.

All right, let me ask you this theoretical question and who knows? Maybe one day you'll take this on. If you were to take over a program today, where would you focus your priorities?

I hope that I would still have the same priority system. I can't imagine that I would change because it's such a part of who I am. That is to focus on the development of the player and the team and let winning be the outcome of the program. I love to win. There's no doubt. But I learned really early that if you focus on winning and you make your goal, "We're going to have this many wins in a match, in a season," you don't know whether it's going to happen or not. But if you focus on the development of the team, the outcome is winning and I would still do that.

I would still focus on the program. I would establish it within the school, within the university, then within the local community, then regionally, then nationally. I think focusing on that order and starting in small steps proved to be very successful and I would think that I would be very similar to that.

Off the court, what were the biggest challenges that you had from an administrative, management-type perspective?

We were very fortunate. We had a super athletic director and an amazing president of our university. Chancellor Danforth – a very familiar name to many – was amazing and fell in love with the spirit of the volleyball team. We had a lot of support and were very blessed that way. The biggest challenges for me were that we were in a top academic institution. The easy part was that the focus is clearly on the student-athlete. They are a student and they are an athlete. We wanted to be first class in presenting both to this student. That was the easy part.

The hard part was that as a coach, keeping your focus on the academics of the student as a priority because you're trying to develop them as an athlete, yet academics is number one. This comes at all of our institutions. It's a fine line balance, but I tried to keep the focus on family, fun, academics, and athletics. The order changes all the time, doesn't it?

If you had been able to continue coaching, if you didn't have your health challenges, would you have ever left the university? Would you have contemplated moving up to a higher division or anything like that?

Well first let me clarify that I don't always consider it a step up to go to Division II or I.

Fair enough.

Having said that, I don't think it's a secret that I had lots of opportunities to leave Washington University over the years. To be honest, it was very difficult for me to say no to a major DI program that wooed me a lot in the last year that I coached. I didn't know if it was the right answer. I love a good, strong, well committed-to program and I don't look at the division of the program at all.

Washington University runs a first class program all across the board, and I love their commitment to running a first class athletic program as well as a first class academic program. I would love any institution that did that, no matter which division it is.

Having said all that, did I have the draw to win at Division I level? Very much so. I was halted in that effort because of my health. Would I have gone? There's a pretty strong inclination that I might have if my health had stayed with me, but did I think it was a step up? No, it was a personal challenge to win at a another level.

Related to that, as a obviously successful female coach, was there any external sort of pressure or feeling that you got from other coaches that you needed to kind of carry the banner for successful women coaches and get to the highest level you possibly could?

Nope, not at all. I saw myself as a coach, not a female coach. I saw myself as a coach and it was my responsibility to give back to coaching. Obviously, I want to give back to women coaches too because I'm a woman, but I want to give back to coaches and I really didn't differentiate. Just like I don't differentiate my own children at home, "I owe the girls more than the boys." I owe coaching. I owe my sport.

What's your thought on the debates that go on about trying to get more women involved in coaching or trying to progress women up the ranks to the higher levels?

I think there's some definite advantages to women coaches. Having said that, I don't differentiate in my daily practices between coaches, but I played sports including competitiveness and including connectivity. Women coaching women can help to connect in a lot of easy ways. I think men can do the same with women, but have to work really hard at learning the intricacies of why women play sports.

That begs the question. Why do women play sports?

Well I think that women play for many different reasons. I think most guys play ... this is my perspective ... most guys play to compete and to hang with the guys, but women play to compete and to be with their friends in a much more social and connected way. They want to have a close-knit team. They want Susie to like them. They want to have this bond that goes far beyond just hanging with the girls. The closer the team, the more they take away from that experience and many of us who have won championships will talk about not getting the trophy, but getting the feelings and the camaraderie that went with it.

When we ended the season, we would often talk about there's only one team that gets to know ... Well there's two teams that get to know when their season ended – the team that takes first and the team that takes second in the national championship. They're the only teams that know when their last match is, so it wasn't enough to be there. You're after a certain feeling that you get to keep the rest of your life and women in my perspective are much deeper about that, stealing that feeling away that they shared with other women.

I liken in one of my books that guys can play a volleyball game at practice and they face somebody across the net and they walk off the court and they say, "Hey let's go to lunch together." A woman can face one of her teammates at practice and walk off the court and say, "I'm not speaking to her again for a week," and it's not like that in my gym. It's not like that in most gyms, but we see that a lot because they're looking for something different or in addition to just the competition.

Right, so it sounds like you would agree with Kathy DeBoer, when she said in her book, boys battle to bond and girls bond to battle.

That's a great quote. I wish I would've said that.

I've had the fortune, or misfortune, of coaching both genders and it definitely rings true for me.

Well good. Yeah, I so much hesitate to say it because I don't want it to be like that. I don't want it to be that I think women should coach women, but I know they get it. I know that they do, but I do think it's a real edge that I'm so competitive.

It's so interesting, huh?

Yeah, and your point about that feeling after the match. It's not necessarily about winning. I can so get that because I coached a team in England a few years ago. We only made it as far as the national semi-finals, although that's as far as that team could possibly have gotten that year given the opposition. Looking back, it was the feeling of, "Okay the team at the beginning of the year set their objective and you battled and you struggled, there were good days and bad days, but at the end you made the objective and you even went a little bit further." We didn't expect to get into the semi-finals. We were happy to get into the final eight and that had been the goal. Everything else was just a cherry on top. It wasn't about having a trophy or anything like that. It was about the process of getting there as a group.

That's interesting John because that process begs me to talk about goal setting on a team. I think that we so often make the mistake about setting our goals at the beginning of the year. Look at it from my perspective. When you win a national championship and you're seeing your team the next year, what are you going to say? We're going to win Regionals this year? We're going to win Districts? We're going to win conference?" No, of course not. It would be foolish for me to say we're going win anything but the national championship the following year, correct?

Having said that, why would I ever set my goals in terms of wins? Why would I ever set my goals in terms of victories against specific teams? Why would I ever set my goals in terms of anything but development?

I remember us setting goals. When we'd play a match against a team that we knew was not as competitive as us, was not as talented as us,

I remember setting goals of, "Let's score on three slides. Let's score on an X tandem with a quick hit. Let's score on four aces. Let's score on a ace to zone four." We'd have a list of 25 goals perhaps that we wanted to score on in that match and that's what our success was based on. Not the victory because chances are, we were going to pull off the victory in 90 percent of our matches. We did over my career, so why would I set any goals to match victories? I never did that. Why not set the goals in terms of always development? Because that precludes winning.

I read that you started every year by basically saying, "Okay, congratulations for those of you returning players. Now this is a completely new team."

That's right. This team has never won a national championship, so let's start the process. I would start every year and wherever I went, I think that's the number one question I got.

Well there's two questions I got.

One was, "Why did you win?" I'd always say, people always didn't know if we won because we had fun or if we had fun because we won. That's kind of a very general statement, but what it means is we presented ourselves as just a really fun team to watch. We're fast-paced. We laugh when things were funny. We enjoyed the process of this.

But that made people ponder and say, "Do they work hard in practice, or do they just have a good time?"

Well it was one in the same. You can do both. That was one question I got. I kind of call it the great mystery of our program, that people didn't know what we did in practice. I thought that was great.

The other question I got all the time was, "What was the magic? Why did your team win repeatedly?"

It wasn't about the number of wins. It wasn't about winning a particular match. It was about the focus on development and that's really what it was. We focused on practice and making the practice and each drill the best opportunity that we can make it and that's really what it boils down to, is the commitment of players and coaches to practice.

Health issues aside, can you look back on any particular difficult

challenges with individual players, with a certain team, with a certain situation that you had to deal with and overcome?

Right away, I remember one situation.

I always talked to my team. At many levels, alcohol is an issue and I talked to my team at the beginning of my second season and said, "You make the decision. I'm not going to babysit you when you're not with volleyball. I have a family of my own. I can't focus on what you're doing in the dorms. You make the decision on what the alcohol issue's going to be,"

I left the room, and when I came back in, this particular team said, "We're not going to drink. We're not going to drink at all through the season."

I said, "That's a wonderful decision. You're going to police yourselves because I'm not going to do it."

That was not only a commitment to not drinking. It was a commitment that we want to take care of our bodies, that we want to perform best, that we want to get enough rest, etc.

That went on for several years because as you know, success breeds success and since the team before did it and did well, we better not break the tradition and it kind of became a tradition. Everyone on campus knew that the volleyball team didn't drink. It didn't mean they didn't go to parties, didn't mean they didn't hold the cup in their hand, but what they had in that beer cup was water very often or a soft drink. The whole campus became involved in, "You know the volleyball team doesn't drink?"

Well, the chancellor of the university said to me one time, "Is it true that our volleyball team doesn't drink?"

There was even a pub on our campus at the time. I said, "It's very true, but I don't have anything to do with that rule. It's their rule."

It was well-respected on our campus and it actually increased our attendance dramatically. People kept coming to see this team that was so committed that they wouldn't party and I would see people, students on campus, and they'd say, "I saw so-and-so at a party last night. She didn't drink anything," like I was policing it, but I wasn't.

Then after about eight years, I had a knock on my door and one of my players came in and she was crying and I said, "Whatever is the problem? Have a seat."

She said, "The problem is this. I drank at a party. I had a drink." She said, "I just sipped. I lost myself and I had a sip of it and I went to the team and I was so upset with myself, I told them that they might find out and I wanted to be the one who'd be honest and tell them. I told them I had this drink and I didn't know what to do with it and they asked me to step out of the room and they all talked about it and I came back in and they said, 'Your consequence is that you have to go tell coach what you did.'"

She told me that day. She cried that that was the worst possible consequence that she could have, that she was so dedicated to me and so dedicated to the team that it would be the most emotional thing she had ever done. I thanked her for caring that much, for realizing that she'd broken some trust there.

I saw her about five years ago. She's about 35 years old now and she said it was the #1 lesson of her life and she never has a drink ever since then without thinking of how important it is to respect any rules that you establish within a group. That stands out in my mind as one of the most important lessons learned during my career.

It's impressive, and you talking about the non-drinking thing bringing people to your matches brings up a question. Were you involved with actually marketing the program to try to drive attendance for any of those things?

Well we didn't have a marketing budget so we were completely responsible for bringing people in the gym. Surprisingly, or not surprisingly, that not drinking put a lot of people in the gym because it became so well-known on campus and then there would be an article in the student paper, "Hey, did you know that the team doesn't drink?" It wasn't ever meant to be a selling point, but you take what you can get. I always joked that there were 18 people at my first match that I coached there. Well 25 people total, and 18 were my family. It really is true. That's exactly what it was and at the last match I coached there, we had 3,200.

Wow.

We averaged over 2,000 in my last three seasons at each match. We were drawing at the time well over the norm of Division I schools and it was amazing. But we kind of became the sweethearts of campus, #1 because we won, I'm guessing, but #2 because of commitment that the players knew and it became a well-known fact, not just the drinking, but the work that they put in at practices. We brought in grade school, middle school, and high school teams to watch our practices on a regular basis.

Did you do a lot of outreach in the community?

Yes, a lot.

The funny one was the year that we had the national championship on the week after Thanksgiving. It was a real dilemma. Do you let your players go home for Thanksgiving, or do you train? We decided to train this particular year, but have a team Thanksgiving meal and to do some outreach in the community. There was a flood in St. Louis that year, so I'm guessing that was '93, the year of the great floods in St. Louis. Our players did all kinds of yard work and carrying furniture out of homes and everything and they were so sore that we couldn't practice the next day before the final. But it was worth it.

We did a lot of clinics and coaches and camps and we did a lot of outreach.

Winding back to the question I should've asked earlier, after a match, what was your philosophy on your conversation, your post-match talk with the team?

Well again, I keep referring back to the match as just a test, so I didn't spend a lot of time right after the match evaluating the test. I wanted to take my time grading the test and talk about it the next day at practice. Didn't mean I didn't celebrate a little bit with the players on victories or cry a little bit on losses, but I really didn't evaluate until I did my homework.

You've obviously seen a lot of coaches and talked with a lot of coaches and sounds like you still do. What do you think are the most important skills in terms of being a successful coach?

I would say communication skills – being able to communicate what your philosophy is and turning it into success and development. That's a very difficult thing to do.

I would also say ask questions to continue learning because successful coaches tend to be ones that will share on a snap of a finger. Successful coaches give away the answers because they're so competitive that they think, "Even if I give you the answer or give you the style that I use or give you the information of my strategies, etc., I can do it better than you."

I really believe that to be true, and I think you have to ask questions. You have to say, "How did you do that?"

Sometimes new coaches are afraid to even ask a simple question that they don't understand. Ask it. I even wish that I had asked more, as I was growing up in the world of coaching. I think I would've been a better coach had I asked more questions earlier and I would encourage that.

You've written how many books?

All or parts of about five or six.

What's on your recommended reading list, aside from those books of course?

Yes, well I always like my humorous books a lot. Some of the books that I did, like *The Volleyball Drill Book* that I did with Jenny McDowell [published by the AVCA] and I really liked learning her philosophy on it too and sharing that. It's always good when you find a book that is written by many coaches, like *The Volleyball Coaching Bible*. You have a lot of experts write together on different topics. I did the setting in that book, but I learned a lot from the other coaches.

I like books that many coaches participate in. One time I did a book called *Competitive Excellence* where I spoke – we all spoke – on winning national championships. All the coaches did. Mick Haley was in there, but it was also Pat Summitt from women's basketball, [Joe] Paterno from football. We all wrote on the same questions by the interviewer. It was pretty intriguing to read the answers and the responses from coaches and to see how alike they are.

Have you read anything good beyond volleyball, even beyond sports, that you think is valuable?

I like to read books on successful businessmen too, and women, and the reason is is because I liken it a lot. The same reason I get asked to speak at a lot of businesses is the same reason it correlates well and that's because we're all competitive. I always liken back to the book called *Made in America* by Peter Ueberroth, who ran the '84 Olympics and was the first successful entrepreneur to make money in running the Olympics and see it as a business venture. How he did it was so competitive and so decisive in his style. I like books like that.

Last major question, what would your advice be to new coaches or developmental coaches early in their careers?

Well, I know one of the big questions is always do you specialize or do you not? I don't really see a problem with specializing early. Unlike probably the norm, I think when you introduce volleyball and you ask somebody to focus on a specialty position, they're going to learn that as well as they can. They're also going to have a drive to learn the other positions. They're also going to be able to understand the other positions and how their role fits into it. Just because we ask someone to specialize early doesn't mean that they don't understand the game and I hear that argument a lot, but I asked my players to specialize when I was at the high school level and I feel like they had a good grasp of the game. I feel like they still could intertwine and play other positions.

At the same token, when I was at Washington University, I would bring players in who were an outside hitter and turn them into a setter with no qualm and didn't see it being an issue. There's an understanding of the game beyond the position and it's our responsibility as coaches to make sure they have that understanding, so I don't see specializing early as a problem myself.

When we're talking six to twelve year-olds, sure let them play all the positions and find out who's going to grow tall, who's going to be quick, who's going to have different skill levels in different skills, but beyond that, I don't have a problem with specializing.

I think starting about the high school level, specialization is okay.

I think a lot of people would tend to agree with that. I know when I was in England and they talked about the progressions there was no specialization for the younger kids and they weren't even introducing the 4-2 system – so a setter specialization – until 15. I think they're along a similar thought line there.

That's good.

The issue that I have often seen is when you've got really competitive coaches with a bunch of 11 year-olds, that they're thinking about winning. This goes to your earlier comment about the focusing on the development and the process and not the outcome. These coaches are specializing their kids at 11 years old because that's how they win, which causes problems with other clubs that don't want to specialize, but can't be as competitive.

Right, yeah it's definitely a dilemma. But if they make ... If they wouldn't allow it, if they made them run a 4-2, it might solve that problem, right?

Right, and I know that discussion has come up in England of, "Do we, at these tournaments that are sponsored by the governing body say, 'The rule is you must play a 6-6 or you must play a system appropriate for that age level?'" I don't think I've seen it actually implemented yet.

True.

All right, is there anything that we didn't touch on that you think is worth discussing?

I oftentimes give a talk on winners and whiners and I think that coaches should be very aware of – that we're trying to coach winners, not whiners. I think in this age of entitlement that we're in right now, it's even more important to differentiate, early in the season, who is a winner and who is a whiner and how you separate yourselves. For example, in speaking about give and take, winners do give and whiners do take. Winners do rest and whiners do never wake up. Winners are focused and whiners are unfocused. Winners surround themselves with wannabe winners and whiners surround themselves with wannabe whiners. Winners ask for help and whiners know it all. Winners give a pat on the back and whiners ask for a pat on the back.

We need to help our young players really understand the differences in being a winner and being a whiner. A whiner stomps her foot after she misses a serve. A winner just runs to the next person and says, "We need you." Give examples on the court of what differentiates a winner and a whiner. Give examples off the court of what differentiates a winner and whiner. Student-athletes are not entitled. They are not entitled to get to play the game of volleyball. It's a wonderful sport that we are totally committed to and if we are entitled to the right to be on the court, we're missing the boat. Whiners are entitled and winners want to work to get there.

I think if nothing else, if we could help players to understand the difference between being a winner and whiner in a team setting, we're really getting somewhere.

6

GARTH PISCHKE

A lot of people have probably never heard of him, but Canadian Garth Pischke has become one of the winningest college coaches of all time during his 30+ year tenure leading the University of Manitoba men's program. This is after being one of Canada's best national team players.

Garth has more victories in men's college volleyball than even the legendary Al Scates. His Manitoba teams have made 26 trips to the CIS National Championships, winning 9 golds, 9 silver, and 5 bronze medals. He also head coached the Canadian National Men's Volleyball Team from 1996-2000. During that time they improved from 21st in world rankings to 10th.

This interview was conducted by Mark in May 2016. As with many players who transitioned from successful playing careers into coaching, Garth had his early-career struggles handling the performance issues of his players. In the interview he talks about how his coaching changes over the years, in sometimes surprising ways.

We normally like to start off with how you came to volleyball originally, how you went into coaching, what was your volleyball timeline?

A lot of my coaching technique philosophy stems from being a player. I don't know if this is a unique situation, but I had very little background in coaching. In getting into it, coaching became an extension of my playing career, and it gave me the opportunity to stay competitive in my personal life. It's something that has really helped me get through life and enjoy life and keep that component in my life. I had some great opportunities, and really was in the right place at the right time when I finished my competitive career.

I don't know if you know much about that, but I had played with our National team in the Montreal Olympics, and then I went and played some professional volleyball in the United States when they used to have the IVA, or International Volleyball Association. The funny thing at that time was in playing in that so-called professional league, we were instantly banned from playing international volleyball again. I kept playing in that league, and the league eventually disbanded around '82 I think it was, or earlier. I was banned from playing international volleyball again until... Basically what happened was the United States, I believe, took the FIVB to court with regards to it. We managed to get our eligibility back.

I was still at a relatively young age – 27, 28 at the time- and I was contacted right away by the Canadian head coach, Ken Maeda at the time, and asked me to be involved with the '84 Olympic team. I was very interested in that. I had been coaching already at the time, but I took a brief absence from that so I could join the '84 Olympic team and play there. From there on I just continued on with my coaching career. Like I said, I think you'll find in a lot of my answers to the questions that you ask me will go back to my playing career, and that's really where I get a lot of my resources from.

To flesh out the time line a bit, you were already coaching in around '83?

Yes, I started in '79. I started coaching at the University of Manitoba. At that time, I was playing in the professional league in the United States. The beauty of that was it was just a four month season in the Summer, which didn't conflict with my coaching, and I was actually a student at the University of Manitoba while I was coaching. Because I couldn't play anymore in Canada, I went back to school and was a student and coaching the men's volleyball team, and playing in the professional league in the summertime.

Since '79, you've been unbroken at the University of Manitoba except for 4 years with the National team?

Yes, that's correct. I have now coached 34 years with the University of Manitoba, with that break in there when I was with the National team.

How many championships have you won, if I can ask directly?

Yeah, I do have a lot of these. In those 34 years, I've won 9 championships, 9 silver medals, and 5 bronze medals.

That's a pretty decent record. Because you're the first Canadian – from the Canadian college system at least – that we've interviewed, can you explain a little bit how the system works for non-Canadians who are listening.

We have a system of four conferences across the country. It's almost becoming a full-time type of commitment, aside from maybe a few months in the Summer where athletes do get the opportunity to go and play with a junior National team if they are good enough. We start right at the middle of August. We start our training, and our competition usually gets started towards the middle of October. Our national championships end up in the middle of March. It goes almost the full length of the academic schedule. Of course, athletes have to maintain their academic eligibility, so they are required to not only pass a certain amount of courses but they are also required to maintain a certain grade point average so they are eligible for athletic scholarships, which obviously they need nowadays because of the full-time training nature of it. It doesn't leave a lot of room for these guys to hold part-time jobs.

The system is similar to the American system?

It is very similar, yes it is, although I don't think they compete as much prior to Christmas in the September to December range, but they do go longer than us. They go to the beginning or middle of May. I think they just finished their championships. It is very, very similar, yes.

You have all scholarship athletes? Or some? How does that work out?

It's different from institution to institution because it comes down to who's raising the money to have it available for their athletes. I know that we've been very fortunate in one of my former players who was very successful in the real estate industry after he left and he dropped me a very large check, which was matched by our provincial government. That has allowed me to have basically 14 full-ride scholarships right now that I can give to athletes.

When I say full-ride, it is different than the United States system because we're only allowed to give tuition to our athletes. We're not allowed to give the accommodation or meals or anything like that.

Tuition is a fairly decent sum.

It isn't for Canadian students. It is for international students. It's really quite modest if you're a Canadian. It's in the $4,000-$5,000 range, but as soon as you're an international student it triples right away.

The NCAA has a lot of restrictions on what players and coaches can do, particularly with regards to training. Do you have the same kind of restrictions or do you have pretty much free run as long as they keep their academics up?

The Canadian system is very different. We have real free run other than we are limited to the number of international athletes that we can have. Aside from that, our eligibility rules are a lot less stringent than they are in the United States. In fact, we can even have professional athletes from Europe come back and play in Canada. We can have athletes come and play when they're 35, if they want, as long as they haven't used up their eligibility elsewhere. It's a lot less difficult for an athlete to come to Canada and play, and a lot more opportunity for those.

We do have restrictions with regards to if an athlete has played professionally over in wherever then they are losing a year of eligibility by doing that, but they could play 3 years of professional volleyball in Europe and come to Canada. We also have a 5 year rule as opposed to a 4-year rule [regarding total eligibility] that they have in the United States.

In some sense, it's a quasi-professional league?

It really is. It's a lot more open to the athletes to come at any particular point in time. It's very important for our developmental system in Canada, because we really have no club system to speak of at the older levels. Once you've reached the university level, there's nothing, no competitive level that's in Canada that would help you maintain your athletic ability, or volleyball ability, other than to leave the country and go somewhere else.

To go back to your coaching... You said that your coaching philosophy was and is informed by your playing career, but were there any coaching influences that you had when you began? And perhaps coaches who have influenced you as the time has gone on?

Yeah, there were, of course, and certainly three of them would come to mind. One is a developmental coach that I had back in my high school days. She was very influential on me when I first started out because she would push me by whatever means she had to to get the maximum out of me. I guess her philosophy was that if this individual is good at the skill level that he is, rather than forget about him and worry about the lesser skilled athletes which in a team concept you tend to gravitate towards as a coach, she forced me to do everything twice. And made me work twice as hard as everybody else because she felt that it came easier to me. That certainly helped me and kept me being pushed.

I was fortunate enough when I started the University to have another very aggressive coach, but someone who just showed the value of work ethic and showed that his philosophy was if you work as hard as the other guy, you've got just as good of a chance of being successful at whatever you do – not just on the volleyball court, but in life. Never to fear that challenge of being successful, and if you wanted to be a millionaire, he used to say, you go out and work as hard as that guy there, and surround yourself by people that have been successful in that area, and you've got a great opportunity to getting to that situation.

The man, of course, who was probably the icing on the cake, was Bill Neville, our coach in the '76 Olympics. Again, he was a very honest and personable individual that you could talk volleyball with for hours. You could go back to a story that you talked with him about five years ago and he would tell you the exact same story. The reason for that is Bill is incredibly honest with whoever he talked to. He rarely would tell somebody what they wanted to hear. He would just tell them a story, and tell them what he felt. He instilled that in me. If you're like that, you're almost always going to tell the same story to whoever you're talking to. That's the beauty and probably the most important thing about being a coach. It's being honest.

We've interviewed Bill in this project. My partner did the interview, but I listened to it. He's definitely a storyteller.

He's phenomenal. It all comes from the heart and it all comes from his experiences. You know you're going to get the same thing from him every time he tells it because it's exactly the way he feels. He doesn't embellish anything. He just tells it the the way he feels, and it's the same thing that's going to come out of his mouth all the time.

So all of those influences were before you started coaching, basically. Were there any that influenced you during your coaching career? Not necessarily from volleyball. It could be also from other sports or in the university environment.

Other than seeing professional coaches in the NHL, or the Canadian Football League, or whatever as to how they talk to people, and how they treat people, and getting to know them, probably a lot of, "That's the way I don't want to coach," came out of those situations. I just wanted to really emphasize the honesty of the way I go about doing things and attempt to treat everybody the same, and to show a real general passion for what I'm doing, because I feel extremely lucky that I found this. Going through school and getting my Master's in Business and thinking that I was going to be an accountant or something down the road and ending up coaching. I joked with people when I first started. I said, "If I'm still doing this after 10 years, will you shoot me?" That never happened, and here I am, some 40 years later, still doing it and loving it more than ever.

The one really constant theme with all the coaches we talked to is just the passion for the game and the passion for coaching – not necessarily in that order – but both of those. Just listening to what they talk about is pretty incredible.

It's been a fun ride. I guess what's been so great about it is the evolution of the game of volleyball in that period of time. I'm not sure other sports that have been around for as long can really say that they've lived through so many changes in their sport. That's what's made it exciting, is to stay on top of that change, and maybe I'm not the kind of guy that has always looked for the change in the sport. Sitting back in 1976, I recall a time in the Olympic final where Tomasz Wójtowicz went up, and the game was on the line against Russia. The ball just happened to go up in the middle of the court, and he came out of the back row and hit the ball, and everyone on the building was just going, "What the heck just happened? You can't do that." Look where the game's come to today with regards to the back court attack.

My point is, my strengths lie in really evaluating where the game is now and learning how to incorporate that into my system, and taking my playing background and realizing what we're capable of doing – designing drills to get to that level. Seeing where the game is right now, and obviously you have to keep on top of current events and what other teams are doing to evaluate that.

A couple of general questions, firstly about coaching philosophy. How do you think your coaching philosophy has changed over the 40 years since you've been a coach. As the game has changed, as society has changed, as the culture has changed, how do you think your coaching philosophy has changed in that period?

I hope that it hasn't changed a lot. I think the same underlying principles have always been there. I think the major changes is changing from a real player's attitude as a coach to more of a coach's attitude as a coach. In saying that as a player, I was a very emotional type of individual. I lived every point, and it was extremely painful every time I lost a point. I think I took that into my coaching career and because of it, I was a very aggressive, in your face type of guy. I think I've learned over the years. I kept that style, but when I was maybe screaming at somebody to do something I was probably laughing inside, going, "This is what I have to do as a coach to get you motivated, to challenge you." In my initial days I was very into that type of style. Down the road it became more of a coaching technique and more understanding that I knew when to back off and when to keep going and which individuals could take it and which individuals couldn't, etc.

Moving from the general coaching philosophy to the training philosophy... You mentioned about drill design. How would you think that your training philosophy or methodology has evolved over that same period?

It's probably changed quite a bit. I really believe for the better, just in learning more and more about the game and being involved with it more. When I first started out, it was probably 90% just competitive drills – just putting guys in situations where I was pushing them to their limits. As I evolved, the other aspect of teaching and training and more technical refinement type of drills has become a real big part of my coaching now to the point of one of the most important things that we do now is our individual training. We really want to break down what an athlete is doing, so that means taking 3 or 4 guys into the gym for an hour or two and really working on the technical part of it. The team drills become more of a competitive situation where you're always playing with a consequence of some sort on the line, just to keep the motivation level very high, to keep the competition level very high. Probably way more emphasis on the individual part of it now than when I first started.

You said that when you first started it was competitive with individuals. Can you give me an example of what you mean by that?

No, competitive with team drills. A lot less time spent on individual type of technical drills, etc. A lot of just pushing guys to the limit, running defensive drills and just forcing them to never have a fear of going after the ball, and to challenge the block in any way, shape, or form when they're attacking. Nowadays, I spend a lot more time with individual groups, breaking them down on different courts with different coaches. We have more support coaching-wise as well, too, which helps that. Really trying to break down into a point where they're improving on certain techniques.

From early on, you were doing 6 against 6 type of drills?

Yeah, a lot of 6 on 6, or 4 on 4, very competitive type of drills. Or success drills, keeping going until you got so many touches of a ball or digs, or things like that. Not a lot of real technical refinement things, which is very necessary now.

The reason I kind of stayed on that point a little bit is my expectation is that at that time there was less 6 against 6 at practice as now. When I asked the question, my expectation is that then was more individual, but now it's more 6 against 6. It's a little bit different than what I expected.

When I first started coaching at the university level, maybe this was a good thing, but we started off with, I don't know, I'll try to give a brief, 1, 2, 3, 4, 5, 6, 7, 8, 9, 10, 11, 12, 13 ... 13 of my first 14 years we made the National final. We were known as an incredibly competitive team that just left it all out there on the floor every time we played. I don't know if it was an intimidation factor or what, but I think we were way ahead of the rest of the country from a competitive standpoint at that particular time. Maybe that had something to do with the fact that that's the way we played.

In feeling that the game was very basic in those days, I really felt that we could be successful with that style of play. I guess part of the situation was the area of Canada where we were in was probably way ahead of the rest of the country, technically, too, just from our development at the younger levels. We tried to take it to the next level competitively and it was very successful at the beginning.

[Editor's Note: Reading back now, Garth used the word 'competitive' in a slightly different context than I was expecting. He meant partly work with multiple actions by a single player, e.g. in defence or attack. I was initially expecting 'competitive' to refer solely to 6 v 6 game play drills. Hence the follow up questions to try to understand what he meant.]

We're talking now about the season. How do you go about managing the different phases of the season, the preparation, the main competition, playoffs, etc. How do you change or not during the course of that time?

We have some very distinct parts of our season, as everybody does. I think the benefit now is we do have the support staff to help us out with regards to that. Unquestionably in men's volleyball, the physical aspect of the game really stands out nowadays. We've been very fortunate at our university to secure full-time people who are involved in the strength and conditioning of our athletes, or so-called off-season. They monitor that throughout the entire course of the year, even during our pre-competitive phase, and then our league phase, and obviously our playoff phase at the end. We have those different phases, and our pre-league schedule phase is a lot different than it used to be. It is the only real time that we have to evaluate our players and get them ready for the season, so we do give everybody an opportunity to get on the floor, to prove themselves, and then once we get into our competitive schedule, there's not as much opportunity for that. It's every game and every set and every point, so it becomes so extremely important.

With the physical preparation part, how has that changed since you started?

It's gone from absolutely zero when we first started to very intense and a very important part of our training throughout the whole season, not just the off-season now. We really monitor it throughout the course of our season and trying to keep up the strength training. There's certainly not a time for gains once the season starts, but maintenance is very important. We also have our athletic therapy staff, and they are strongly involved in that as well too, so that they can monitor what the athletes can and can't do given the fact that they may be injured during the course of season.

Overall, you it sounds like you have a fairly large emphasis on weight training.

Yes. Yes, we definitely do. It's a real big part of the game that we feel now. The men's game certainly. Obviously, the level of attack, but the back court offense, the serving, and the strengths, and the blocking is just a real big part of the game.

What about the on-court training? How does that vary through the different phases, if at all?

We try to keep up our individual training throughout the course of the whole year, but certainly as we get into competition we spend a lot of time on working on things that we need for the upcoming weekend with regards to our opposition. A lot of that stuff comes from statistical stuff and video analysis of the opposition and ourselves, and improving on what we feel we've done. As coaches, you try to think that you see the whole picture from the last weekend's game, and sometimes you go back and take a look at the stats and go, "Wow, I missed something there. Let's take look at these things and take a better look at the video and see if we really did miss something." I do find personally from time to time you do miss some of that stuff and have to work on certain areas based on what the stats show.

Do you use live stats and live video during the game with the apps, especially Data Volley, now that lets you do that relatively easily?

We don't, unfortunately, have the staff to be able to pull that off, so until our budget is increased, we basically are looking at the stuff after the game. Although we do have some statistical things that we are taking of both ourselves with regard to tendencies and stuff. Nothing from a video nature, no.

You mentioned about preparing for other teams during the week. How much do you tailor the training during the week towards the next opponent? And which part of the week?

Certainly the last couple of practices prior to our Friday/Saturday matches we are offensively and serving-wise very tactical in what we're trying to do to exploit the weaknesses of the opposition. Defensively, we do make some changes there, but really we try to go with a system that tries to force the opposition to put the ball where our strengths are. We probably stay with that a little bit more. Tactically from an offensive standpoint, we really try to exploit the opposition's weaknesses.

In the last couple of trainings before the match?

Yeah.

Do you ever use scout teams? One side of the court is playing in the same way as the opponent, or the way you expect the opponent to play?

We try to, but we are limited with the individuals we have on the other side of the court, on our B team, our scout team, or whatever. So if the opportunity does present itself, or where we're coming up against a left-handed hitter, and we happen to have that, we will really try and use that type of thing to our advantage. I don't feel we really have the individuals that can really do exactly what the opposition is doing.

I ask because it's something I think about relatively often. I personally spend a fair bit of time on the scouting for the next match, but almost never do it in a scout team format. It just doesn't feel right to me. I'm interested in how the coaches think about it.

That's exactly why I said that, Mark, because I don't feel that in our situation ... Maybe in a perfect world you could find individuals who actually do that stuff. What I really put a lot of emphasis on is not just visualization in what we do as players, but watching videos and seeing what the opposition does from that. As a player, I spent a lot of time without anybody training me to do it. I spent a lot of time preparing for matches with my eyes closed and visualizing what I was going to do, based on what I knew the opposition was going to try to do. Defensively the same thing – visualizing that person going up and hitting that shot and putting myself in a position, whether I was going to block it or play defense against it. I really believe that that type of training is very, very effective. I spend a lot of time with my players – and always have – in buying into that and believing in themselves, that they can reproduce what they think in the volleyball court after they've gone through it and keep going through it until you are successful with it from a visualization standpoint. To try to get other people to do the same thing as the opposition, I find that hard to do.

In a broader team sense, what strategies, what things do you do to develop the team concept. Or probably now we would call it the team culture?

I think a lot of it comes from work ethic and believing that you are going to be the team that works harder than everybody else. I really try, as part of my overall philosophy, I really try to give that information to my athletes. You can be successful, but it takes hard work. Your chances of being successful are very, very high if you're willing to work hard, but work the right way. Obviously you want to put yourself in a position where you're learning from people that know the right way to do things, or have already done it. You don't want to bang your head against a brick wall too hard. It starts to hurt after a while if you don't know what the heck you're doing. If you got someone who has been very successful at that level, and has learned from going through it, you're going to learn a lot faster that way. Just being so open-minded. Not many people win the lottery. It happens from time to time, but most of the people who are successful get there by working hard, and are not afraid to work hard.

You do most of your team-building work in the course of the daily work, you would say?

No question about it. I really feel that I've never had a sports psychologist with my team because I feel that I'm a sports psychologist. I feel that every little thing that we do is geared towards the team concept, and the building a foundation where we're confident when we step on the floor. Whether it's through drills, or whatever we do, that we're confident in the athletes that we have around us, and the coaching staff that we have around us, and what we're going to do on the floor. I think that's been a real benefit for us, that we don't have to go sit somewhere and listen to a guy for two hours telling us about goals, etc. We do that on a daily and hourly basis right in the gym in our practices or wherever we are.

That has come up once or twice in other interviews. The team con-

cept, the team culture is not some kind of intervention or some team trip, but it's everything you do every day.

It's everything you do. I try, and one of the things that I'm constantly telling my athletes is, I have an open door policy. The reason for that is I want you to know exactly where you stand on this team every minute of our season. The door is always open if you have a question. You don't question me during practices. What I do in practices is there, and I have a reason for it, but if you want to know why we're doing something, why you individually are not involved in something, you need to come and see me.

I can guarantee you I will have an answer. I can't guarantee it's the answer you're going to want to hear. The answer is always going to pertain to the betterment in my eyes of the team and where the team has to go. If I don't have an answer, shame on me. I'm not doing my job. I need to be open and honest with the players with regard to that, and they need to know that they can always find that out and find out where they stand, and what they need to do to get to the next level, whether that's possible or not, but at least know what they need to do.

How do you go about managing situations where there might be conflict between players? Or between players and staff, which can also happen? Or with unusual personalities that happens from time to time?

We're always learning in that situation, because in today's world things are changing all the time. Unfortunately, I guess some of the problems I feel happen when you don't get all the information on what's going on. People aren't telling you something. I always feel that I can talk it out somewhere, somehow with those people that are involved and impress upon them that this is the way it has to be for us to be successful. I can say that with a fair amount of confidence. I can also tell them, "I'm not always right, unfortunately, but I think I am most of the time." Someone has to make these tough decisions. Unfortunately, I guess, if you can't make any headway with regard to that, there comes a time when you have to part ways. You have to always be doing things for the greater good of the team, and you can't mold things around certain individuals to be successful.

Does it happen that often in the college environment that you might have to cut a player for those reasons?

It does not, no. It really doesn't. In our situation, college players are also students, and it may be different in a professional setting. I don't know, but in your professional setting your hands might be tied, too, where you can't get rid of players if they're under contract and are getting paid so much. I don't know. Certainly, in our situation we've been very fortunate that the athletes are here to learn and to buy into the system, and they certainly have a lot to gain by being on the team and being involved with the team. Very rarely does it come to a situation where you just have to part ways.

I want to ask about qualities and skills of a coach. We're talking about the different qualities a coach has, technical qualities, tactical, personal, communication skills, I could probably list 5 or 6 more. What do you think are the most important qualities for a coach?

I think a lot goes back to my discussions of Bill Neville there, and honesty and being able to portray the same message to everybody all the time. If you're ever saying one thing to somebody, and then 3 days later you say something else, you're in trouble. It's never going to work that way. You got to be sending the same message all the time. I think one of my strengths is very motivational in trying to get the most out of each and every individual. I feel that honesty and delivering the same message all the time is a big part of that.

On the weekend you have the game that you play, and you win or lose. Which do you think is the more important part of the coaches work? The practice, the preparation leading up to the game? Or the management of the game – timeouts, substitutions, changes of tactics, etc.?

I think they're both very, very important. If I had to say I had a strength, my strength is definitely right in the game. I think that's where I've been very successful, in changing the flow of the game, in bringing players back into the game if they haven't started well, in controlling emotions during the course of the game. I think that's always been a very positive part of our game, and has led to us playing our best most of the time. That's the exciting part of it for me. That continues on into the course of the season.

I can honestly say that some of the more successful seasons that we've had were years when we've come in second. When we just didn't deserve to be there, but we over-achieved, or played to the best of our ability when we had to, and maybe somebody else didn't. Those were, to me, some of our most gratifying years. We had years when we won national championships and I would just rub my brow and go, "Phew, I'm glad that's over with because we should have won by a landslide with the talent that we had." The fun years, and the really successful ones, were the years when we squeaked into a bronze medal or managed to make that final when we probably shouldn't have been there.

You talked a lot about having been a player and that informing your work. Is there any disadvantages to having been a top level player?

At the beginning, yes. We were very successful as a team, but I don't think I was as good of a coach at the beginning as I probably was later on, and that's because sometimes I didn't know what to say. I just wanted to sub myself into the game and say, "Just let me show you," when I didn't have an answer. But I guess my passion is always front and center. The players knew how serious I was about every play. That certainly rubbed off on players. I think that was a frustrating time for me that I managed, with time, to deal with and to get better at.

Coaching is a really complex activity. Which are your favorite parts, or which is your favorite part of the whole activity?

I guess being at a university setting is, you only have these guys for a brief period of time – 4, 5 years or whatever. It goes way beyond coaching. You know and I know that we know these guys better than their parents do over that course of that time because we spend so much time with these kids. We are very impressionable upon them and it's how many times do I get guys coming back to me going, "Coach, those were the best 5 years of my life and I really enjoyed it."

This gentleman that donated this huge sum of money just said, "I learned everything from you. I learned all the challenges that were out there in this world that I really felt I could be successful at it, no matter what I did."

I knew if I was going to go out there and work just as hard as I did on the volleyball court I was going to be just as successful in real estate or teaching or being an accountant or whatever their challenges were after they left us, or whether it was with the national team. We had many,

many successful guys at that level too. I really feel good about those guys leaving the program ready to take on the rest of the world.

That's a really interesting point, that your favorite part is the overall influence on lives. I think that's fair to paraphrase what you said.

Yeah, definitely.

Do you go about your coaching with that in mind? Or is that an outcome of the coaching?

I definitely have that in my mind every time I'm talking to a kid. Maybe that's just the experience factor now, but as passionate as I am about coaching and coaching the sport of volleyball, it's a short part of their life, a very important part of their life, and they're learning a lot from this situation. They have a great opportunity to learn a lot of positive things from this situation. Regardless of whether they're the main guy who's getting 50, 60 sets a game, or whether they're getting subbed in for one or two plays a match, it doesn't matter to me. I want those same guys to be just as successful, and I have to treat them with that respect and keep them motivated so that they are going to be just as successful and confident when they leave.

You've been coaching, obviously, for a long time and for almost that whole length of time in the same place. In 20 years I've been in 8 different places or something like that, so it's not something that I really comprehend very well. It's interesting to me. What is your ongoing motivation to keep coaching?

I ask myself that question all the time. I think it's probably the beauty of the sport of volleyball. Getting back to this evolution of where the game has gone and how much it changes all the time... It's better, and we get better athletes all the time. I can say that back in – and this wouldn't be the same in other countries – but back in the '76 Olympics, we had a couple of guys on the team that were, in my opinion, good athletes and the rest were good volleyball players. In '84, we had guys on the team – and the same is the case now – these are guys that could have been successful in a variety of sports, regardless of what they've taken on. Their athletic ability is so much higher. That has certainly helped in Canada for the progression of the game of volleyball and what we can do on the court. That has been a very exciting part of it.

I think I was tapering off for a while, and then all of a sudden my son came to the university and I got to coach him for 5 years, and certainly my motivational level kicked in a lot more at that point in time, too. Rally score, how has that changed the game of volleyball? As coaches, we used to be asleep for the first 8 points of the set and then you could always come back if you were good enough, even if you were down 7 to nothing. You could still win 15 to 8 if you wanted to. That's not the case today. If you get down 2 or 3 points, you're scrambling to get back into the game. That's been a motivational part of the game as well too, and kept the juices flowing a lot more than they used to.

I like it now. My perspective is a lot different now based on what I've been telling you with regard to where I want athletes to be when they leave the program. I've learned a lot more in that regard and how to mold these young kids, so it just makes it a lot more exciting.

You've touched on a couple of things there that I want to circle back to. One is about the rally point system, and how that changed the game. How did that change the way that you trained? The way you thought about training? Were there some specific things that you stopped doing or started doing in response to that rule change?

When it first came out, I think everybody was a little concerned about making mistakes on the court. "Oh, it's going to cost us a point. We can't afford to make a mistake." We started off really conservative, and I think we found out that that's the worst thing you could possibly do, to change your game by becoming conservative. You had to be just as aggressive, and you had to be just as aggressive with the serve prior to allowing the net cord to be ... when they changed that rule too. Of course, that obviously helped. You still had to play the game aggressively, but you had to play the game aggressively right from the beginning of the game. You really had to focus in practices having short little games of 4, 5 points to keep that intensity going right from the beginning.

The other question is about coaching your son. I wanted to ask a little bit about this because I'm a relatively new father. My son's 2½ now. I spend a lot of time thinking about the similarities between the two activities – fatherhood and coaching. You have two children playing volleyball, yeah?

Yes, I do. My son no longer plays. He's now working in the working world, another world, but he did play his 5 years here. He played some National B team at that level. He was first team All-Canadian for two years. That's an interesting concept, in coaching your kid. My daughter, she plays on the world tour in beach volleyball right now.

The question that actually comes to my mind is what you learnes about coaching from being a father, or what you brought from coaching to being a father.

I think you learn... Fathers are always very protective of their children, for sure. As much as you want to say it, you want the best for your kid. You want to do everything you possibly can for them. Fortunately, I started coaching him from a very early age. Technically, he became very good, very young, so that helped him stand out above the rest of the kids. That's an important thing that made it easier for him, because he was better than most of the other kids. When you're dealing in a team game, and whether girls are different I don't know because I haven't coached girls, but we all know what guys can be like. At any time if they think somebody is getting preferential treatment, they're going to say something and they're going to make it difficult for that individual. You got to make sure that he is working as hard or harder than everybody else and that you're giving him as much criticism as you to anybody else. That's important for him. It's more you start thinking about how to make it as comfortable for him by not treating him differently, or you are almost treating him tougher than everybody else.

What I had in mind was actually a different kind of question. Were there occasions as a father – not in the volleyball sense but just raising the kid at home – where you said to yourself, actually this is a situation I've had coaching the team, now I know what to do as a father in this situation – in the playground, or playing with other kids.

I think one of the things that comes to mind is – and maybe this is a little bit different than what you're asking – but we have this sport in Canada called hockey, and every father that's ever watched a hockey game on TV is a flippin' expert in the game. Most of them obviously haven't had an athletic background or been through this. We just hear horror stories time and time again of the poor kids driving home from the game because their father's just grilling them on every little thing that they did wrong and totally destroying that father-son relationship. I've heard stories of kids that they'd rather walk home and carry their hockey equipment home than get in the car after the game because of what's going to happen to them.

From my perspective, when we were away from – well after a game driving home, because we drove home together, or if we were away on a family function – I just avoided that whole situation and made sure we weren't talking about anything like that. It was more of a professional type of relationship where there is a time and a place when we talked about it, and hopefully the same time and place as I would do it with any other individual on the team.

It's my personal experience with reading coaching books, reading stories even, the emphasis is always on the wonderful successes that that particular coach or player had. It's often overlooked the mistakes that they made along the way that they learned from to get to the end point. I think it's useful sometimes to be aware of the mistakes that are made along the way. I wondered if you have one or two mistakes that you made and learned from that you would be prepared to share.

I wouldn't mention any names, but I think if I did make mistakes, it was just being a little too aggressive with certain individuals on the court in a game situation and in trying to motivate them, and hopefully I learned to a back off when I found out that some individuals couldn't take that. I think that's unfortunately a trial-and-error type of situation that I don't know if we can avoid, but because we always have to learn how to try to find the right buttons to push, and sometimes you don't push the right ones. Hopefully we're smart enough to realize that. Having said that, it hurts. It hurts when I know that I've hurt somebody's feelings and I have to work real hard at trying to rebuild that relationship that I want to have with my players. It goes beyond just a coach-player type of thing. I don't breach the respect that I know I want to have for that individual.

In terms of staff, you intimated as we went along that the resources that you have available have increased, have improved over the years. What staff do you have now and how do you manage them in terms of roles and responsibilities?

It still has a long way to go, and I think that unfortunately, even here at the University of Manitoba, we are now behind quite a few of the other institutions in Canada where they are starting to hire full-time assistant coaches. Still a big part of my job is trying to raise a little bit of cash just to keep around a quality assistant coach, because there are way more demands on us as coaches now with the statistical stuff that's going on, the video analysis going on, the extra practices that we want to run in the afternoon. There was a transition period where strength and conditioning was really important, but we didn't have any staff other than me and my assistant coach to implement those programs. We do now have full-time people that are involved in that. That has certainly helped.

The next thing is in managing those individuals, of course you have to make them feel that what they're doing is being appreciated as well as giving them tasks to complete on their own. I don't want to be the overbearing individual at the head of the program that is telling everybody what to do all the time. I'm just trying to give them an opportunity where they have their area that they are going to report on and that they feel confident that they are being given that opportunity to make some decisions.

In practice, how do you delegate or assign the responsibilities in practice in terms of perhaps designing the drills, running the practice, providing feedback, etc.?

Certainly I talked before about the individual practices that we do run. My assistant coach is very involved in that, and I pretty much give him carte blanche as to what he wants to do with regards to it. We talk about what we need to improve upon, but he is running it and giving a lot of the real skill breakdown. Hopefully our discussions have kept us on the same page with regards to that.

As far as when we get into our team practices, that's pretty much my baby for the most part, and even though we have talked about the drills going into it as to what we are going to accomplish, very often those drills get changed because of what I'm seeing and what I think we need to work on in making a change or whatever during the course of the practice. A lot of that emphasis still stays with me.

As an aside, how often, how much would you change practice from the original one that you've designed earlier in the day?

Quite often, actually. You get into a drill and it's just not working the way you want it to, or you see something else that is a glaring area that you think you need to improve upon, or an individual is doing something that's just wrong and you have to stop it and give him some individual attention at that point in time to make sure his concentration is still there, and to send messages to everybody else that you better keep doing what you're supposed to be doing or you're going to be the next guy that's going to be singled out to improve in a certain area. I do go off on tangents quite regularly. Not major, but I will go on a slightly different direction quite a bit.

That sounded a fair bit like a code for coach-on-one, is that fair to say?

Certainly, that's what it is. If you see an error, you want to correct it. Not a punishment type of thing, but more of a correction type of thing. "Okay, wait a minute, you've got the line here and you're not utilizing it, so let's stop the drill and you're going to hit 10 balls down the line. Now you're going to be comfortable with using that shot in the course of a game. You haven't been, and you've been staying away from it in this wash drill that we're doing, so I want you to have that confidence so you can use that shot in this drill."

That's a really good point. That's something, not even error repetition, it's a situation repetition. Going to a situation two or three more times as a reminder, as a teaching tool. It's something I use a lot and I think is really important.

It doesn't take a lot of time out of the drill, but it really reinforces and can build the confidence of that individual to use it, in whatever area it is. I find it very successful.

I had one question that I wanted to ask you because I've spoken to you a long time ago about this particular topic, and I think it could be of interest to people. That is the IVA you mentioned before. I remember a conversation with you about some particular parts of IVA that you enjoyed and that maybe we could even learn from the way the game was played then. Maybe you can just give a little brief glimpse of your experience in that league.

I absolutely loved the IVA. I really enjoyed being able to have the opportunity to play in that league. What I really enjoyed about it was something that at that time was not in international volleyball, and that was the extreme specialization of the game. Since then the game has evolved a certain amount to that with the libero and certain individuals just involved in serve receive and the places you play on defense, being more specialized, etc.

I always felt that maybe volleyball would go completely to this situation where there was no rotation involved in it. I loved the challenges that went along with it. It was difficult because with no rotation there were matches where on four consecutive days I'd hit 110, 115 etc. balls and your arm was about 8 inches longer at the end of the season. You're playing against the same guy on the other side of the net for the whole match and he got to know every shot you had, and you got to know every shot he had, and it just became an unbelievable 1-on-1 battle with this other individual. I loved those challenges, and I thought it was great for the game.

That was of course side out scoring, so it could go on for some time.

It went on for a long time, yeah. The games were shorter. They were 12 points, I believe, at the time. The tiebreaker game was the first one to 6. It was cut down a little bit that way, but in side out scoring obviously they could last a long time.

If you talk to guys now about hitting 110 balls I think they would just go straight to the physio.

It was quite a challenge. Maybe if there was a rally scoring component to it now that would make it certainly a little easier. One of the interesting things... The first year I went to the IVA and Bill Neville was our coach in El Paso. We got down there and just had a 2 hour practice to get things started. After about 45 minutes, me and Tom Reed, and I forget who else was with us at the time, we had to go to Neville and say, "Look, Nev, this is not working. You can't run these type of drills when you've only got 4 guys hitting the ball." We were fried after 45 minutes. There's nothing left. You've got to learn how to adjust things a bit here. He did and things went well after that.

I had the same experience. For some period I coached for a beach volleyball team, and all of my drills were for 12 people and I suddenly had two and practice was pretty much over in 25 minutes. That was day one. By day two I said we have to fix some things.

I have just two rounding off questions and we're done. The second

last one is about a reading list. Do you have a couple, or one, books that you recommend for coaches?

If I have a major weakness, it's the fact that I have believed in myself all the way through my coaching career and I've learned from watching and really haven't done a lot of reading in the area. I couldn't even recommend one to be honest.

No problem. You are not the first person who said that.

Do you have any general advice that you would have for young coaches or developing coaches who want to pursue coaching as a profession or even just pursue it as an activity.

It's a very tough profession to get into, and timing is always a big part of it, and being at the right place at the right time. You certainly have to learn skills to be successful, if and when you ever do get the opportunity. The most important thing is learn as much as you can from clinics and camps and whatever, but also to be involved as a coach as much as you can, whether it's at developmental levels, because you have to learn those skills of being a coach. You have to attempt to be involved with successful programs to be noticed. You probably won't be noticed if you're not out there and hanging around with a successful program or successful coaches. You will learn from that situation too. To get an opportunity, those are the key components of what you have to do to get into this profession.

I think hanging around is probably an underrated quality. Being around a lot gives people a chance to see you, to meet you, to learn about you and it happens often that the time comes to hire an assistant and the first person that comes to mind is the guy who is around at every clinic, at every practice. That can be the start of a career.

Yeah, it has to be, and it's not just a straight education thing. You can't just go out and read all the books and go to all the clinics. You got to get to know people and you got to be available, and people have to have seen you being involved, and even giving clinics yourself if you get the opportunity. Learning how to give that knowledge to other people and showing that you can do that, because when you do get your chance you have to be prepared for it.

Is there anything that we haven't covered that you think is important that you would like to be on the record about?

The one thing that I didn't touch on was just how to manage a particular team. I've had this question many times. Do you like to do it the way the Japanese do it? Do you like to do it the way the Dutch do it? Do you like to do it the way the Brazilians do it? My philosophy has always been let's get in the gym, and let's find out what we can do. Let's try and formulate our system around our strengths and see what areas we can improve upon, but I don't like to take square pegs and try and stick them in the round holes. I like to see what we're capable of and develop everything around our strengths. I think that's a very important part of coaching, trying to find out what your best can be and be realistic with where you can be with that team.

We talked about this with Anders Kristiansson, the Swedish coach, and he made the point that we spend a lot of time talking about weaknesses and improving weaknesses and that if you spend a long time on that, it has a negative psychological impact on people. It is important to spend time also working on your strengths and pointing our your strengths. I really like that idea.

That is part of the team culture in having that positive feel going into whatever your doing and, "Hey, this is what we're good at, so this is what we're going to make sure we can do every time we step on the court."

7

TOM TURCO

American high school coach Tom Turco is a legend in New England volleyball circles. His Barnstable High School program has won 17 Massachusetts state titles. Along the way, his 2003 to 2007 teams put together a 110-match winning streak. That's one longer than the 109 match streak the Penn State women's team ran off between 2007 and 2011.And it's not like Tom schedules easy. In the interview he talks about how he always looks to schedule good competition. His teams were just that dominant in that span.

Not surprisingly, Tom has received high level acclaim for his achievements. In 2008 he was named National Coach of the Year by the AVCA. In 2012 the National High School Coaches Association (NHSCA) made him their National Volleyball Coach of the Year.

Tom attributes a major part of his success to the mental, off-court training he has been doing with each of his teams going back 20 years. It seems to be working pretty well!

This interview was conducted by John in December, 2015. Tom and John crossed paths many times when John was involved in Juniors volleyball in New England, though it had been probably a decade since they'd seen each other at the time of the interview.

Okay, the first thing we'll start off with is just to have you go through what got you into volleyball and how you progressed through your coaching.

I got into coaching because my profession, the job I got paid for, was called adaptive physical education. So Phys. Ed. for special needs kids. I had taught that for six, eight, ten years. On a personal level, I felt that I was successful working with kids with special needs so I was curious to see if I would be successful working with mainstream kids. That's how I got into coaching. The only job that was available was the JV job for volleyball. I played club at Bridgewater State College [in Massachusetts] for one year, but that was ... Club volleyball, men's club volleyball, at that time was basically how many guys I could fit in my Cadillac Coupe DeVille and drive to a nearby college. Didn't get much training.

I coached two years of JV, and then in 1988 I became the varsity coach.

This is Barnstable High School. You're still there.

Yeah, well you know what? It's funny. I went to the AVCA Convention – which is a great convention to go to because of the styles of the volleyball coaches – and the topic came up of what drives coaches out of coaching, why they change jobs. It's not parents. It's not kids because they always turn over. It's who you work for – the school system you work for, and your athletic director. I've been lucky to have good and supportive people.

It's interesting to hear you say that because when we interviewed Marilyn McReavy-Nolen, when we talked about advice for coaches coming up on the career side of things, she actually specifically said look at the administration and look at who you're going to work for, as opposed to anything to do with the team or the players or the parents because the administration is going to be the ones that are supporting you and maybe helping you develop through your career. So it's good to hear some reinforcement of that.

Yeah, absolutely. I mean, every coach has to deal with parents. If you've got a strong administration, it just makes it easy. But when you mentor coaches, you have to say to keep that communication open with your athletic director. It doesn't eliminate problems, but it certainly helps. When you get their advice on certain situations, two things happen. One, they're notified that there's not a problem, but there's a potential problem. The second thing is he's invested in the decision. That's part of their role – advising coaches on what they should do and shouldn't do. If you go against that advice and things don't work out, then you are dealing with it on your own.

While you were coaching volleyball, you were teaching P.E. along the way, right?

Yes.

When did you form Cape Cod Juniors?

I formed Cape Cod Juniors in 1990.

What was your motivation at that time?

My motivation then is the same as it is now and that was to help my high school program. When I first started to coach, my first year was an absolute disaster. My second year was better, but we really were kind of a good mid-line, second tier program. I asked a friend of mine who worked in a high-level club at that time, Mass Pats, and he just said, "Look, you can compete at the local level by not having a junior-level program or having athletes participate in a junior-level program, but you can't go to the next level unless you do that."

In Cape Cod, there's ten different high schools. We have our compliance rules that we've got to follow so we had enough kids in the area that we could sustain compliance, so we started Cape Cod Juniors. It just became the kids' opportunity to be there. Our coaching staff is also from high schools.

Just for clarity, what are the Massachusetts rules in terms of restrictions on who you can coach and how many players from your team can be on a team together in a club?

Okay, the rules are you cannot have more than 50 percent of your current candidates as members of your individual roster. If I'm coaching my 18s team I can have three kids my roster from varsity-level and so forth for all the other coaches in the program.

Then, because I run the program, I don't have more than three varsity-level kids on any one program just to err on the side of caution. It's a funny thing about volleyball. It's pretty self-policing. They changed the rule recently where prior to two years ago, you could only have two members of your team on the court at one time. There was a rule proposal and it was changed to three players.

In volleyball, that made a huge difference. That was huge. I mean, I actually got back into coaching [club].

I know in certain states, you can't coach your own players. They can play together, but you can't coach them.

Well, it differs.

This year I've got a lot of kids in my program. Some years we'll have 250 kids come there, so when it gets down to the ratio it's pretty easy. They have their try-out guidelines. I put three in each pile so people can't mess that up because you really don't need to. It's funny because my graduating seniors are not considered my candidates because they have no eligibility left, so I'll take six of those. I'll take my six seniors, three underclassmen, and a couple other kids, but I named my team Cape Cod In-Compliance because that's kind of a joke.

Cape Cod Juniors is basically a regional program, right? You don't really do much in the way of national or inter-regional play.

No. We're called a club program and I don't know what it's like in other states, but in New England juniors there are open teams where they have real referees, while at the club level they have the kids ref. The talent down the state is okay. It's not great, so we'll have two top teams and they'll go in the top club level. If they win that, they go up to the open level. We start much later than everybody else. We start January 3rd this year. Everybody else started... I mean I had kids after our state championship, the next morning they're at club tryouts.

You do have players for your high school team that go and play with the open level clubs?

Yeah, I have two this year. I had three last year and I've got one kid that's just actually a freshman this year, but she was all-state. She's probably one of the best players in the state, as a freshman. Really kind of scary, but she goes all over. She travels the country to most of these high-performance camps, she improves, and she's got the goods to back it up.

In my recollection, you primarily coached your 14's team. Has that been consistent?

Well I started coaching 14s a while ago. In the 90's and early 2000's eighth graders were not considered candidates, so I coached eighth graders that were coming in to my school. Then when they changed that rule, I didn't and I just ran the club. Then three years ago we had 20 teams and I only had 19 coaches, so I had to coach a team. But I kind of got my staff to give me the good ones. I said, "I'm not taking one for the team here. I'm taking the best kids in the club and then we'll divide everybody else up," which was okay with them.

It comes from that. I basically know what kids are going to be playing and I'll have a pretty good team. I'll take my three candidates that I've got to develop throughout the year, throughout the off-season, and they'll play for me.

I can completely understand as a high school coach, especially if there are restrictions on coaching your own players, the appeal of coaching the 14's teams – getting an early start on the kids that are coming into your program the next year.

Yeah, well we've got 12's now, but we have a totally different attitude and approach to 12's. It's an in-house program and then we couple with another club so they'll get some competitive experience. But there's no medals, there's no first place. When they become 13 then they can join the insanity. The most important thing we can do is give them fundamentals and some sense of competition, but they've got to like the game. These kids, if they're going to up to New Hampshire with all these type-A parents and you missed a call, man! That's going to turn more kids off. It's worked for us. It's definitely worked for us.

Let's wind back the clock a bit to your early coaching days. Before we started this, you'd mentioned Bob Schneck as being an influence of yours in terms of going to one of his clinics. Who else would you put in that list of people that influenced your coaching along the way?

Joel Dearing in the beginning. Those were the two local New England coaches who I went to their clinics. Schneck was... I mean he did a defensive drill that we still do today. This was 25, 26 years ago and I was silly enough to volunteer for this defensive drill on a Saturday morning at a state coaches clinic. I thought I was going to have a heart attack. I went out in the hall afterwards. The name of the drill was Touch Two and it was just this unbelievable defensive drill. I felt balls just flying by my face and that was the last one I volunteered for.

Joel was just like the gentleman of the game. He's just one of these great guys, but that just gives so much back to the sport. I knew him when he was at Roger Williams and then he went over to Springfield College and I got to know him then.

Then I mean, a couple high school coaches that helped me along the way, more so with the mental part of the game than anything else.

You're still coaching, so I would assume you're still evolving at least to a degree. What can you kind of look at from the early days of your coaching that has really changed, and what has been pretty consistent?

I think the skill level has changed. The skill level has gotten better. We have a lot better teams out there. I think the thing that has stayed the same is our mental approach to the game. All those bits evolved throughout the years.

Actually, you'll notice these guys out here that know a lot more than I do about the X's and O's, from basically fundamentals. Each team is different and so there's a lot of ways that they could take and we went in a lot of different directions.

One consistent thing is we adopted ... We use this book. The name of the book is *The Winner Within: A Life Plan for Team Players* by Pat Riley. Since 1994 – I'm sorry, 1995 – we've used it as a textbook. There's 12 chapters, so there's 12 sessions that we spend in the classroom. Each session takes an hour and a half out of our practice, and it's evolved to where the seniors now teach whatever class it is, whatever chapter it is. It was a home run the day we started it, and it continues to be just a huge part of our program.

This must sound like blasphemy to some coaches, but you actually sacrifice court time for classroom time?

Yes. The time we spend in the classroom is as important, if not more important, than the time we spend on the court. Absolutely, 100 percent it is. He talks about, "Do you want a good team, do you want a great team, or do you want a together team?"

Okay, so I mean we take 12 sessions out. We're in a classroom. Everybody's sitting there. The whole class is arranged in a big circle. Everybody can see each other and you're in a non-threatening environment. Say the chapter is "The Innocent Climb". That's the first chapter. They talk about trust. It's an awesome environment where you can ask, "What does trust mean to you?"

You're just fostering this whole communication between players and players, and coaches and players. Throughout the entire season, you can weave anything you want into this. How could you do that other than calling a "team meeting"? You call a team meeting, because there's something wrong. There's something the coach want's to talk about.

Instead, where here and it's like, "Okay listen, before we start this... Last night's match. Give me the good, the bad, and the ugly." Now they can get some communication going and closure going or open up some discussions on, "Yeah, the good was we finished out really strong. The bad, well we could've had higher energy." All this stuff you want them to be talking about, but you never get the opportunity. They're not going to talk about this on the bus or on their social media sites.

Anyway, that's me. I could go on forever about that. I couldn't imagine doing without it. This is based upon their goals. Right after my selections are made, the very next session we send them into a classroom by themselves. Coaches are nowhere and the seniors will lead a goal-setting meeting. At the end of the meeting, they'll come and get us and we will either accept the goals, reject them, or modify them and the first day I tell them, "These are not my goals. These are not the coaches' goals. These are your goals. We're going to embrace them. We're going to do everything we can in our power to get you to these goals, but they're your goals."

Riley talks about, "This is a covenant." He says, "A covenant is an agreement that binds people together."

I mean, that's just the entire focus of everything. For me to go in there and say, "You know girls, our goal should be to win a state championship." Honestly, they could care less what we want. It's important what they want, so this is the thing that drives them.

We'll go through the whole thing. They understand the process, but Riley says, "There's only two ways in regards to a covenant. Either you're in or you're out. There's no life in between the lines."

I'll go around to each, "Okay, you want to win a state championship, goal #1. In our out?" I say, "Don't look at me. Look at your friends. These are your goals. They're your teammates' goals."

Then I'll go around a second time and I'll say, "This is easy to say in August, tough to say in November. Regardless of playing time, or roles that are assigned to you as far as this team by the coaching staff, in or out?" You've seriously got them now. I add, "If you're not sure, don't tell your teammates this because losing a starting role and still being in takes some character. So think about it."

Then in the end you get a kid like Colleen Kenney who was my starting outside hitter in 2012 up until two matches left in the season. Her numbers were going down and I sat down and I explained it to her. I said, "I got to do what's best for this team and I've got to give Ciara a shot."

So Ciara goes in, lights it up. This kid [Colleen] did not play until the state semifinals when Ciara was struggling. Back goes Colleen, and Colleen was like this possessed volleyball person. She had eight kills in ten attempts and she was just ridiculous. She started the state finals and played very well there.

On the way home on the bus, the seniors – Colleen was a junior – the seniors said, "Coach, that was just an unbelievable move that you made, benching Colleen to motivate her."

I said, "Look, that had nothing to do with it." I said, "I don't bench kids to motivate them. I bench kids because their performance is going down." I said, "Here is what made this state championship far more of a possibility and a reality in the end. Colleen Kenney was true to her word that she was in regardless of the playing time or her role, because she came in early and practiced and worked hard and supported Ciara, etc. If she went the other way and criticized Ciara, this would've been a harder road for you guys. But she didn't."

Anyway, those are the things that ... Forget what offensive system you ran or ... We do all that stuff, but it's like these are the important things in high school sports. How together can your team be?

That's my Colleen Kenney story. It happened this year. It happens every year, but it's nice when you can – in this environment of those 12 sessions – tell those real-life Colleen Kenney stories. Then it becomes expected behavior. If you're on the end of the bench complaining and moaning, you're going to stand out in the wrong way and people are going to know it.

When do you schedule these 12 sessions?

Well, I take a look at my schedule. They're all pre-scheduled. Sometimes we'll move one or two. I will schedule them before an easier match on my schedule. If I'm playing a Top-5 team – and we play a real tough schedule – I'm not going to do it then. But if we're playing an easier league opponent, or if we have two practices prior to a big match, I'll do it then. We don't practice weekends, so sometimes it bunches up a little bit. We're in the post-season a lot. Well, we have been for the last 27 years, so there's always a week before when I can finish up chapters 11 and 12. We always finish those two chapters after the regular season.

So they are interspersed over the course of the year, rather than being all in pre-season.

Yeah. Seriously, we only lost one match this year and in that match, it became very clear that serve receive was something we had to drastically improve on. Believe me. There was a couple moments [while going through one of the 12 sessions] that I'm looking at that clock going, "We got to work on serve receive, we got to work on serve receive here!" We finished the session and it all worked out.

Going back to the idea of changes, obviously this mental stuff has become a big part of what you're doing. Have you changed the way you do training over the years?

Yes and no. We changed ... You're learning every day. Just because I'm in my 60's doesn't mean I stop learning. One of the things that stayed consistent is something I learned at the AVCA Convention. A coach – I don't remember who it was – said, "If you post your practices by the minute or by the segment, it reduces anxiety in your players." So they'll walk in and they'll sit there for a two hour and 45 minute practice. Post it.

You change, the philosophy and the work ethic doesn't change. We have some basic rules we've always had since my disastrous first year of coaching. I have a saying that still ring true and it's, "If you walk anywhere in practice, you run, and we run as a team." So if you're on my team and I say, "I need you to go to that court over there and work with Coach Martin," and you walk over there, we stop and we run. That's stayed the same. If you don't go to the floor for a ball, then we stop and we work on it.

Very rarely will we stop practice and work on conditioning because we're too tired to run to a station. Usually, it's when they go out to get a drink of water that the seniors will say, "Listen, I am not running because you are walking."

This year we developed a thing called Serve Receive School. It was just something that I heard Russ Rose say in one of his interviews about fundamentals, and then Bill Belichick [football head coach of the New England Patriots] from the past. In an interview, he talked about the biggest fundamental to football really is tackling. "You got to get the guy on the ground." So it was interesting because he said he and his coaching staff had their players work on tackling for a half hour every single, right back to the basics.

In our Serve Receive School, we went back to almost how you train 12-and-under's and we just did it for 20 minutes a day. That was the Serve Receive School and that made an absolute huge difference on our team, on our game, and our performance. The fundamentals. Last year we needed to work on hitting a lot. Not this past year, the year before. You're only as good as your athletes, and our athletes struggled last year. We hit a career low of .123. That's pretty hard to do. I mean, you got to try real hard to hit .123 as a team, but we did.

We emphasize defense. Our whole team philosophy is defensive-minded. Even at hitting .123 as a team last year, we found ourselves with an opportunity in our state semi-final match, but it didn't pan out.

You get to a certain level where it's defense just isn't quite enough.

Yeah, I mean you rarely look at it and go, "Wow she's set a record in my league. There's a school record in digs." Of course she did because we couldn't put the ball away!

Yeah, I think my partner Mark hates dig stats just for exactly that

sort of reason, because you can get digs for things that are not going particularly well.

Correct, yeah. But you can't tell the kids that.

No.

You got to say, "If you have the best defensive team in the state, then things are going to work out for you in the end. Work on that," where you're actually saying to yourself, "Well, you know what? If Kara puts that ball down on the first contact, then we don't need the dig that involves us."

Are there any sorts of games or drills that you used to do that you don't do anymore? Philosophically, you just have gone in a different direction?

We used to do a lot of Touch Two in practice – that drill I referred to before – but we don't do a lot of that now. We do try to do drills like ... Russ Rose one time said that, "If you expect your players to perform in pressure situations in a match, then you've got to manufacture pressure situations in practice," so we do a thing called 8-ball.

When my son was coaching a woman's club team at San Diego State and I got an opportunity to watch their Spring practice one time, they did a thing called 8-ball. They just did it as a warm-up. It's two groups, one of them on one side, one on the other side. Basically it's a cooperative ball control drill. You have eight balls, eight minutes, and once the ball hits the floor, or a kid nets or a kid carries the ball, then you'll go to the next ball. When you're out of volleyballs, then they will run a sprint. That is a drill they absolutely loathe in practice, seriously.

We used to play Guts a lot. I can't remember where I got it. Guts was a game that everybody gets a ball. It's is a serving game. A Guts serve is a serve that when you are on match point, or after a timeout, or after a substitution. That ball's got to be in. You got to put that ball in play. Everybody gets a ball, everybody gets on the line. One missed was one team line sprint. Two misses was two team line sprints and so on and so forth.

Then you go to the other side of the net and that would be Game 2, just a little bit closer to the end result. Each individual misses it is two team line sprints and so on and so forth. I mean, if you're going to play in this program, you should be able to serve a ball into a 900 square-foot area. But as the years went on, I changed that. I don't think we played Guts this year, where we used to play every single day. Now they go to ... If you miss a big serve at a big time, you probably won't be serving for awhile. We're going to send you to exile island for a little while and just work on it, and then you can come back.

That's only at the service line.

Just to sidetrack one thing real quick, because some may not understand the rules, what's the current set of rules for high school volleyball in terms of substitutions?

Well, we in Massachusetts are one of only two states in the union that play NCAA rules. Everybody else plays National Federation rules. Each state governing board can adapt the NCAA rules. So to answer your question on substitutions in NCAA, it's limited to 12. [Current rules actually allow 15] We, as a governing board, changed it to 18.

So you have lots of subs.

We have lots of subs, but it's a silly rule. I mean, come on. I argued that as a state association we want to limit our players' playing time? We want to say, "Nope, sorry. Nope, you've got to sit because we're out of subs."I think this whole limited subs, that's all about how long the officials have to stay at the match.

The traditional argument or trade-off is it comes down to a participation versus more playing time for the players that are actually on the court. Depending on what level you're at and your focus, I could see the arguments going either way.

Yeah, well I don't know. I could've played eight kids this year, easy.

They're just different dynamics. There's definitely different dynamics in college than there is in high school. To keep kids in, you got to play them and if I lived under those rules, then I'd be a little bit more selective, a little more careful. I'd have to think ... You're assuming they're going to be on the floor, have some role – especially a senior.

Let's shift the conversation to that. You do your try outs at the beginning of the year, and we'll get to that process in a second, but

you basically suggested that you would not keep a senior that you did not think was going to get at least some measure of court time during the year.

No, and that's advice I got from a hockey coach at Barnstable High School who had won a couple state championships. I asked him, "What's your philosophy on selections?"

He said something that I thought made perfect sense, "When they become a junior and they're a junior trying out for the varsity – if they didn't make the team as a freshman or a sophomore, but they're an incoming junior – then you've got to look at their junior and senior year and you've got to, within reason, see them as a day-to-day player or a possible starter." You know he's talking about himself, but he says, "If I don't, I have to cut them."

His thing was it's not fair to the player to come to practice every single day without a possibility of playing. He said, "They all want be a participant and be part of the team, and then they become just a big pain to everybody." That was his thought.

I thought that it would be unfair to do that too. I think there's a lot of activities that kids could be doing. In a school like Barnstable, there's a drama club, there's cross country, there's a lot of clubs and things that they could participate and be an active participant in. When I went against that advice one year, of course it bit me in the tail.

Amidst the state championship celebration on the floor, I had this grandmother come up to me and say, "Do you realize Suzie is a senior?" [name changed]

I said, "Sure."

She said, "Do you?"

I thought, "Oh, this is Suzie's grandmother wanting to have my head on a platter because she wasn't the starter and she only got in there for a couple serves."

It's hard. Let me tell you something, when it's all said and done and I leave coaching and somebody asks me the question, "What was the most difficult part of coaching high school?" It's going to be, "Having to cut kids."

I had to cut a girl. It was the last sister. The first sister got a full ride at a DI school in New England. The second sister was just a tremendous player. Third sister ... I didn't see the playing time. I had to cut her. It just goes on and on and on, and it's the worst part of coaching. It still bothers me.

All right. In terms of the junior varsity, do you set a limitation in terms of how many you'll take?

That's entirely up to my JV coach. I may come down and throw a safe card in there. I may say, "I know the kid," and I ask them, "What are you looking like?" They kind of go the opposite. They'll keep those kids that are good, but not going to make the varsity so I've got to make that decision whey they are juniors.

Lucky you.

Yeah. You know what? My A.D.'s got a real healthy way of looking at it. This is a program that you've got to take every year as just that one year. Kids coming in and playing, and the kids know it. There's no real surprises or disappointment. It's a rejection, but knock on wood, the number of calls my athletic director has gotten in this regard in the last 15 years – zero.

Because they know. It's like my high school. When I went to high school we had a state championship hockey team. Me not making the team wasn't going to be a surprise because I didn't play hockey. I'm just saying, if this was a 10-10 team, you're going to get a lot more parent complaints.

How integrated are the varsity and the junior varsity programs? Do you work them together at all in any fashion, or are they run separately?

Well, the varsity's got three full courts upstairs in the main gym and the JV and the freshmen share four courts downstairs. The integration comes with the coaches because the JV and freshmen, they practice from 2:30 to 4:30. The varsity, we delay our practice and they go to study hall from 2:00 to 2:45.

We had an issue with them coming in late to practice. They had to go to NHS meetings. They do their turtle projects. We've got a lot of very smart kids. We just changed it saying, "We'll delay our practice. You can have 45 minutes to get all your extra things done academically. If you need extra help, go. If you need to work on a project, go. If you need to study, if you need to go ... Fine, but you're going to meet in the library. Come 3:15, it's go time." That's really helped.

But anyway, to get back to the original question, my JV and freshman coach will go 2:30 to 4:30 and then they come up and they participate in my practice from 4:30 to 6:00. They have one job. Then they have one job they volunteer for [helping with varsity], but they want to do it because it helps them be better coaches.

As my JV coach says, "I just take everything you do and bring it down to these guys. I get a much better understanding on what you're looking for in both behaviorally, work ethic, and skill-wise."

That really helps. She's a real good motivator. She works these kids really hard, but has a good way about her so when they come up to me, I don't have to re-train them. That's the thing that I really love. These kids come in with great transition skills, great defensive skills, and most of all, good work ethic.

She's a huge asset. She was born in the Philippines and was a defensive player in high school and is a kickboxing black belt teacher – one of these coaches that works the kids, but the kids like her. I looked in to one of her practices once through the back door because I had a late class and she was in the middle of a practice. She's banging balls. She's saying, "You've got to dig these balls! You've got to dig these balls! If you don't dig these balls, he's going to cut you!" I'm like, "Okay. I think I'll slip back out the back door." But it wasn't in a mean way. It's just, it was a Marylou way.

The kids saw me and they just started laughing.

Do you hire the JV and the freshmen coaches, or does the administration do that?

I do, then they get to go through the administration process. My administration is really good. Marylou's been with me for 15 years, and Jessie played for me in 2006. Then she played in college and got a teaching job at the high school. She's now a freshman coach.

Have you had a lot of turnover in these positions over the years?

Jessie's been with me ... For let's see, this will be her fifth year. Not a big turnover, all said and done. I had JV coaches in the 28 years, five years, three years, seven or eight years, and then Marylou's been with me for awhile. I don't know the math, but anyway something like that. I usually have a shelf life of five years. I'm good with that.

If you were looking to hire today, what qualities would you be trying to find in these assistants?

Great question, I love that question! Number one quality to me is loyalty. Not blind loyalty. I mean if you've got a suggestion, make it, definitely. I want you working with me, but loyally. I had an assistant coach one year. I was afraid to leave the gym. If I gave him a drill and then I left the gym just for five minutes and came back, he'd have them in a huddle.

We were on the bus one time and I went back to this kid, Terry. I said, "Terry, listen here. You need to remember in today's match, you need to stay outside the block. Read the block, stay outside and get that dig."

"That's not what coach told me."

I asked, "What?"

"He told me, 'If you don't like the answer Coach Turco gives you, come to me, I'll give you the right answer.'"

I thought, "Wow. This is going to be an interesting conversation at the front of the bus."

If your assistant coach understands your philosophy, and is working with you, and accepts their role, and the kids know that, it's a much better coaching situation. I've been blessed to have that coaching situation. If they're going to cast doubt with the players that you don't know what you're doing, then that's going to have that effect.

Like they say, assistants make recommendations. Head coaches make decisions.

I relinquished more responsibilities this year to my assistants than I ever have because we had this crazy libero thing and my freshman coach Jessie was a libero in college. This whole libero thing just confuses the heck out of me."You're running this, here it is. This is what I want. I want Danielle on the floor as much as possible, so in, out, in, out. You figure it out." That's what I did because basically she's my libero coach and the kids like that. She's got a real calm way about her. When the kids come out, whether it's a switch or a libero, they go give some love to their teammates and then they go sit next to Jessie and Jessie will coach them up a little bit.

Let's talk about a little bit about season planning and execution. We'll start with try outs. How long do you normally run them for?

We run them through three sets, three 3-hour sessions.

I'm assuming for the varsity anyway, the primary try out is for the kids that are coming up for junior varsity and any questionable juniors from the prior year?

No, I never ... Although getting back to your A.D.'s advice, he was like, "Are you going to keep this kid?"

I said, "Well I kept her as a sophomore, I'm going to keep her as a junior."

"Wow, do you want to think about it?"

I said, "As long as her attitude's okay, then we'll figure the rest out."

But it is the cut year. The kids coming in as juniors that didn't make the varsity know that this is the cut year for me.

It gives me an opportunity to look at freshmen. I aim to not predetermine it. You know your talent coming in, but sometimes the kids that you don't think should or will make it just stick. I had a kid, Caroline Brodt. Caroline was in try outs as a freshman. She spent the entire summer doing strength and conditioning. She kept doing this bigger, faster, stronger program, and it just made her strong. There was no way I had her even penciled in as a member of the varsity. She had the base skills. She had this tremendous work ethic, and put the time in, and yeah, she made the team. She started this year, and was a big part of this year's championship team, and will probably set for the next three years.

You kind of get an idea of who's going to be on your team, but you don't know for sure.

Is it basically a mass try out for varsity to begin with, and then you say, "Okay we take these kids for varsity and then we're looking at the rest for JV and freshmen?"

This is what I do. You have to come out for the varsity. You have to go to the varsity try outs if you are in the 10th, 11th, or 12th incoming grade. If you are a 10th grader, then you are eligible to try out for JV. Here's the hard thing. You get these kids that never played volleyball in their life thinking they're going to come out as juniors and sophomores and it's just ... We weed them down. I'll require all 10, 11, and 12 graders, but any 8th and 9th graders, they can come if they want. We have some kids that are skilled and if they want three extra days of volleyball, that's fine.

I kind of weed them down and have them go down with my freshman coach for the last two days. I keep the kids that I actually have to give the news to, which ends up with my returning varsity players. We got them in 10th grade, and then my 11th and 12th graders, and then they battle it out. Then we do the cut process at the end, which isn't my favorite day. We do it face-to-face. I mean, if we spent nine hours together in a gym then I at least owe them a face-to-face meeting.

I'll have Marylou with me. You either give them the good news or bad news. What we do is try to ... It's hard. It's a difficult situation. The first time we did it, they went back into the hall, grabbed their stuff, and left, and I'm like, "That was bad," because then they had to ... I don't know, you've got to kind of preserve their dignity. If they've been part of this program and been coming to camps since they were in the second grade and now they're 16 years old and they get cut ... So if you enter in this door, you exit out that door and then you can deal with it how you choose to deal with it.

How do you run your try outs in terms of what you're doing over those three sessions?

First of all, you get baseline data on skill because you've got to. Same thing we're going to do on Sunday [for Juniors tryouts]. Same thing we're going to do at camp. They get their index cards and you test them on passing, serving, attack, defense, serve receive, setting, blocking. You have a baseline. I'm going to be honest with you. This is the A.D.'s request – and not only my current A.D., but A.D.'s before him. "If the parents come in, you've got to show that the cutoff line was a cumulative point total of skills."

What does that mean? Okay, so my middle hitter can't pass, but boy oh boy I'll tell you, she can put the ball inside the attack line! So would her cumulative points be less than an okay kid? Not if you evaluate properly.

Basically, the A.D. wants you to try to have everything be objective rather than subjective, at least on some level.

Yes. Basically over the years my A.D.'s have not been questioned. They sometimes are in other sports. A lot of sports it is harder because of the volume of participants. We have had very little feedback on our selections. I have been fortunate. I think parents respect that I am going to select players that I feel can play at the championship level.

I understand how difficult it is for a parent when their child is not among the selected players. They often handle it in a very positive way, reinforcing to their child that they are proud of them for taking the challenge of trying out for team that they might not make. Not being selected is a rejection of sorts so this type of positive parenting has a huge benefit for the prospective athlete.

Anyway, I get the cards and then I watch them play. The last four hours – three or four hours – it's just play. A lot of play. I want to see how competitive they are. It gets down to ... If you're watching balls hit the floor or you're not making plays, then you put a scoreboard up and I can tell you the kids I want.

So the team's together. You're in a preseason. What does your schedule look like?

Well, I run a play date. We have 14 teams come in. Every team in there competes in seven, 45-minute matches. I get right into it. Some years, you get into things that you think your team is going to be in need of. Like had I coached better, I would've seen that my serve receive needed some help [this year]. But I learned the hard way there. At the end of seven 45-minute competitive sessions against some of the best teams in the state, it answers a lot of questions.

When does that play date happen, relative to when you start preseason and when you start the regular playing season?

Our team is selected on a Friday. In this state, we always open up on a Thursday so we'll go two sessions on Thursday, two sessions on Friday.

The first session [Friday] is the final try out session, and then the second session, once the team is selected, that's the goal setting session. Then our first practice is on Monday and the play date is on that following Saturday.

All right, so you've got a week of ... Are you doing double days at that point? This is still before school starts right?

The state rule is you get ten sessions, up to and including Labor Day Friday, so Labor Day Saturday is our play date. Labor Day Friday, our last session, we've got a team from New York, that comes in and we'll do a five-set match scrimmage. That's our last practice session, and then they play.

When you're doing your double days – assuming that you're not doing one of the classroom sessions in there for one of your sessions – how are you breaking out what you're working on in each of the day sessions? What are you working on in the morning, and then what are you working on in the evening or the afternoon?

Well, because it's really a short amount of time, I get right into what I think my rotation is going to be. We have our play date on Saturday, so there's four practice days. You'll have like four practices left, and then you've got scrimmages and then you get your play date. We give them Labor Day off, and then Wednesday will be our first match. I've got to get them right into what I think it's going to be and that's trial and error.

I say, "This is where we'll start. It's been my experience, it is not necessarily how we'll finish. This is all production-based, so it's what I think could happen." But you know what it is? They buy it, hook, line, and sinker. This is all about they truly believe that everything that happens in practice and everything that happens in the season is to get them to their end result.

The last time I was questioned about playing time was about ten years ago. The last request from a parent for a meeting was in 1999.

Wow.

I mean, the communication level is really good and the kids. If they get something they want to talk about, we'll sit down and talk about it.

Just to get a little bit more specific, you're doing two sessions

today. Are the morning and the afternoon sessions going to be different? For example, would you do skills in the morning and play in the afternoon or the other way around, or do you just kind of mix them up in both sessions?

No, we'll mix it up. We'll do a progressive conditioning thing to start off each session. It's called the UCLA drill. We usually start off with that, and then it depends on what your needs are. I mean, this year coming in I'm graduating my two middles and my right side, but bringing back some really good outsides. So we're going to be spending a little bit more time working with our outsides and transition and block and things like that.

Sometimes when it comes down to winning, it's not your top three players. It's your players five, six, seven, and eight. In the high school level, if our eighth player is solid and their eighth player is a little sketchy, we'll find out. I mean, our level is going to be different because not everybody's really good at the high school level unless you're one of these top teams in the nation. It's going to get weak somewhere. It's going to get watered down somewhere down the process, so developing those players is huge, I think.

How much conditioning do you actually do with the team?

Well we do this UCLA drill. This is a drill that I worked at camp with this guy named Wally Martin. Wally Martin was a middle hitter for UCLA. He was a pretty interesting character, but he told us about the drill that they did at UCLA and that they added a minute on to each day and that's what we do. As far as conditioning goes, we do that, but I like the philosophy of the approach. One time he said, "You can build conditioning into every drill. If all your drills are up-tempo and these kids are moving and you're demanding during the drill, then the conditioning takes care of itself."

In-season what is your normal playing schedule during the week?

Well, we play three matches during the week.

Monday, Wednesday, Friday-type thing?

Yeah, but see I'm allowed to make my own schedule. A lot of volleyball coaches in the state are, if you've been around long enough. I play three a week. One of the better teams in the state this year was Notre Dame Academy from Hingham. I'll call them up, "Hey, what do you want to play? Listen, let's just find a Tuesday because that gives us a prep day on Monday." Then both of us will schedule easy games on a Wednesday and then a more competitive match on a Friday. I'm in a different situation. I'm in a league of three. I mean, I love it because I get to make my own schedule.

According to MaxPreps, we had the second toughest schedule in the state. When I make my schedule, I want one really good match a week.

Moving towards the end, I want to schedule the better teams in the end.

Right. Are you still playing two out of three?

No, three out of five.

They changed that. All right.

Yeah, well two out of three. God, we haven't done two out of three in ... You know what? We stopped doing that. It was weird. When I first started coaching, it was traditional scoring, side out scoring, and you would play two out of three to 15 and then in the tournament you'd play three out of five.

Then we went to rally scoring and the matches were, I mean the sets were, to 30 points.

I can still remember my assistant coach saying, "Hey Tom, relax. The score's three to three."

I'm like, "God, you're right."

It's like, 30 points, oh my God. Then we were still two out of three. When the NCAA went to 25 points a set they went to three out of five. I'm on the state board. This whole thing is about the biggest fight we had with officials because, "How much more time are we going to have to be there?"

Anyway ...

So if you're playing three times a week, what's your main focus during the two days a week that you get to actually do practice?

Well it depends. Don't forget, that's where you're sacrificing some practice time because you want to the classroom sessions, so I'll do one a week maybe. Then on the second time around with an opponent, you get together and do film study. With film study, that's another hour in the classroom and so it's basically preparation in facing our opponent that we've seen before.

These are high school kids. You start doing this film prep, film study. They don't always get a lot of information, but psychologically they're prepared. I mean, they talk about it all the time with their matches – the scouting report. We talk about our opponents' strengths and weaknesses. We watch them on the film. They walk into a match a little bit more confident. I mean, that's just an added bonus into actually what they understand, but ... Do you have Hudl out there?

I haven't used it, but I've heard of people who do.

Yeah, I mean one of the things with Hudl is as the administrator you can go on our their Hudl account, click on their roster, and see how often, how many hours these kids have spent watching the film. Coaches really get into this. I'm like, "I'm not doing that."

Here's what you should do. I talk to the girls, I say, "You can do that. I really don't care. Here's what I care about. Come into this film session and listen and follow directions, okay? When you're home, do your homework. When you're here, we'll figure this thing out together."

I mean, this isn't the USA national team. This is Barnstable High School and kids have to get good grades.

How has your offensive system developed over the years? I'm assuming from year to year it's going to vary depending on the players that you have, but how much have you say incorporated the back row attack and brought the right side attack into play over different years?

Well again, it depends on your resources. The basic thing that we try to do is turn the ball around fast. We try to go from first contact to last contact in the quickest amount of time, especially in free ball. In free ball, we feel that teams should be punished for giving us a free ball so we try to do that.

In 2013, we set a lot of antenna high shoot sets to our outside. They were very athletic, they were very fast. They can make the adjustment in midair type of thing. We're known for our middle attack and which is kind of different than any other team anywhere in volleyball I guess. I mean, my middle this year had 478 kills on a state-high 962 attempts. Yeah, so you got the point?

Yeah, that's a lot of attempts for a middle.

It's a lot of attempts for a middle, but you know what? She had 26 kills in three sets in the state finals.

Yeah, that's a good night.

We've always hit back ... We brought our team out to California in 2007 and the guy goes, "Well you sure do like the middle." You know what? Nobody does that. Next year we won't be getting 473 kills out of the middle, but if that's your best offensive weapon, that's where we're going. She had incredible timing with her setter and she ran a great slide, so she was really a right-side hitter. You do what you do with what you get.

If this was a poker match ... I'm holding a good hand, I'm playing that hand.

I've got a couple aces, but I've got a couple three's and six's in my hand too and I'm like, "How do you bring them up?" My middles next year will be getting the ball a little bit. We're going to make sure that they're solid. They're going to be as good as they can be, but we'll focus on the outside.

How many kids do you normally carry on the roster for varsity?

I carried usually 14 because there's always kids that are injured. Then I brought two kids up from the JV so we ended up with 16.

And how many of those would normally get a fair amount of playing time?

Ten, eleven maybe.

How do you keep the rest happy?

They keep themselves happy because they buy in. Their role of significance comes in practice. I'll meet with them in the beginning of the year and I will define their role as I see it at that point. "There's not going to be a lot of playing time. It's really important that you go home and share that with your parents, that you're going to be working hard and it doesn't mean you're not going to play, doesn't mean you're not going to be given the opportunity. It means that as I see it right now, playing time will be limited, but you're going to work hard to help your team achieve your goals. Remember those goals? Your goals?"

For us, it hasn't been a problem. Are they happy? Probably not. The real true motivator for a competitive athlete is playing time.

Where you're in trouble is when you have a senior who isn't playing. If you keep them and don't play them, you may get problems.

What's your philosophy on captain selection and what you give them for responsibilities?

Okay, here's ... I have a unique a look at this. I say, "If you are a senior on this team and you've gone through the process and you're in good standing, you're a captain, okay?"

Here's my look at it. It's like going to Vegas. Play Roulette. Cover the table. You can go down there with 100 bucks and throw it on number seven or you can spread it out and your chances of success will be greater, so the way I describe it and explain it to my players is, "This is something that you're given as an opportunity to lead."

I've done it. I've selected two out of six. Wrong choices. Now I've got them. They weren't the leaders on the team. Everybody leads in a different way. Do I get a lot of grief, or have I gotten grief at times from opposing coaches and referees? Yes, but I just looked them in the eye and said, "I promise you I will never have more captains than I do state championships."

I mean, what does it mean? It means the kid can put it on their resume. It means I've got a tremendous amount of leadership in kids that had I selected them would not have been the selections. Then the kids that I thought would be great leaders didn't turn out to be great leaders. When it comes down to it you, as the coach of your team, set the tone for practice, set the tone for the year, set the tone for everything. It's you. The others can't help.

I've had this discussion with my son, who's coaching in college now. His goal this year is to develop a better culture and have discussions. He's relying on his captain. It's like, "Justin, I don't give you a lot of coaching advice, but I'm going to tell you that this ... You are the person that runs the show. You're the person everybody's looking at and you can utilize and mold and shape good senior leadership, but you set the tone for practice. The rules? They're not going to enforce rules – locker room or otherwise. They're not going to. You're the person who's going to enforce the rules and dish out the sanctions." That's my thing on captains.

I want to talk about what you do in matches in a second, but first before we get there, what if any technology do you employ with the team in training, aside from when you talked about doing video scouting. Do you use anything in training?

No.

Some coaches do. A friend of mine does. The technical part of the game is far outweighed by the mental part of the game in our program. So yes, so we work on fundamentals – on serve receive and setting, attack and things like that. Yes, we have used our iPads a couple times, but our program's not built on that.

Let's go to matches. Do you have a kind of a match day routine?

What do you mean?

Well do you have a specific time you meet with the team ahead of time or things that you do for preparation or whatever?

No. We prepare them prior to the match. Don't forget, it's a high school setting and it's JV and freshmen and JV play. We have a routine where the varsity sit in the same spot in the bleachers and they watch the JV match. At the end of the first JV set, they'll go down into one of the empty courts in the field house and they'll warm up, stretch, and hit. They do that by themselves.

As far as ... I say very little. I mean, we've covered everything in practice, and they know what's going on, and they're a team that ... I mean, although we prepare for teams, it really comes down to how and what we do – what happens on our side of the court, how much energy do we have, how much of the fundamentals of covering our hitters, the little things.

Any player can change the momentum of a game. Any player. We never say, "Who's going to be that player?" They know that. It's part of what they do. It's part of who they are.

So from that perspective, when you're coaching during a match, are you focusing primarily on your team?

Yes. I have one resource, Marylou. She's always to the left of me [closest to the score table] because if I've got to make a comment about a player's play, it's to her and away from the bench, if you understand what I'm saying. Then she'll watch the other side.

She'll let me know, "Listen, they're over-playing the three, the outside hitter's coming way inside the court. You could shoot a ball down to the floor and get a point and get out of this." She's keeping an eye on that, what defense they're running, what open lines there are, and our kids are good as far as taking direction. Then Jessie does the stats on the iPad, and she runs the libero situation attacks and defensive players, and I look at the scoreboard.

How many stats does Jessie take? What sort of stuff is she taking for you?

Well she takes all the NCAA type of stats.

Okay, so it's the full?

Yeah, it's called iStats or iVolley or whatever.

She's really good. I used to do them all at home. I used to get home, go down to my office, get the video out, and do the stats. It would take me a long time. That's when I hated away matches because I'd be there until one o'clock in the morning. So when we first got into this iStats... Jessie's just a real calm young lady – terrific person, just real calm. So rally goes bang, bang, bang and I turn to her and I say, "Did you get that?" She goes, "I got enough." When we started, I took the tape and I kind of corrected her. I did mine the old way, looked at what she had, it was within ... She got like a 98 percent. I said, "Good enough."

Once in awhile, I'll write out a stat and she'll add her own, "This kid had no kills and this kid that came in for a couple plays did have one kill." But she's good. This stats stuff is getting better, but it's inconsistent. I mean, this kid got recognized in the paper. She had 72 digs against us. Seventy-two digs! We only had 65 attempts!

I asked the coach about it.

"We had one of the kids doing it on the clipboard."

I said, "When it's free ball over, it's not a dig. It's got to be an attack."

But anyway. Blocks are the funniest ones. In the state championship match, 18 recorded solo blocks against us. I'm like, "Wow! That's amazing to me and we only had 11 errors the entire match." [In this case blocks are counted as hitting errors]

Yeah. It seems unlikely. Eighteen solo blocks in any match seems extremely unlikely.

Anything that is blocked back... Like I said, they're getting better because Jessie actually runs a yearly session at our state coaches' clinic on stat taking. A ball is blocked back and continued by the offensive team is not a block. A block is a ball that is blocked and ends the play.

Just so you know, that even at my level here [Swedish professional league], we have our issues with the stat taking. You'd think it would be a lot better, but we still look at the numbers and go, "I don't know where they're getting these things."

The only stat that I wish, that isn't a stat in the NCAA, but is to me, I tell the girls, "It's the biggest stat of them all." It's when we attack a ball and it is blocked and we pick that ball up.

I mean, that's got to be something because that's ... Actually, as a coach, that's a team that understands and that's a team that actually... If you go up and you roof somebody and that little back row player digs that up, that's a momentum turner, right there. I mean, you just absolutely roof somebody and that kid brought it up and continued to play on that side. That's unbelievable, and that still amounts to no stat, am I correct?

Yeah, well there's so much to blocking that it doesn't ... I mean, you don't count block touches that allow you to get a really good dig. You don't count when your block takes away the right part of

the court and channels the ball perfectly to your libero. So yeah. That's just part of the game that doesn't get measured.

Some of the tough blocks are never touched. You put them right into that dig alley and you did the job.

End of the match, do you talk with the team very much or do you leave that?

No, not at all. Basically, especially if we lose... It doesn't happen very often. I'm not bragging. It just statistically doesn't happen very often. I think the safest thing a coach can say is, "Hey, tough match. I'm sure you're as disappointed as I am. We'll take a look at the film and we'll talk about it tomorrow."

They don't want to be yelled and screamed at. They don't want to be. A real good program, a real good team, they're as upset as you are.

Listen. Your kids cool down, and I don't know about you, but I tell my players occasionally throughout the season if I see you in school – or now I'm retired, I might just shoot you a text – after I see the match on film, because the match I see on film is sometimes a totally different match than I see while I'm looking at the scoreboard. Sometimes these kids make these great plays that you miss in the excitement of it all, I guess.

You'll see these kids that won't get their names in the paper, but they'll bring that ball back up at an important time. They might have six digs in the match, but one of those is just a game changer. It's important for them to know that what happens during a match, I don't get it all. I don't get it until I see and I watch the film.

You talked about the thing you loathe the most in this whole process is doing cuts. What other challenges have you found in your coaching? They can be either kind of general, broader things or some specific things that have come up along the way.

I think the challenge, which is an easier challenge every single year, is getting them to agree on the course that they want to take as a team. I mean, this whole ... Like I said in the beginning of the interview, and I'll say it until I stop coaching, this whole Winner Within segment of our season is huge – getting these kids on the same page, keeping them on the same page. The challenges for me are much less. I think that's the most solid part of Barnstable High School Volleyball – recognizing what we need to work on. Sometimes it's a loss that takes that. Certainly it's a challenge. Set distribution gives them a challenge. Yeah, trying to put all the pieces together. It's like a puzzle and trying to put the pieces together and make this whole thing work. That's talent-wise.

I love the coaches that you beat. A while back ago I had a coach call me, "We're coming to you on Thursday."

"Yeah, it should be a great match," because they were ranked #1 in the state.

He says, "If we play poorly and you guys play out of your minds, it should be a competitive match."

I'm like, "This is good!" If I kept this guy on the phone long enough, I knew he was going to say something to motivate me.

He says, "Tom are you there?"

I said, "Yeah," I said, "I'm just writing this down. I pulled over on the side of the road and I'm writing this down because I want to get this exactly the way you said it." I said, "That's fantastic. You just made this much easier for me."

"I didn't mean it like that."

I said, "Okay, let me read it back to you."

So like I say, these kids don't need to be motivated in the big match. But it just kept me up a little bit later that night looking at film. That's all I could say. I don't how that got in the conversation, but that was the question.

No that was good. Flipping from challenges to what do you look back and feel most proud of?

One of the greatest moments for any coach is to see their team through to their goals. When you can see your seniors for 17 times do the happy dance at the end of the season, that is one of the most satisfying things out there. The things that I'm most proud of I think are the fact that they've been good role models to our girls throughout the years. The top students – they won that AVCA academic award over the last five years – but at the end of the season, the fact that they developed goals that others might not have thought of doing, carrying on the tradition, for them to say that they want to be a state champion just puts the whole season at a different level.

It puts everything you do at a different level. And the fact that I've never once had to sit the team down and ask them, "Should you reassess your goals?" I'm sure that would be the worst thing that they'd ever want to hear. They have to do certain things for that not to happen and that's sacrifice. They've got to sacrifice complaining about playing time, they've got to sacrifice things that they do to get to the level that they're at.

Two final questions. One you've already sort of started to address and that's what's on your recommended reading list?

Let's see, *The Winner Within* by Pat Riley.

I've mentored coaches. It's funny because there's a coach who's a very good friend of mine, and he called me for five years, three times a week. We'd spend an hour on the phone and I was happy to do this because coaches mentored me when I was that age and I talked to him about the book.

I said, "Did you do *The Winner Within*?"

"I did a couple chapters."

"Listen," I said, "I am not accepting one more phone call from you unless you make a commitment to do this *Winner Within* and do it the right way. Make it part of your practice. Make it part of your program. If you do that, then I'll continue to do everything I can do to help you win a state championship."

We're in different divisions, by the way.

He said, "Okay, all right," and he did. Strangely enough, he won a state championship.

During that season this coach had an incredibly talented group of players. He recognized that in order to guide his team to their ultimate goal they would have to be a more together team. He readily admits that *The Winner Within* provided that guidance, and is glad he did it.

Like my wife says, "Tom reads a lot of book."

I say, "This is the best book I've ever read."

And she'll say, "It's the only book he's ever read."

Two separate coaches from another Cape Cod high school – Bourne High School – teach *Winner Within*. It doesn't mean that there's not teams out there that have done *The Winner Within* that don't win state championships. I'm saying your ride is a lot smoother ride with this.

Related to that mentoring, aside from telling them to read *The Winner Within* and follow it, what other advice do you generally look to give to developing coaches?

Always invest in your Athletic Director. He's your direct supervisor. Keep him apprised of the weather report out there, and if you see something potentially brewing, then sit down and ask his advice or let him know because athletic directors are really grateful when they have a clue of what's going on before they get a parent phone call. If the situations hits the fan, and they heed your advice, they're part of that decision.

You've got to keep that communication open with your players. I mean, *The Winner Within*, that's key to us. You can't get many more opportunities to communicate and get things talked about and said than 12 hour and a half sessions in a classroom, in a room together.

I mean, you spend a lot of time with these guys. When you think of the amount of hours that you spend with your team, it's more time than they'll spend with anybody.

8

CRAIG MARSHALL

Australian coach Craig Marshall is a fixture on the world beach volleyball circuit. He has coached teams on the highly competitive World Tour for nearly two decades, with eight podium finishes and a World Championships medal. He has also coached multiple medal wins on Continental tours, including a historic clean sweep of medals at the 2016 Asian Championships. He coached the Australian men in the 2000, 2004, and 2008 Olympics tournaments, and was on-hand in 2012 as well.

This interview was conducted by Mark in July, 2016. Before this one, we had done interviews with indoor coaches who also did some beach volleyball coaches. Craig, however, was the first primarily beach coach we talked with. He brings a new and different perspective to the Market Wizard project, as a result.

The first question is about your volleyball history, how you started in volleyball, how you started in coaching.

Volleyball for me wasn't a sport that I knew anything about until I went to high school, grade 8. That would have made me 13? I went to a school in Brisbane called Craigslea High School and that was the school in Brisbane and in Queensland that had volleyball people attached to it. Volleyball was something that you did when you went to Craigslea. Now, all my friends went to another school, which was Aspley, which was Aussie rules based [football], and I was an Aussie rules guy. I reckon in a way, I'm lucky that my parents made me go to Craigslea because I didn't really want to go there. I made some friends there, and got into volleyball.

Obviously I'm very short – 170 centimeters [5'7"] – so volleyball was something that I had to work really hard at. I'm not a naturally talented guy. I have to work really hard at things. The doors of opportunity opened up for me in volleyball quicker than they did in other sports. I was playing open age stuff when I was in year 10. We had the first National School's Cup in Canberra, so I had all those opportunities. That kept me going. I played for my state. I played my first senior national champs when I was 17 or 18 – 1989 – in Sydney. That was around the time also that the first national team started, full-time national team. For me, volleyball was just something that I played, loved playing. Obviously, playing as a setter I got to experience teamwork and leadership and running an offense and how to use your brain. I really enjoyed that. It was physically challenging for me because I had to learn to jump really high and move really quick to make up for my lack of height.

Coaching became something that I did while I was playing, so I went and did coaching at the schools. I coached some under-19 teams that I was part of. The last year I did at school, I ended up really coaching the team because one of the teachers wasn't available. I had some people along the way that helped me get better, and I reckon I was 19 when I first captain/coached at A-grade club level. I was thrown in the deep end because Darren Donaldson had to go to the national team, and from 19 I was coaching and playing virtually all the way through from then on.

Then beach volleyball just became an avenue of helping out some players that wanted to go further while I was still playing. We used to train indoor at nighttime and I used to train them during the day for nothing. I had doors of opportunity open up at national camps and the like. I went and coached at a few world tour events. One in Brisbane in the early '90s. One in Melbourne in the mid-'90s. My first real world tour opportunity came in '98 with the national team. They invited me to go and tour, but I didn't have a particular team. I was there to help all the teams. After that year, I came back and a guy that I was working with back in Brisbane had had knee surgery – Matt Grinlaubs – and I came back and spoke to him and just said, "Mate, I think I can get you to the Olympics in 2000 if you want to have a crack." Everything's grown since then. I relocated to Adelaide – my first real full-time job. Been through the ringer and the system from there.

So 18 years with the National Beach Program.

Nineteen. This year's my 19th year in a row on a world tour.

Okay. You've seen a lot of things in that time.

I've seen a lot of change and a lot of things, yep. Seen some great teams and some great players.

You managed to get Matt Grinlaubs to the Olympics in 2000. What teams and what successes have you had since then? They got what position in Sydney?

Seventeenth [with Josh Slack]. I had Lee [Zahner] and Julien [Prosser] as well in that cycle, who got a 9th. I had two teams going in that cycle. I was paid a small amount to be [Prosser and Zahner's] project coach from the middle to the end of '98, through the Olympics. Real eye opener for me. I wasn't that much older than Lee or Julien at the time. They were more experienced than I was on the international scene. I had to learn how I could add value to them in the areas that they weren't so good at, and how I could learn off them.

Julien Prosser and Lee Zahner who are probably considered to be the best team we've ever had in beach volleyball. Most people think that. After the Olympics, when my job with them finished, the very next year they actually won their first world tour event in Germany and then they finished up as a team at the end of that year. From that time, Matt retired with family stuff and Josh [Slack] kept playing and picked up a new partner, Jarrod Novosel. They ended up getting four 9ths in 2001, but Jarrod was just not committed enough. He was good enough, but the world tour, you've got to really throw yourself at. There's no half going. He wanted to still work full-time. His business was really good. He relocated from North Queensland to Brisbane, but once I took a job down here to Adelaide, I said to him, you guys have got to make this work and they couldn't. Josh said, "No, I need to come to Adelaide." That's where Andrew Schacht came into the picture.

Again, a guy not dissimilar to my age, but a guy who we, if you like, stole his Olympic spot in 2000 because up until Matt and Josh got together, they were the second best team in the country. That was probably the best coaching experience I ever had with those two guys. I had one guy who I'd taken from nowhere to get somewhere in beach volleyball, who was still learning, still had a lot to go on. I had another guy who tried to do it one way, and it didn't work out for him. I thought he was playing way out of position and had some areas he really needed to change. He just came in with an open book and said, "I've tried it one way. It hasn't worked. I'm prepared to try it your guys' way and see what we can do." Those guys went on to win multiple medals on the world tour, and play two Olympic games, with 9ths in Athens and Beijing.

The two events that stand out for me outside of the Olympics for them was a silver in Canada in a 2007 world tour event where we lost to Ricardo and Emanuel 18-16 in the third – maybe it was 19-17. Two great sideouts from Emanuel/Ricardo in the advantage period in that third set. That's the team they are. Best team I've ever seen. We were so close, and it would have been so good to beat that particular team because that was the team that we liked playing the most. Then we were third at world champs in Switzerland in that year – actually 3 weeks later. That made it a pretty special time for the team, because at the world champs four years earlier, Schachty [Andrew Schacht] hurt his back and essentially paralyzed himself for a couple weeks. He couldn't really move. He actually did it in a game against Karch Kiraly. We all know what a great player Karch Kiraly was. We were actually looking forward to beating him, even though he wasn't at his best, but beating him anytime. In the third set Schachty went down, so he owes me one for missing the chance to beat Karch.

Josh and Schachty were that type of team that were prepared to be open to a different way, be open to a different style, be open to a different way of training, be open to a whole bunch of things. Then at the end of that 2008 cycle, Schachty retired. Josh, he retired as well, but he came back about a year later and tried some things with the younger guys. A year's a long time. It's actually pretty hard to come back after taking some time off. I think it was a lot harder than he thought it would be. He had a few injuries that he couldn't get rid of. Playing with a younger guy, it was difficult to get to that standard because he was so competitive. While I think he brought the guys along, he just fell at the last Olympic qualifications. It was a golden set, the set to 15 against Japan for us not to qualify. We lost that, were literally a third set away from the Olympic Games.

I look back now and go, that was pretty courageous. Chris [McHugh, Slack's partner] had some surgery during that cycle. The surgery was quite significant. He had a blood clot in his arm. Which to be honest, he could have lost his arm. He could have lost part of his arm. He came back from that, so there was all those interruptions, and he had something similar going on surgery-wise with his foot. He had a little surgery on that in the last year. It affected all those competitive opportunities leading into that one big tournament with the Olympics. I'd look back now and I think it was pretty good to get that far.

Then this cycle with Isaac Kapa and Chris McHugh – actually in 2013 – they had more top ten finishes at grand slams than we had any Australian men's team do in a season. They ended up with a 9th at the world champs in Poland in 2013. In the Netherlands, at the world champs in 2015, they got knocked out by Bruno. Actually in both of them. We all know how good Bruno is. For me, he's the favorite to win the gold medal at this Olympics coming up. They won a 3rd in Klagenfurt in August 2014, with Kapa with a labral tear in his shoulder, which he'd been carrying for the last 3-4 months. Pretty significant.

We had to go through a whole bunch of scenarios to get to that place because he was struggling to deal mentally with his injury and stuff. Chris really stood up at that event, and Kap fought his way through to third in Klagenfurt, which is the Wimbledon of beach volleyball. Everyone wants to do well there. They run a great event. I actually couldn't get any of my other teams to get a medal at that event before. We went through the heartache and the devastation of elite sport by losing in Cairns for this Olympic cycle qualification. That's hit everyone pretty hard, and things didn't go our way. We had some injuries at the event. You can't rewind it. You can't redo it.

You have one chance.

You have one chance, and it wasn't our chance. We've got a really good culture going with men's beach volleyball here at the moment, but it's too early now, still in the infancy stage of the collective group going on.

I've also coached women's teams in my time. A whole bunch of different combinations, with the obvious ones being Angela Clarke and Tanya Gooley-Humphries. My wife [Kylie Gerlic] played. I ended up coaching her a little bit with Angela Clark. Last cycle I had a lot to do with Louise Bawden and Becchara Palmer. I'm considered mainly a men's coach, but in my mind I just end up coaching where the gaps are, where people want me to coach. Just lead the way.

This is our first beach volleyball interview. Some readers don't necessarily know the system for beach volleyball, particularly in Australia. Can you give it just a brief outline of how the system works there and how it fits in with the world tour.

We have a national program based in Adelaide, in South Australia. When you talk about Australia in regards to weather conditions, you go, "Why South Australia? Why Adelaide?" It has its cold moments in the Winter and where I'm from, Brisbane, is very much tropical and a little bit more suited weather-wise to beach volleyball. But the reason why we're here is really because of the high performance mentality. SASI, South Australian Sports Institute, have been a great investor in high performance beach volleyball history through Steve Tutton, and so forth. When people ask my why South Australia, because they're the people who want to help us the most.

We have a men's side and a women's side of the program. We have elite players and development athletes. We have right now a development part of the program with both males and females. In our time we've gone through a bunch of different systems, but we are pretty much about getting international results at the top end. We spend a lot of time traveling, where we're away from Australia for long periods of time and it's not just us. It's Brazil. The world tour is 75-80 percent based in Europe, so the cost for us to travel is more significant than for the Europeans. When we're actually going, we're really moving from week to week to another venue where a lot of the Europeans will play and then you go home for two days. We go to another venue. We just don't know any different. We hear a lot from Europeans going, "I don't know how you do it." My answer is it's what we have to do if you want to play.

I think the younger athletes get caught up too much in talking to the Europeans. I feel like the more experienced players that I've coached have gone, "That's what you've got to do." This is how we do it, and we love doing it. It's a big commitment – beach volleyball – because you're traveling internationally, you're traveling 4-6 months of the year. That means that the athletes are full time. They have to earn their income from beach volleyball. We encourage our development athletes to work or study, but for our elite athletes, who's going to take a person, let them work part-time where they're only around for 5-6 months of the year?

It's not viable to be a world-class beach volleyball player and try and do a little bit of work on the side. You can study remotely but you have to earn your income through the sport, and if you're good enough, there's good money to be had. But it's cutthroat, because it's like every other international sport. It's not an easy situation where you can just turn up and then suddenly be good. You've got to put your time and effort in and that's something that separates beach volleyball from a few other sports, is that if you don't want to put the time in to get good, then you're just going to be one of those good athletes that came on for a little while and fell off.

What support is the program able to give athletes to live?

All of our elite athletes get some support, what we call living support. They get some money to help pay for rent and things like that, to make things viable for them. We do offer all the resources through sports science, sports med, all of that stuff they don't have to pay for. The coaches are full-time. This is their job. That's what they do. They're 24/7, taking phone calls at midnight, coming to trainings early in the morning, traveling overseas with them. In all my time in the sport, I've never seen in Australia teams supported like they are now. They definitely get the best of the financial and the human resources side of things. Some of the coaches that are part of the system have been around for a while. We've gone through the rough and tumble times and some of the players don't have to experience some of that stuff anymore.

Going back to your coaching. Who were your initial influences as a coach, and who influenced you as you went through the journey to reach today?

On the coaching side of things, actually, the people that I connected with the most were the people that were prepared to see something in me, and I try to do that as a coach. I remember Gary O'Donnell. He always challenged me. I loved it. I found that he was always challenging me, but encouraging me at the same time. Darren Donaldson was a guy full of energy, and I ended up moving to a club team with him and he was really full on and I loved that. He was always saying it wasn't good enough. A lot of people struggled with him, but I really enjoyed his energy, and he was technically good at things too. He worked really hard at it.

I remember Phil Borgeaud when I was younger. He had a good head on his shoulders. I was under 17. I was about 15, and he was challenging me and stuff. He was the guy that at a national camp, at the trials for the national university team that I was at you know, 170cm. I know some of the players would have liked me to play, who were in the national team, but I clearly wasn't going to get picked. Phil took me aside and said, "Look. I heard a lot of really good things about coaching with you. Have you thought about giving up playing and just coaching?" I was 23 at the time. I was thinking I like playing. I like coaching. But I like playing and I wasn't ready to give up playing. Ironically I did a lot more coaching as I was playing then. I look back at the conversation and go, it just helped me let go of some of my ambitions around playing.

I remember Peter Hastie when I was really young. He was always challenging us on how you saw the game. In a beach volleyball context, I'm not a traditionalist. People like him really helped me. Then the rest of the influences were really the guys I ended up playing with. Influences I have as a coach were the players I've coached, and some of the coaches, but the guys I remember the most are Russ Borgeaud, Matt Grinlaubs, Paul Arnicar – people that weren't massive names, but for me, they were high quality people who had this really competitive will to win. They were very different personalities from me, but I really liked people who didn't give up, or could see that something was possible. Who could see that good things that were possible rather than, "Oh, it's not possible because of this." Playing with a 170cm guy on your team means you've got some limitations at the net. Most of those guys saw me as an advantage because of other areas, rather than a disadvantage because of my blocking ability or things like that.

There's people here. Andrew Schacht and Josh Slack are working here now as coaches and have an influence. Steve Tutton and Alexis Lebedew. All of those people have had an influence on me through how they interacted, or how they've had to go about things, not just what they say or what they've given me. I don't actually spend a lot of time worrying about other coaches' philosophies, because I have mine and I'm comfortable with why I do things. The methodology is different, but the philosophical approach for me is a bit strange.

In terms of your philosophy, you've been coaching now for 25 years. How has your philosophy changed over that time?

Massively. In the early days, I was coaching younger people, really just coaching to win, to be honest. I had a certain way I wanted it to be done, and I was very clear on that, but it was about winning. It was winning at all costs. It's quite funny. Now, I'm at the peak end of the high performance arena. There's no higher standard than international beach volleyball. Winning is as strong for me as it was back then, but philosophically it's different. More now than ever, I'm about volleyball being the vehicle for growth, and for people to grow and become the best they can possibly be. That may not be winning on that day. Their best may not be enough to win that day, but it doesn't make it a waste of time. I'd like to think that the players that I've worked with over time have walked out of the sport better people than when they started with me. Not just better players. For sure, they're better players, but actually better people. That's really important to me.

Do they become better people through something that you do specifically, or through the process of becoming better players?

A bit of both. I'm asking them to leave their heart and soul to this thing that we do. If I don't get to know them, if I'm not connected with them, and I'm asking them to give their heart and soul and I don't care how they go that day, either winning or losing, then it doesn't last very long. It just doesn't last very long. To win a world champs medal doesn't happen in a year. You've got to do it over years. Qualifying for the Olympic Games doesn't happen in a season. You've got to prepare for that. You're talking about commitment from people over years and years and it's very hard as an athlete to see, "Oh, you want me to bleed and work and do this today for a possibility of something in four years time." For me, that connection as an individual becomes very important.

In terms of getting better at volleyball, volleyball's more than just a physical game, whether it's indoor or beach. For you to be really successful at the international level, you've got to be a thinker. You've got to be a strategic thinker. You've got to be a technical person. Players have to make adjustments in the moment during games. Players have to deal with their ineffective methods over a preseason and work at it. They've got to be open to constructive feedback. The reality is that they need to grow as people to be able to grow as volleyball players too.

If you're just about being good on the day, you're putting a ceiling on things too much. I've actually worked with athletes who people have said to me, "I don't think they're going to be very good. I don't think they're going to be as good as we need them to be." One quote was, "You're working with camels. You need a racehorse. Those camels are great camels and they can go as fast as they can but they're not going to match it with a racehorse." I listened to that and I just said to myself, "I hear you but I'm going to back my camels in." That team ended up with medals at world champs, and [qualifying for] two Olympic Games, and winning medals on the world tour. But when you compare them to the very best team in the world, maybe they weren't racehorses, but they beat them 50% of the time they played against them.

I just think philosophically for me, they've got to walk out of the system, either when they retire or when they choose to leave, they've got to be able to take all the learning that they've done and implement it as part of their lives moving forward. It can't just be lost within the sport. I learned how to be resilient and how to deal with pressure, but now I'm in my life and got my kids and I'm under pressure, but I don't know what to do now? For me, it's all transferable. That's something that I philosophically have grown over time. Maybe it's my protection, because at the international level you don't win all the time. I don't. My teams don't win every single time we play. That's something that I've learned along the way. I'd rather see teams try and reach their very best rather than just be as good as the next team they're playing. I enjoy us playing the very best teams in the world.

I know some coaches don't. I know I've had conversations with coaches and they find the biggest events to be stressful. I actually enjoy them, but not all the players do. I will admit not all of the players have enjoyed all those high end situations, playing against the best team in the world. Ricardo and Emanuel had a ridiculous win-loss ratio going on there for a while. Our philosophy at the time was if we can learn how to beat them, then we're in a position where we can beat anyone.

We understood that the game still has to change or the tactics need to change for each different team, but if we can get some of the physical, technical, mental and emotional areas set to beat the best team in the world, then we're putting ourselves in a good position. We weren't great against some teams, but against Ricardo/Emanuel, it seemed to be something that we really thrived on, because we put a lot of emphasis on learning from them – not just how to beat them, but actually learning what they did, and philosophically taking some of that stuff with us, and then going, "That's how they might act in that situation." We don't care how they act but, why were they acting that way to handle the pressure, or to be tighter as a team in a final.

We took some of that stuff with us, and then philosophically said we want that to work for us, but we have to do it our way and act our way. I think that really worked for us rather than I hear all the time, "I want to be like that player. I want to be like that team." I don't believe in that. I'm not a firm believer in copying. I think you've got to do it your way. There's a lot to learn philosophically from the very best teams that go around. The hardest thing is to crystal ball gaze where the sport's going, or where the teams are going in the longer term and try and get there as quick as you can. That's not so simple to do.

I haven't thought it all the way through it, but I have developed a theory that the jumps that happen in men's volleyball in this particular moment in history have to do with individuals. An individual comes in with a particular skill set, or a particular way to play the game, and that is the thing that inspires the change in the game. In the past, and the obvious example is the USA men's team in the 1980s, it was a coach-driven situation. Now, with the men's indoor teams, I see a change in the way teams play on the back of N'Gapeth, Kovacevic, couple of Brazilians, Saatkamp, for example. That is what is making volleyball – men's volleyball anyway – evolve a little bit.

It's probably the same in beach volleyball on the men's side, when you look at the quality of people that have come through. The style of game, everyone plays a bit different. Everyone has their own way, but there's a general way that beach volleyball gets done, as is there is a general way the indoor volleyball gets done, and the key is in how does each team do their own detail. The attention to detail becomes really important.

I talk philosophically about my approach to volleyball that there are four key things that I look at when I'm coaching to build something great. Teamwork is the big one for me. It's where I'm a bit different to other people in beach volleyball. I believe good teams are really important, and everyone sees that, but individual players become really critical. There's so many good individual players out there, and Australia in men's beach volleyball hasn't had the pick of the bunch. We haven't had the best player in the world play for Australian beach volleyball so teamwork becomes really critical.

The second thing is what I call structures or culture or standards. Those things aren't based on what the guy next to you is doing. But actually, your team's got to set some things – where you want to be in a certain period of time. If you want to be somewhere in four years time, then what's it going to take? What are the standards you've got to have? The culture you've got to have?

The third thing for me is you've got to work hard. That seems obvious, but I reckon there's a difference between just turning up and doing the work and working bloody hard at what you do. At times I'm a bit over the top but, I think people have got to work really hard to get where they want to go. That's what I introduced into beach volleyball in this country, around strength and conditioning and the types of training that's possible if you want to beat the best teams in the world.

The last one, like I said a bit earlier, is that attention to detail. If you don't want to have that attention to detail, I don't think you can match it at the top end. That attention to detail is dependent on what people think, but the best teams I worked with are the people who are prepared to go into the detail.

What detail are you talking there?

The little things. Every little thing. The way your body language needs to be when you're playing in a final, or the way we go and communicate under pressure in a game, or how we go about improving our offense on a particular part of the game rather than just generically going, "Give me the ball." What drills are we doing today? Off we go and do it. If you don't have a real strong purpose, and you're not prepared to look at the why's and the attention to detail around it, to me, it's not really preparing yourself for the ultimate performance or for the goals that you're setting.

There's still a bit of work for me around that with this different generation of athletes. They like to say, you tell me what you can give me and I'll tell you what I can give you. I'm more like, "No, you tell me what you want to achieve and we'll talk about how we're going to get there." That's where the attention to detail has to come out and everyone else says, "Let's see, we'll have a look and see how we go." I'm a bit like, "We're not going to get there that way. Let's put some detail into this."

The commitment side for me is the structures, culture, standards. It's a bit different because, like I said, I think the athletes these days in our system have it better. There are more resources for them than any other groups ever had. I must admit earlier, because the athletes had to fight a bit harder to find their own way, there was a little bit more commitment from them. That's why it's a really hard conversation to have because you can't compare other people's commitment with the people around them. All you can do is compare where do they want to go and where they are, and that's going to determine how much commitment you need. It's different for each different individual for sure.

You also mentioned the training methodology and how has that changed over the time. You said you've gone from win at all costs to more of a player development idea. What about training methodology? That must have also developed over time?

Oh, massively. In the early days of beach volleyball, or as I was hitting that international area and trying to get teams to fast track really quickly, I looked at what the USA and Brazilians were doing in the late '90s and realized we didn't have the time to get as skillful as them in the time frame that I had with the teams. I said, "What's going to make the difference?" I definitely took a very physical approach then. We determined that we'd be fitter, stronger than all the other teams, and so we trained to be different than the other teams. We did stair runs and I included conditioning stuff without balls and did stuff that I knew no one else was doing, and took a very science-based approach with it – with the physiology people. My experiences were limited in beach volleyball internationally because I was just traveling, not seeing what our opponents were doing in their hometown. I knew that physical training wasn't massive back then, so I took a very science-based approach, tested the athletes once a month, challenged them on where they were at compared to themselves, and kept just pushing the physical barriers. Because I did psychology at uni, I was at that point going, "There's a psychology component to every time they're physically doing this."

It doesn't just happen physically. You've got to mentally go through a lot of things to get there, so in my mind, we were physically and mentally preparing. We did a lot of work on skills, don't get me wrong. A lot of work on skills, but I just did that to get enough of that happening to be able to play a game that I thought we could beat the best teams with, rather than trying to beat them at their own game.

I was big on coming up with offenses that were going to beat some teams and where I thought the game was going. Defensively, we were trying to use some of our strengths and just accepting that some of our weaknesses were going to improve, but never be a weapon. The methodology around training for me, as I got more into international beach volleyball, as the standard of the athlete went through that. With Josh Slack going through it, I got a different athlete coming out, so I worked even stronger around the technical, tactical areas as I went further and further. All the conditioning stuff I do now is pretty much with the balls, which is common sense.

I'd like to do a little bit of that other stuff, but there's never a perfect time to fit it in now. The season goes so long. The younger athletes, I don't know, tend to be different. They're taller. They're leaner. The athletes I had back then were in the low 190s [6'3"+]. They were a bit more resilient. The athletes I've got now are in the high 190s or the low 200s [6'6"+]. They break easier and you have to put a lot more work into them to get there.

You said they break more easily. Is that a function of the type of athlete that's now playing volleyball? I have this conversation in my head a lot. The way that we trained, or the way that teams trained in the '80s, is just insane. Indoor teams would train 6, 8 hours a day. They would do plyometric training in addition to their court training. We train now perhaps one-third as much. But we have the same amount of injuries.

It's a two-fold thing. One is because the athletes are not doing the same amount of loading, and current athletes that I have right now have not reached Josh and Schachty's loading. Josh and Schachty had way less injuries than the current group that I have now. There's a loading component you have to get to, and it's a lot more simple than we think it is. You can't go from here to there too quickly. Everyone gets that, but you also can't then give them a break and then expect them to start back. Every time you take a break, you've got to gradually work your way up, and we're just less patient now in high performance.

The coaches or the players or...?

Everybody. There's just more urgency. "Give me now. Now. Now. Now." There needs to be a little more patience if you want to build it up. The groups in the past had a better training age, maturity. They just had more loading and they were used to it.

Even if the players now started playing at a younger age?

It's not just their playing age. It's their training age. The other thing is, there are different athletes coming through the system. I look back and think, if we go back to 20-30 years ago, there weren't the guys at the same height playing the sport as there are now. Or not as many of them.

They're different makeups of athletes, and that requires some more patience. Particularly when they're younger. All the emphasis in Australia is what I specified earlier, and that's actually a negative in terms of injuries and stuff because what ends up happening is we put them in situations where they're getting better technically, or whatever, but physically they're not ready for it. They're not able to handle it.

The art of coaching is to get the mix right. There's so much science in sports, but the art is not always there. The art is getting the science into the mix and making good calculated risks, because that's what elite sport is. You've got to take risks, but they've got to be calculated risks. You can't just go, "I just want to do this or do that." You can't be in the middle of a game and just make a substitution and say, "I want that to happen." It's got to be a calculated risk. That's the art of coaching. There's calculated risks that are happening as much – more so – before the game happens than during the game itself. Training people, when you lift their load, how much? You could put all the science you want. We do a lot of stuff. For example, every session we run here, I can tell you how many jumps Kap or Chris has, and what type of jumps they are.

Using Vert?

No. Vert's not good enough for that. I can't tell you how high those jumps are yet, but I will soon with a catapult GPS unit.

Oh, okay, so you're using the catapult GPS.

That's where I want to go. As of next year, I reckon I'll go down that pathway.

That's what you're using now?

No. I'm using a pure performance analysis person to count. And stating [taking statistics on] everything that we do. Everything Kap and Chris does has a number in every practice, so we can look back and go, "This is how many jumps they had," but the thing about that is, we know in beach volleyball, a jump float jump is different to a spike jump, which is different to a jump serve jump and the Vert doesn't tell you that. The Vert's okay, but it's just not enough. We use that performance analysis coach at every training session to not only statistically do the passing, 3-2-1, and spiking, but also all of the jumps, the type of jumps, and all the things we considered important, like covering and things – tooling the block. We try to put numbers to everything that we do. It's a lot of data and hard to analyze. We're still in that place of saying it didn't tell us everything. If I look at it longer and harder, it will. The athletes that continue on in the next cycle, like Kap or Chris, are going to learn so much better for what we've done this cycle or over the last 2 years because that's when Josh [Slack, Performance Analysis Coach] started.

Your methodology has changed a lot. Can you give a brief outline of a training session in 1999 compared to a training session now in a typical month before you go to world tour. One in 1999. One in 2016.

In 1999 it would have been like... Warming up would have been do whatever you want. You know best. When you're ready, all right now, and then it would usually start with some critical skill technical area. Back then, it would have been setting. I would have done setting for, I don't know, an hour easy. Different types of sets. A lot of coach throwing balls in, manipulating where the ball's going and all that sort of stuff. We might have then done a bit of hitting on the back end of it, and then try to see if we can play a set or something, and that would have been it.

Now, it would start with very clear direction or the coaches have a very clear direction, where training's going and the players have no clue. We're doing some of that stuff where we just literally go, "Okay, what do you think training's going to be about? Okay, guess what? Clear your mind because things are going to come at you today and you're going to have to go with the flow." I know all the theories say tell the athletes what's coming. Prepare for it. We've worked another way. Sometimes it's better for them to be resilient enough to go, "Okay, we have a fair idea of what we're working on," but how it comes across or what we're asking them. We want them to think in the moment.

Then I get them to warm up, and usually now... I'm a big fan of doing shoulders first because I think that a lot of injuries occur early in trainings because people aren't physically ready to do stuff with their legs. I've never had a situation where people haven't been ready with their shoulder. I've always been a firm believer about getting your shoulders done first and then usually then doing some stuff with your legs after that. It combines. The volleyball comes into it, and then I like to take over now and go, “Okay, I’ll add something in.” I might do some relays with the balls, or do something that gets them going. I like to do some of the jumping, get them through some jumping stuff before they go and hit at the net themselves.

I want to get two things out of that stuff. One, I want to make sure that they’re doing stuff that isn’t always totally specific because I want to put them in some awkward situations. The jumps are volleyball jumps, but I might get them to get up off the ground, take a step, plant their right heel in the ground, jump high. I might get them to do different plyometric type jumps on the sand and stuff that they wouldn’t have to do, that aren’t totally specific to the game. Some long, some up and down, both legs, practicing landing. Two, knees are always an issue so I’m always big on controlling how things get from a controlled situation to an uncontrolled situation before I’m asking them to do that stuff with the balls.

Then training, depending on what we’re working on, but I very rarely will be throwing the ball into the drills. I like to then create a scenario where it’s happening from the players. Then we’ll set up different types of drills based on what we want to get good at and we’ll try and include, depending on the numbers we have training. Sometimes it’s two. Sometimes it’s four. Sometimes it’s nine people. I normally come up with three or four different things that we work on in the session. It is way more intense physically, speed-wise, the way the players are moving and going from where they used to be. We get a lot more contacts in the two hours that we might train. We train a little bit longer now.

A little bit longer. More intense and longer.

Back in the ’90s yes, but where I was at in the 2005 era, we trained a little bit longer because I had more people at training. Back then, I only trained two hours at a time, but not as intense as those trainings when I ran it a bit shorter.

And now you don’t have the stair runs that you did a different time.

No. I’ve done a few different conditioning things over the years on the sand, but moving in and out of poles and some agility and it has certain rest periods and has to be flat out so it has a conditioning component to it. I haven’t gone down that pathway for a while now. A long time. Everything's done pretty much with the balls now. We definitely had some volleyball stuff actually in our weights program but on the court now would be 100% with the balls. Our conditioning work is set up in the drills.

You have a long competition period and a long training period so you're working 11 months of the year, 12 months of the year?

Different years, different times. The advantage of an Olympic year is the Olympics are over and then I actually have more time off at the back end of an Olympic year than I have in other years. There are some athletes who want to touch the ball more. Some don't. Kap and Chris, for example, we'll do 4-6 weeks of lifting with no balls early in the preseason.

Preseason being January? February?

Oh, no. October, November. It's pretty much straight off after the world tour. They get about four weeks off and then that preseason starts. This season, that'll happen in September. September, October, November, December will be our solid preseason once people commit back into the next cycle. Whereas Josh and Schachty I would have done more ball work with them.

So there'd be 4 weeks off, a preseason, a preparation period of some type, and then you're going from about December until August?

Then we were in a really awkward phase for me, where we got our national tour happening and we're still working on our game. It's not an easy mix. I've never found it an easy mix. I've never had my teams perform at their best in January and February because their best needs to happen in May, June, July, and August.

It is awkward that they're playing real competition, but not important competition?

It's not easy for them and it's not easy for me, because it's important for our sport to be growing beach volleyball. But it's hard to get up mentally and emotionally for the national tour. If the game's tight, it's not bringing the same levels of emotion. I want teams to try things on the national tour in competition. You get a scoreboard and you have things in front of you, so losing has its impact. Everyone says, they should win all the time. The reality is, particularly now on the national tour, we've got all nine senior guys so we've got four and a half to five teams that can play pretty good, so they all like to beat up on each other, which I like.

I'll want them to make sure that they're not restricting themselves or putting a ceiling on where they're going. I like them to try things, do things, work on things, not just go out and go, "Oh, we're here to win and that's all that matters." It's not an easy mix for me because then every time you're playing on a weekend it affects the training week, affects the lifting that they're getting done. It has its physical side of things, it has its mental and emotional side, but the other bit for me is that we travel so much and then the national tour's asking us to go away on weekends. It's more and more time away from their loved ones, and that has its impact too.

How do you manage all that? With a really big spreadsheet?

No. You got to put a competition plan together with each team or each athlete. Everyone's a bit different, but the national tour only becomes really useful from a playing perspective if I can get all the good players to play in it. We have a culture right now on the men's side where we commit together and we talk about making the national tour good, because we're going to commit as a collective group. That worked really good last Summer. Our domestic side of things is nothing like Germany or USA or Brazil, or anything like that. We're miles off that. Our advantage or our strength about preparing on the world tour is really around what we can do in our daily training environment in preparation for the world tour. That becomes number one.

How important is weight training during the competition season and how do you manage that?

It is critical because we have such a long season and it's spread out. It's not just every week, but it is mainly that four months of the year. If you can't start there, you've got to build people up to there. For example Josh and Schachty, that year in 2007, they won a silver in Canada. Then three weeks after that, they won the bronze in world champs. The week before world champs, we played in Marseilles. I made them lift heavy twice that week. I made them lift heavy once the week before. It was power-based stuff, but it was pretty heavy, to the point where we did one of the sessions the day before we played. But it was all part of our plan.

The players very much had prepared over the years for this, so it wasn't like asking them to do something that they couldn't or wouldn't. They're very open to that. I haven't got there with the collective group I've got now, to that degree. They're still not as physically mature as those guys were. You've got to get up to that. It's really important if you want to last the season, and most of our bigger events happen at the middle to the back end of the season. You've got to be prepared to perform where you're not peaking at certain events physically.

What I did in the last season and will continue to do is taking the next step, that we lift everyday.

We have daily exercises everyday, which include some of the equipment in the gym and stuff. So the guys go through a 45-minute daily exercise. That will happen every single day, and then some of the major lifting stuff depending on phase on of the season. During the season, it's power-based. Preseason, it's strength-based. I find it really important for injury prevention as priority number one. Then performance, priority number two. I see it as really important. You've got to build that over time. In your situation, where you're talking about different development players at different levels, I can see them doing different programs based on an 18 year-old and a 29 year-old. I believe in specifics for individuals around lifting, as specifics for individuals around training depending on what position they play and things like that. It's the art of coaching again. The art of planning.

In the formative part of your career at least, you did a lot of work in the indoor teams parallel to beach. What are the different challenges between each? What are the first things that stand out to you as how to work in those two different environments?

There's some obvious physical differences. Playing on a hard surface where there's no give, you engage different muscles to jump at different times. Indoors you can move faster or react quicker, where on the sand, if you measured the speed, it'd be a little bit slower. The distances you have to travel in beach volleyball could be bigger.

The first thing that I notice from going from walking on hard surface to walking on the sand, is it feels different. Kinesthetic senses take over and you've got to re-engage. As beach volleyballers say, once you get your sand legs, then I think transferring from one to the other or back and forth is actually not as hard as people make out. I had Matt Grinlaubs and Josh Slack playing indoor with me and training beach volleyball to go to the Olympics. I saw that the indoor games that they were playing and the style of game we wanted to play, and then competing and playing indoor, was a really important part of preparing them for beach volleyball. It's different now. Not necessarily for the better.

Different in what way?

A lot of the players that we have now, we touched on this around injuries. A lot of the players we have now, patella tendinopathy, a few issues around their knees. The more they're doing on the hard surface, the worse that stuff becomes. I think there's something to gain by playing a high quality indoor game that could transfer over to beach volleyball really good, but the athletes have to be resilient enough to do it and it has to happen at the right time of their careers. The time it would be best to happen is when they're younger, but they're carrying more injuries from indoor. It's just a complicated situation. I've got a really talented young guy. He's 21 this year or next year. His knees are bad. I can't put him indoors. His knees get too sore. He's a pure beach volleyball athlete, right? He would really prosper from some indoor competitive opportunities. But if we give him that, he's going to take weeks and weeks to recover. It's just not possible. It would really help his competitiveness, his thinking, his ability to tool the block.

There's so much to learn from both disciplines, but the other thing for me is just that teamwork or specificity side. Beach volleyball has a specificity side, but it's nowhere near as specific as indoor. A middle blocker in indoor volleyball is not required to be a great setter – to set quick balls or something. The way I teach beach volleyball is the blockers have got to set great. They've got to transition set and they've got to be able to run the rhythm of the offense. I like people to see themselves as setters. Beach volleyball, you're a setter at certain stages in the game, but then you're also a transition hitter or blocker or defender. There is some specifics and it's usually around defense.

Where it's a little bit different for me, is that beach volleyball requires you to just bring more of the skills of the game into one person at a higher level, at that elite level than indoor asks of different players. People play defense and stuff, but some of them go off and the libero plays. I know in beach volleyball, people are at the net blocking more often now than specifics, but they've got to transition set the ball good or we're wasting our time.

What about in terms of the player-coach relationship, for example?

I would say that because you don't coach during games, the coaching relationship for me becomes really important around understanding, and you'd say it happens in indoor anyway, but philosophically understanding what we're trying to do and how we're trying to get it done. Training and discussions – meetings – become really important because the players have to make all the decisions during the game.

I want to upskill them in the ability to work together and to get on that same page, because that's where teamwork becomes absolutely critical in beach volleyball. You've got to make decisions with another guy in the moment. If you're not thinking exactly the same as the other guy, you have no time to debate or discuss. You can analyze it after the game, but in the moment you've got to have a unified front heading into one direction. The reality is Plan A won't get you through to the end of the game. If the other team's on their game, Plan A will get you a good start, or get you good things, but they'll adjust, and so you can't just go in and just do this and it will be enough.

"No plan survives first contact with the enemy." Helmuth von Moltke

It takes time – months, years – to get all of that out. I call it evolving or growing, fertilizing the ideas because you can't start with everything. You've got to build the foundation and work your way through it. You've got to see your jigsaw puzzle and then build it for them. I see it building for them because I don't think players can do it all on their own. It's too hard.

I don't think that players can do it all on their own. I also don't think coaches can do it all on their own.

The players are the most important. They're the center focus of it.

My experiences are the players are good at seeing the here and now times, and okay looking a little bit in into the future, but terrible at visualizing where it's going longer term. They just want to do what can get us something now, but it may actually end up heading in that direction where you really need to go slightly in a tangent, in another direction. They'll get ultimately where you want to go.

That's a really fair comment because my experience is that some players that I've had are much more aware in the moment of the game. They're much better, much more able to read and understand and solve problems than I am from the side.

Correct.

Not to mention the timing issues. They're faster anyway. But they're much less able to see the big picture, where they fit into everything and how things progress. Perhaps that's a good, decent explanation of what the differences are.

I think ultimately an indoor coach wants to be in the same position as a beach volleyball coach leading into a game anyway. Where I might make some decisions during the game, but the players are going to make most of the decisions anyway. There's just more information that you're allowed to feed into the game tactically and...

Allowed to is not the same as required to.

We're just not allowed to. We're just not allowed to offer anything during the game at all.

My pre-match preparation has changed. In some areas, it's changed a fair bit in that I base my preparation now more on learning how to read the opponent instead of when X happens, we do Y. That's part of developing those decision-making things. Players often want to be told what to do.

It's easy. If you take some of the decision-making out of it, then it makes it slightly easier to implement, but it doesn't mean it's going to be successful.

It also changes the lines of accountability.

Yes. But I find that the best players just want to get a bit more information so they can make some calls during the game.

I watch a lot more beach volleyball than the players do. I'm watching week-to-week a lot more games than they do. They're looking after themselves physically, trying to get away from the game. I'm trying to absorb myself into it a lot more. They know that I see a lot more than them. I've talked to them about tendencies and I just emphasize these tendencies aren't what they're going to do all of the time. These are the tendencies that I believe they're going to use under pressure. That's the most valuable information that you can give in beach volleyball, because if you just tell them what they do, a good team will do a lot of different things, and you end up chasing your tail. The players can feel that pressure on the court. It doesn't mean the score's tied, but they can feel the pressure, and this is the moment that tendencies appear. There are some tendencies that we've got to determine that they're either really good at and we've got to stop, or they're not so good at and we've got to create for them. Easier said than done.

You talked a lot about culture and the way that the culture of your program has developed, and that the culture of the group right now is very good. What processes, what things do you go through to develop that with the group?

It's different depending on the number of people. A lot of my work has happened in teams. A lot of it's come down to having that open discussion within a team about what you want to achieve, where you want to go, and therefore help show how they're going to get there, and therefore what they've got to do. We've used sports psychologists and different things, but I found the connection between the coaches and the players to be the critical one to developing the culture. People coming outside in have good intentions and they have their methods, but ultimately, you can write something down on a piece of paper and call it culture but that's not the culture. It's got to be what you're living and how you're getting it done. It's got to align to the beliefs of the people and their values and morals as well. That's not easy.

The current group of men that we have, like I said, we've got nine of them. We've got four and a half teams. We've influenced the way each team plays, but in terms of the culture, we've actually written up our own way the group works.

We the staff, or we the group including the players?

With the players, with the two coaches and the performance analysis coach, but it actually happened specifically. I did a specific thing and took a risk. I took one of the players aside and asked him to do a presentation. I knew the quality of the guy and I knew what he stood for. I knew it was going to resonate within the group. He's not the best player in the group, but he's the unofficial leader of the group.

He made that presentation and all I asked him to do was to make a presentation about what you think it means to be an Australian athlete, and what you think people should cherish, and what makes Australians great when we compete. From that discussion, and the things he put out, we videotaped it, and then I wrote up some notes from what he presented and put it around to the group. We had a discussion about it – a debate. One of our guys is not from Australia. He's actually changed his nationality and he gave his impressions from the outside looking in. Ultimately, that discussion created a document that we were already starting to live, but then it became something we talked about.

We called it the Australian way. We called it *Our Way, the Australian Way*. Now, we weren't saying that everyone that plays beach volleyball had to do this because we weren't talking tactically. We were just talking about things that we considered important within the group. Now, that grew legs everyday to the point where we went gold, silver, and bronze at Asian Championships this year. That's never happened before. We had all the podium at Asian Championships and that document was something that people referred to. We did it *Our Way, The Australian Way*. That, in itself was just a way, but with each group you've got to work out what type of people they are, how they operate, what's going to work. With Josh and Schachty, the more formal it was, the more structured it was, the more pedantic we were, the better. With Kap and Chris, the more unstructured it is, the more it's an open discussion, the better it is. We had a sport psychologist coming and trying to do culture with them, but it was too structured for them. A really good document. Lot's of different points, and all that good stuff, but they didn't live it.

So what you have now is only appropriate for this particular group?

I think right now, it is. Most of this group is going to continue on the next cycle. I can see it evolving with that. The question is, what do you do when a new person joins the group and didn't start from scratch. The difference that we're doing right now is we've got a squad going on, and we've got teams within the squad. Each team has their way. I'm not suggesting we've got it right, but beach volleyball in Australia needed something to unify it, because domestically it wasn't working. The teams are really competitive with each other, which I like, but I'd hate to see that fall down. I don't know if it happens in indoor and the one team philosophy, but we've got multiple teams trying to achieve something. This cycle we had the Olympic qualification process with the Continental Cup where you needed two teams to play for your country. That was the reason why we did it.

And only one of those two teams would actually go to the Olympics.

Then the committee's got to make a decision on who goes. They all don't go. We had to do it for Australia, not for a single team. I don't think if we hadn't had the Continental Cup process there, I would have taken this approach. It was, "We're in this environment. What am I going to create that's going to help us achieve some objectives?" The one thing that didn't work as good as it can is when you've got a group and a methodology, people can hide within the group. "I'm not so good at this." "He's better at that." He'll do it." I was very conscious of that in January, February, and made that really clear that no one was going to hide in the group.

Now, in the end, we didn't play great in the Continental Cup. We had injuries and other issues. We still didn't play to our potential. Part of me goes, maybe deep down there was a little bit of 'if we don't win, they will' but it didn't feel that way at the time. I've got to look at it all. I still think the key in beach volleyball is your team and the culture of your team and your four keys around that, which is the attention to detail, the teamwork, the hard work, and what I call commitment / culture / standards. The four keys have to be there, but what they are for each team is up to them. I wouldn't have a team that doesn't focus on those things. We're trying to improve those things.

You mentioned earlier that you were not a traditionalist in beach volleyball. Is it fair to say that you're an innovator?

I like to try. That's how I like to see it, but that's for other people to determine, whether I'm an innovator or not.

All right, I'll say that you're an innovator. What are the things that drive that innovation? What's the personal quality or is it a competitive necessity?

It really stems for me around what the objective is. I work, and have worked, with a level of athlete – and some people might take offense to this – but the level of athlete that I work with in beach volleyball is never the best volleyball athlete in the country. Never. There are always better volleyball athletes. They're just playing with the national indoor team. Doesn't make them better beach volleyballers, but there has been players that I would like to see come to beach volleyball because I think it would have made us better.

The reality is, I match up the potential abilities, physically and mentally, of the athletes that I have, and where I think their growth can take them under the time frame that they're prepared to give. Then I have to work out a style of game that's going to be where I think the best teams are going to be at that time. Then ultimately that's how the innovation works for me. If I have the best athletes in the world, then I'll try and beat everyone at the way they play. But I've never had that. I've always been in the situation of trying to come up with a way that we can play the game that's going to make it really difficult for the other team, which is usually not playing the way they're playing.

Offensively is where people can see it the most. They may be saying, it's too risky and they'd probably play better if they played safer. The point for me is yes, if all I wanted us to do was get to 15th in the world or 10th in the world. But if we're trying to beat the best teams in the world, I'm prepared to take that risk. I've always seen it that way for me. Maybe that's the reason why the consistency isn't there all the time, is that we're playing a game that's always at the edge, if you like, in terms of where you need to be physically, mentally, to be able to execute it consistently.

I was talking actually with my dad today about football and if you're playing a game that's inherently a little bit risky, you need to be at the absolute best to be able to perform because you have nothing to fall back on. You have to have maximum attention at all times. If you have an inherently risky game, when you're 99 or 100 percent, you're great. When you're 98 percent, you're in a deep hole. That is how I think about the French indoor team. Their 99 and 100 is fantastic. Their 98 is just a very good international team.

Maybe if they didn't go there, who knows, right? They've won some big events lately. Who knows? They might even go all the way to the Olympics, but we all know that they've got to be on their game to deliver it. If they took a less risky approach, they've probably got no chance of winning the Olympic games. For me, I look at that and go, "Good on them." I reckon they've copped some criticism too for it.

The individuals in the team certainly do.

I feel that over my career, that's been the case. When it hasn't looked good, when it hasn't come off, the criticism is definitely there. I had a text the other day. The Netherlands women qualified through their continental process and I sent their coach a message saying, "Good on you. Congratulations, you deserved it as I know he was going through some philosophical stuff to get there." He didn't have to, but he sent me back a text and said, "Mate, a lot of what I've learned philosophically has been through what I've seen your teams do over the years and I've taken a lot from there." I'm not in the game for recognition from anyone else or even the players. I'm just there to try and get them as close to their goal as they can, and their goals are not small. They're not something that they can just click their fingers and get there tomorrow. I don't think it's risky from where I sit, but other people do.

The Hawthorn Football Club play what would for other teams, because of their skill level, be really risky. Now, I reckon that's the reason why they've won three in a row and potentially, even with all the injuries they got this year, are in a good position to win four in a row. Only one other club's ever done that in the history of Australian Football League. Because they're prepared to be innovative, to take the game on, to back their skills in, there's actually still a chance of being in their premiership window as they keep talking about. If they just tried to do it okay, I don't think they'd be in there right now.

I think the biggest impediment to innovation is a fear of consequences. Not the consequences of losing, but sometimes it's worse to look bad than it is to lose.

There are definitely players that think that too. "I don't want to look like a fool out there. I don't want to stuff up."

What's then the advantage that you have, or the background that you have, that makes you not fearful of looking stupid?

I won't say there isn't that fear.

What gives you the ability to overcome that fear that other people don't have?

I've been through different parts of my career where it's been easier or

I've been a lot stronger. I've been a lot stronger about my philosophical approach and prepared to back it in. But now I've got a family. I've got a wife and three kids. I need to feed them. This is my job. If I lose this job, I don't have another job sitting waiting for me. I found that really hard, to be honest.

Since I've started a family, I've caught myself saying, "This is my job." Originally, when I was coaching internationally, it wasn't even a job. I wasn't even getting paid that much. I've fought through a lot of stuff. I just keep coming back to, what are you here for? You're not here for the job. It's more than a job for me. It's what I do. I'm doing it with other people who are putting their heart and soul into it. I go, "If we're going to do this thing, let's do it with everything we've got." It's just staying true to yourself, staying true to what you agree with, and it's easier said than done. There's a lot of emotion attached to everything that you're doing and there is that fear.

Someone said to me, "Courage always happens in the presence of fear," and I like to see it that way. It's just about being bold and showing a lot of courage. That is what really sport is all about. I'd call it calculated risks. That's what you're there to do. If you're just there to play it safe, you're only going to be mediocre. Mediocre just doesn't excite me. It just isn't my thing. It's not what I do it for. I'm too competitive.

The thing is, like I said to you, beach volleyball's one of those sports where the way the system works now, there's only ever one team – and often not even that many – that doesn't lose in a week. There's 31 other teams in the main draw, and another 20 or whatever. They all lose. If you don't like losing and you can't handle losing, beach volleyball's not for you. Or you can be that one team that wins every game every week. The only problem is, that's getting harder and harder to do. There's no one dominating like there used to be.

It's hard to win. You're going to have to accept that losing and winning are all part of the deal, and I reckon there's as much to learn from winning and losing as long as you are prepared to see that this is all an opportunity to grow. That's philosophically where I've got to. Beach volleyball's the vehicle that we're doing right now to grow. I've been through some horrendous personal things that the players have been through at tournaments. Things that I can't talk about, but they're ridiculously full on. I sit there and go, "So what do we do now?" It's just winning and losing? It's more than that. For me, if I can teach people skills that can help them in life, being resilient, dealing with stress, dealing with pressure, if you play down everything and you're not there to win all the time, then you're avoiding the stress and the pressure. You're actually not evolving into the growth that you want as a person anyway.

You have no chance to win and you have no chance to grow. Then it's a really hard life, to travel eight months a year, to not win and not learn.

Exactly. Ultimately, it comes down to the question, how do you keep yourself there, or how do you take the risks? It's the degrees of it. For me, I've got to stay strong to what I believe in, what morally and ethically is really important to me, what philosophical approach.

You ever find yourself compromising those things?

All the time. It's always a compromise because there's always something in the system that's not aligning. To what degree do you compromise? I always feel like there's a little bit. This cycle was a really good example for us. We took on a team that was formulated through discussions with myself and Andrew Schacht. Because of the way the funding was working in Australia, Kap and Chris needed to get results behind their name really quickly. In 2013, they got more top ten results in grand slams than any Australian men's team we've ever had. We had to compromise to do that. We didn't get the foundation that I wanted right because we had to get results immediately. The first international event they played together was Asian Championships and they won it. Australia men's team had never won an Asian Championships before that. Then they played a whole Australian summer where they didn't lose a game. Everything that was going on was teaching them that we're winning, but we weren't getting the foundation stuff right. But we got to get these results to keep the funding going. In the end, we didn't qualify.

That compromise cost you in the long run?

It's difficult to say right now. It wasn't the only thing, but I can tell you now, if I had that team again, I would have done things differently earlier, and I would have told everyone you're going to have to accept that they're not going to deliver results early. We would have been in a much better position if people could have looked ahead further. That's really hard because people that are giving out the money don't want to. They want to see that the money's having an immediate impact. It's not how you deal with longevity, or how you build to the very top. It's not a linear progression.

How can you improve that situation in the future?

I think that the future lies in people management.

The management of players?

The management of staff. The management of the players. The coaches need to manage the players. Management needs to manage the coaches. It needs to be at a personal level. They don't need security because there's no security in elite sport. They need support. They need encouragement.

In some way, there shouldn't be security either.

No. In the first two years of this cycle, Schachty was telling me, the insecurity around the future is driving us to get the results. Which we recognized as a real positive, but on the negative side, it didn't allow us enough time. We didn't have enough time with the athletes for the few things that were going on to build a foundation consistently. It almost felt like we had one year, and then we had to start again. We never grew like with previous teams or the better teams that I worked with.

I think that it's not what gets said, but what doesn't get said. If I ever stepped into a management role, and you are my coach, every week I'd ask you how you're doing. Every week I'd ask you what you need from me.

That would annoy me after a while.

It would, but you know what? That one time when you really need something ...

There's an open door that I can actually ask.

Correct. Where if that wasn't there, you might decide in three months, "I really need something, but am I going to go to this guy and ask for it because I'm not sure how he's going to react because I've never done this before." If I made it feel like I'm here for you, at least we could work out what we could do. That's the people management side that I'm learning along the way, that I'm getting better at with my players and my staff and how we're working.

My next question is what are the most important qualities of the coach? By that I mean, is it technical? Is it tactical? Is it organizational? Is it communication? Is it empathy? What are the things that are most important?

In my job, the way I see it, you've got to be what's required in the moment. You've got to be able to fit into that moment and deliver what's required. Empathy's critical, and how you teach yourself empathy is an interesting one. You can never be in someone else's shoes. You can pretend you know, but it's really hard to say 100%, I know exactly what that guy's going through. But we always think we do and I've learned over time that a coach needs to be confident. Players get their belief system through the coaching group. Sometimes you're missing things because you've got to be confident. You've got to act like you know, and so you say, "I know what you're going through."

Brené Brown does a TED Talk on vulnerability. She talks about vulnerability as important or critical for innovation. If you're not vulnerable, then you're not prepared to take the risk. She says that major companies are not prepared for people to be vulnerable, or for their company to be vulnerable. It's never a good sign for people to come across as being vulnerable, right? It comes across as weak. I've been trying to teach athletes that there are right times to be vulnerable, and within your team framework you can be vulnerable. You can be innovative from there.

In that talk she talked about empathy. I'm not sure I'm going to get this exactly right so this is the way I see it. There is a big dark hole, and you've got your friend down in your big dark hole. There's nothing down there. It's just black and it's dark. They're down there and they can't get out. Then you're talking to them from up the top down the hole going, "It looks dark and cold down there. You must be hungry. Here's a blanket. Here's some food." You throw it all down there and people see that as empathy. She said that's not empathy. Empathy is going down in the hole, sitting there with them going, "It is dark and cold down here." That's empathy. It's really hard sometimes to know or to actually go through what people are going through.

We didn't qualify in this Olympic cycle, and it's devastating. Each person is taking it in their own way, but a coach needs to be able to find a way, to do everything they can to possibly empathize with that, because they're going through their own stuff as well. People are so different. Empathy, and therefore communication and what comes with communication, is conflict resolution, and upskilling yourself on how to be part of that. Because if you don't have a team that has conflict, you don't have a team. You don't have a high performance team. You need to have conflict. You need different ideas, but if the strongest personality always gets their ideas across, it's not always best for the team.

You've got to work out a way where people feel comfortable about putting ideas in there and there is some conflict resolution. The obvious thing to coaching is tactical or technical. If you don't have a tactical or technical background, you can still be a great coach, but you need to get someone who's doing that. If you've got unlimited resources financially, and you can buy the right people in, then I'd consider you a great coach. In my area, we don't have those funds, so I feel like you've got to be at least great at those areas.

Technical and tactical?

Yeah. I always think you've got to be working with the players to keep growing and improving it. Sometimes if you feel like it's all coming from you – they'll only be as good as your ideas. A good coach broadens or gets people thinking, at least helping the team grow. You've got to be a good facilitator. There's probably a hundred other things that I think are important but I'm not good at them.

You've made a pretty good list. I asked for one and you've given me six.

That's my team performance plans where you've got critical, important, and whatever. It's green, orange, and red depending on the importance. Ninety-five of my things are green, where they're all important. You've got to deliver them all. It's my way.

I have a new favorite question that I'll ask that is of particular interest to me because I've just become a father. Is there anything that you've learned about coaching from parenting and/or is there anything that you learned about parenting from being a coach?

I'll give you an example. Kids can push your buttons or push you to the extremes. You love them and so they're always testing you. I have a son who's six. He's full of energy. He's got that little bit of spirit in him. He will push the boundaries, which at times is really fun, but at other times he doesn't know the difference between when Mum's really needing to get things done and when she wants to joke around. He can get quite loud when he doesn't think he's getting his way. The more we're going, "Mate, we can't do this," the more he's shouting back. I found myself after a while shouting at him to stop shouting. That is stupid, but any parent that's really done parenting will know that they've had moments where it just gets too hard and you're shouting at your kid, "Stop shouting."

I learned a lot in regards to, if you want athletes to do something, then you've got to be able to show them or act that way. A classic is I go to the nth degree sometimes. This cycle, this last 12 months, I wanted my athletes to get their skinfolds measurements down. We gave them so much education, so much everything and it was going down but not to the level we wanted. So I said bugger it, I'm doing this myself. And my skinfolds dropped well below the target zone and I kept it there for the rest of the cycle. It wasn't meant to stick it to them or anything, but it was stuff I learned from parenting that if you want, you've got to show. It just can't be enough to talk about and leave it. You've actually sometimes got to do it. If I want my kids to do homework, I've got to sit down with them and help them do it. I can't just tell them to do it. I can't even just show them. I'm going to have to be invested right there.

What I learned the most from parenting is just keep it cool, but you're going to have to get involved, really involved – sometimes – to keep people going. I got my sum of seven sites down to 36mm. And kept it there for the whole time until the end of the cycle. Our target was was to get 45mm and below. The players didn't quite get there. I educated them, and I followed a plan, and things we'd try to do for them. In the end, some of them took a great deal of inspiration from that, which is good, but all I wanted to do was go through the experience myself and know how hard it was. When they're talking about it – it's really hard – I wanted to feel it too. When they were saying they were struggling at something, I can say, I get it. I'm struggling too but if you want to be mentally strong and show your resilience, then this is how I do it.

What's your favorite part of coaching?

I'd like to say it's winning at the big events, but to be honest, even if it sounds cliché, it is seeing a team and individuals within that team evolve and stick at things for the longer term. I'm less excited about a great training session. The players love it. I actually get a bit more excited at the average training sessions because we have to go through a lot more. For me, it's that evolution over time. Not particularly just one thing. A win, a tournament win, that lasts for a few days, but it doesn't stay with me for as long as that feeling that you're having an influence on people and making them better.

It's very subjective. You don't have to be everybody's best buddy to be a good coach. The players don't like me 24/7. I'm a challenger. I'm always asking for a bit more. I'm always challenging them. It can wear people down. There's got to be some times where you can just be there and pick them up and back away. I'm not the guy that just needs them to like me.

You've been doing this for a long time and also a long time in a single job. What's the thing that continues to motivate you to continue? I can feel that your motivation is still very high.

I'm not finished.

It used to be because we weren't the best in the world, and it used to be because I haven't won that Olympic gold medal, or that world champs gold medal. I'm a bit more pragmatic about it now. I still don't think I've reached my best. I still think I'm learning. I'm a better coach now than I used to be. That's what I believe. I cop rubbish from my older players, who are now working with me, who ask, "Why didn't you coach this good when you were coaching us back then? We could have won more." I just feel like I have more to offer. I don't get everything right completely. We're not the best in the world.

Every year they see a lot of different things. I don't do the same thing. I just feel like there's so many more ideas in my head that I haven't implemented yet that I still want to see, that I still think I can help. Whether that's at the elite top end or the development level for me, I'd like some players that are more evolved by the time I get them at the elite level. Part of me is saying I'll need to be that guy that brings them along so someone else can take them a bit further. It's what I do. It's what I am. I just don't feel like I've achieved everything that I've got, that I'm capable of giving yet. Although my future's still in the hands of what other people think of me.

Your future in a job, but not as a coach.

I see it this way. I have a family. I have a wife and three kids. I have two kids in primary school and one who's 3 years-old. I need full-time work. If I don't get employed as a coach, I'm going to throw myself at something else. That's what I'm going to do. I can't see myself working full-time at something else and doing coaching on the side.

All in or not in.

That tends to be my way. All in. I'm not ready to give up coaching. I'm not going to walk away.

You mentioned a TED Talk earlier. In terms of reading or other resources, what can you recommend to developing coaches, young coaches? Things that have resonated with you.

I like reading biographies or autobiographies. I sometimes find it better to be talking with other people about some things and then sometimes they might say, "I saw this thing on Youtube." Otherwise, I don't find myself going there every day. Nothing like what I imagine you might do in that you're constantly evolving, talking about volleyball on blogs and social media. I don't have a lot of space in my life. I just feel like I'm so into something that I'm doing, but when I tour and I'm on those planes and doing stuff, I find it really hard to watch video all the time of the games, so I tend to read books or do something else. That opens me up to seeing things. Every book I pick, there's always something in it for me. I don't know why. I'm picking something up off it and I find it really good. I just don't do it as often as I would like.

What is a recent one that you really got something from?

Confidence Gap by Dr. Russell Harris. Great book. It resonated really good with me. It talks about why people have negative thoughts and that it's okay. It's part of our evolution, but you can deal with it. It talks about strategies. I found it really resonated with me.

For people that don't know me, when I talk about something, I'm always talking about what we can do better. They see that as a negative. Even though I've got a solution on how it can be better, they still see it as a negative. I don't, and the book really helped me with that. That I'm not actually strange. I'm actually normal. I just felt that particularly people that don't know me really well think I'm pretty negative. I really struggled with that for a while. I really did, because I thought, "But I'm pursuing something and challenging. If someone's going to take that away from me, I'm not going to become the coach I want to become." I felt like if I want to keep particular people happy who influenced whether I had a job or not, I can't be who I want to be. I found that book really good.

What piece of advice could you give for the same young or developing coaches?

Be clear on why you're doing it. If you're doing it for recognition from others, I get that and that's okay. You're only going to be disappointed because you cannot influence what other people think of you. You can have a little bit of influence on it, but other people have the right to think whatever they want.

The best thing I would say is be clear on your philosophy. Be prepared to change your strategies and your methodologies, because that needs to evolve, but you've got to keep bringing it back to your philosophy all the time, and remember you're not just doing it for you. Coaching is one of those things that your ego cannot override what the objectives are.

As a player, you have a right and are expected to have a bit of an ego. As a coach, you can't go there, because you're the guy who they need to go to under pressure that's got to show some emotional detachment to it to be able to make logical, rational decisions in the best interests of not just one individual, but a group of people, because we coach team sports. Your philosophical methodology becomes really important that you stay true to, because that's what's going to take you there. Like I said, in the early days for me, it was about winning. But my philosophical approach when I look at it was always about teamwork. Teamwork has been my number one thing. I really like teams to work together to achieve. Even in individual sport, they have a team of people working behind the scenes. It just comes down to being clear on your philosophical approach. Be clear on why you're doing what you're doing because it shouldn't be for you. If you want to do it for you. you should be a player.

CONCLUSION

The eight interviews in this book are just a sample of what we've begun with the Volleyball Coaching Wizards project. As hopefully you have already recognized, the coaches we're speaking with come from a wide range of cultural, sporting, and sporting cultural backgrounds. With such a diversity of experience, it would be highly unlikely for us to be able to draw a single conclusion – or even a range of them – with respect to coaches and coaching.

In a sense, the objective of the project is not provide a coaching template anyway.

When we consider these eight interviews in conjunction with the 30+ more we have completed at the time this book goes to print, though, there are a few things we can say with some certainty:

Volleyball Coaching Wizards are passionate about volleyball, coaching, and competition.

Volleyball Coaching Wizards concern themselves with the development of their athletes at every level.

Volleyball Coaching Wizards have fascinating stories to tell.

The approximately 40 Wizards interviews we've done so far for the project is just a start. We literally have hundreds more folks on our to-interview list, and that is likely to continue growing. A major driver of Volleyball Coaching Wizards is identifying coaches who deserve to be recognized for their efforts and success, and from whom we can learn. That's an on-going process.

More books will follow this one. In the mean time, we are regularly releasing content in different ways. Follow us to get the latest excerpts, commentary, and updates.

Facebook: https://www.facebook.com/VolleyballCoachingWizards

Twitter: https://twitter.com/VBCWizards

YouTube: https://www.youtube.com/+Volleyballcoachingwizards1

Blog: http://volleyballcoachingwizards.com/content/blog/

Podcast: http://volleyballcoachingwizards.com/content/podcast/ and on iTunes.

ABOUT THE AUTHORS

John Forman is the author of the well-respected Coaching Volleyball blog. He currently coaches in the U.S. at Midwestern State University, an NCAA Division II program. This follows a stint as head coach of Svedala Volleybollklubb in Sweden's top women's league. Prior to that, John coached in England at both the university (BUCS) and National League (NVL) Division I levels. During that period, he spent time as a visiting coach with a pair of German Bundesliga team. John previously coached at NCAA Division I schools Brown University and the University of Rhode Island, as well as then NJCAA member Dean College. He was also Juniors club director and coach in the New England area for several years.

An oft-published author, John has multiple books and literally dozens of articles across multiple fields to his credit. In 2011 he published the book *Inside College Volleyball*, which focuses on US collegiate recruiting for prospective players and their families.

John is a member of the American Volleyball Coaches Association (AVCA). He holds a CAP II certification from USA Volleyball and a Level 3 coaching certification from Volleyball England, as well as a PhD from the University of Exeter.

Mark Lebedew is an experienced coach active in professional leagues in Europe where he is currently coaching Polish club Jastrzębski Węgiel. That followed five seasons coaching Berlin Recycling Volleys, during which time they were 3-time German champions and 2015 CEV Champions League bronze medal winners. His prior professional coaching stops include SV Bayer Wuppertal (Germany), VC Pepe Jeans Asse-Lennik

(Belgium), Tonno Calippo Vibo Valentia (Italy, assistant coach), and VC Franken (Germany)

At the international level, Mark has head and assistant coached the Australian men's national team, and assistant coached for Germany, and participated in Olympic Games, World Championships, World League, and zonal championships.

Mark is author of the At Home on the Court blog and a member of the American Volleyball Coaches Association (AVCA). He holds a German DSB A license and an Australian NCAS Level 3 accreditation. He has travelled the world delivering courses for the FIVB since 2009. Mark partnered with his brother and father to publish *My Profession: The Game*, an English translation of the last book written by Russian volleyball coaching legend, Vyacheslav Platonov.